Jesus loves you! ♡

Dr. Tabatha

RISE UP!

Most SuccessBooks® titles are available at special quantity discounts for bulk purchases for sales promotions, premiums, fundraising, and educational use. Special versions or book excerpts can also be created to fit specific needs.

For more information, please write:

SuccessBooks®
3415 W. Lake Mary Blvd. #950370
Lake Mary, FL 32746
or call 1.877.261.4930

Visit us online at: www.CelebrityPressPublishing.com

RISE UP!

SuccessBooks®
Lake Mary, Florida

CONTENTS

CHAPTER 1

FUNDING MY DREAM

By Lisa Nichols 13

CHAPTER 2

THE WONDER OF POSSIBILITY

By Lan J. Shaw 23

CHAPTER 3

SHATTERPROOF: A STORY OF RISING UP

By Susan Rucker 33

CHAPTER 4

HEALING TO BE WHOLE
A WOMAN'S JOURNEY THROUGH TRAUMA AND GRIEF TO
ACCEPTANCE

By Dede Shepherd, ND, PhD 45

CHAPTER 5

"WHAT I DIDN'T KNOW"

By Dr. Fred Rouse 53

CHAPTER 6

IT'S TIME TO TAKE FLIGHT

By Racquel Berry-Benjamin 63

CHAPTER 7

BEYOND THE ODDS

By Frank Brese 73

CHAPTER 8

HARRIET AND ME

By Karol V. Brown 81

CHAPTER 9

CREATIVE RESTLESSNESS

By Nick Nanton 89

CHAPTER 10

"BRAVER THAN I BELIEVED! ...AND SO ARE YOU!"

By Dr. Teri Rouse 99

CHAPTER 11

**OVERCOMING CHALLENGES WITH
FORETHOUGHT, FLEXIBILITY, AND FAITH**

By Francis X. Astorino 109

CHAPTER 12

ADOPTED ON PURPOSE

By Elizabeth Gibson Dunn 119

CHAPTER 13

SURVIVING IN BALTIMORE

By Patricia Carpenter 129

CHAPTER 14

MY PATH TO *LA DOLCE VITA*

By Dawn Mattera Corsi 137

CHAPTER 15

SURROUNDED BY OCEANS OF GRACE

By Dr. Collette Wayne 145

CHAPTER 16

DEFY THE "NO!" – MAKE ROOM FOR THE MIRACLE

By JeNae Johnson 155

CHAPTER 17

A VOICE FOR CHANGE
RISE TO THE CHALLENGE TO MAKE THE WORLD A BETTER PLACE

By Julie Meates 165

CHAPTER 18
THE POWER OF VOICE
By Debra Lee Fader 175

CHAPTER 19
WHEN YOU HIT ROCK BOTTOM, THERE'S NO WAY TO GO BUT UP
HOW TRUSTING IN THE UNIVERSE CAN HELP YOU RISE UP
By Debra Stangl 185

CHAPTER 20
PHOENIX RISING: RESILIENCE AND REDISCOVERY DURING SEASONS OF GRIEF
By Dr. K Bloom 195

CHAPTER 21
LOVE YOURSELF FIRST!
By Ann-Marie Emmanuel..205

CHAPTER 22
COURAGE TO BELIEVE IN YOURSELF FOR OTHERS
By Jennifer Perri 215

CHAPTER 23
TURNING PAIN INTO PURPOSE
DELIVERING THE VOICE AND CHOICE I DIDN'T HAVE
By Dr. Tabatha Barber, FACOOG, NCMP, IFMCP 225

CHAPTER 24

GAME, SET, BALANCE

By Dr. Heidi Gregory-Mina 233

CHAPTER 25

TURN OFF YOUR AUTOPILOT!
I DIDN'T KNOW I WAS ASLEEP UNTIL I WOKE UP

By Rhonda Lynn Davison 243

CHAPTER 26

**IT'S DARKEST JUST BEFORE DAWN —
NEVER GIVE UP!**

By Paula Willey 253

CHAPTER 27

THE WOMAN WHO SMILES

By Sabrina E. Green 261

CHAPTER 28

RISING STRONG
REVOLUTIONIZING BRAIN HEALTH, ADHD, AND ANTI-AGING

By Simone Fortier 269

CHAPTER 29

ENDING THE CURSES

By Gina Jones 279

CHAPTER 30
I'M NOT GOING OUT LIKE THAT

By Lorena Belcher 287

CHAPTER 1

FUNDING MY DREAM

BY LISA NICHOLS

Write yourself a check first.

I'd heard this advice again and again from successful people. The idea made sense. I understood the concept, but I struggled to take the action.

I felt a constant battle between this advice and the truth I felt was for me. I found myself saying on repeat, "Writing yourself a check is just something wealthy white people do. That isn't available to a single mom. That isn't for an African American woman from South Central Los Angeles. That's only something for privileged people. Not a girl who grew up between the Harlem Crip 30s and the Rollin' 60s. Not a girl who got into three fights a week just trying to get home from school. And definitely not someone who, when her teacher asked her what she wanted to be when she grew up, said, 'Alive.'"

Your perception is your reality, and before I could start my transformation, I had to break away from these limiting beliefs I was operating under. As nervous as I was, as much as my trepidation and fear tried to make me disqualify myself, I finally committed to giving my dream and myself a chance.

The first check I wrote was for $110. I was convinced that within two weeks, my water and lights would be shut off and there wouldn't be enough food in the fridge for my son, Jelani.

With a shaking pen, I wrote a three-word phrase in the memo line

13

– *Funding my dream.* I mailed the check to Wells Fargo, and then I waited. I watched the lights to see if they'd flicker off. I opened and reopened the fridge to make sure there was enough in it. After a few weeks, the most miraculous thing happened. Nothing. Nothing bad happened.

So, I wrote myself another check. This one was for $125. Again, in the memo line I put that same phrase – *Funding my dream.* Again, I waited nervously for the bills to start piling up. But again Jelani and I got through. We still had lights, water, food, and a roof over our head. We were OK.

In those early days, I could already feel my perceptions starting to shift. I was training my mind that putting myself and my dreams first was something a single mom of color could do. I challenged myself to make each check for five percent more than the check before it. (Now, I didn't do too well in math, so I wasn't exact about this, but I took my best guess every time!)

I realized that if I wanted to keep writing myself those checks every two weeks for bigger and bigger numbers, I was going to have to make some changes. I was going to have to sign up for some inconveniences in my life. My grandma used to say that your conviction, what you're passionate about, and your convenience don't live on the same block. They're not even in the same zip code.

I was enthusiastically signing up for that inconvenience. I was willing to relocate my mind and my body so I could relocate my possibility, my finances, and my son's future. I was willing to let any form of who I had been die away, in order to birth the woman I knew I was becoming.

Now, most people get to that point and hesitate. They won't allow themselves to become who they want because they're too attached to who they were. But I knew what I was doing wasn't working for me any longer, and I was willing to let go of everything and everybody (if required) to change. To put myself and my son on a new path. To find and fund that dream inside me.

One of the hardest lessons was realizing the doorway out of scarcity thinking and a limited mindset was only large enough for me to fit through. If I tried to carry everybody with me, nobody would make it. I knew with unwavering certainty that I would be more valuable to my family and my community if I was willing to put myself first. Teach myself. Develop myself. Condition myself. And then come back and contribute to their lives. The doorway could fit all of us, but each person had to go through one at a time.

All that was left was to live that idea. I was beginning to truly understand the phrase, "I am my own rescue." To write an even bigger check to myself, Jelani and I moved from our three-bedroom house to living with a roommate who smoked. I had to slip towels under the base of the door to stop smoke from filling our room as Jelani and I slept side by side in the same bed.

I wrote myself another check, and in the memo line, I put that now-familiar phrase – *Funding my dream.*

Weeks went by. I stopped going out to dinner, and I wrote another check. In the memo line, I put with a bolder, steadier pen – *Funding my dream.*

Months went by. I stopped getting my hair and nails done…another check – *Funding my dream.*

I got a second job…lots of late nights and lots more checks – *Funding my dream.*

I sold my new Nissan Altima for an old Ford Explorer…another check – *Funding my dream.*

My mom always used to say money burned a hole in her pocket, and all I knew was that money was hot and it went away fast. Growing up, I had heard that you usually run out of money before you run out of month. So, I didn't want to be tempted by the balance. Therefore, every month, when Wells Fargo would send me my statement in the mail, I never opened it. I didn't want to be distracted. I was too busy funding my dream. I left the unopened statements in a neat pile.

I skinnied down in every possible aspect of my life. I saved and sacrificed and learned how to live each year on a 'bare necessity' budget, so I could keep writing those checks to myself. And in every memo line of every check every time – *Funding my dream.*

For three and a half years, I wrote checks. I meal prepped. Did my own hair. Did my own nails. I lived an inconvenient life. I made daily sacrifices—for me and my son.

Wherever I drove with Jelani, I had to dodge the Golden Arches. I knew if he saw a McDonald's he would want to go in, so I had every location of every McDonald's memorized. I would drive the long way around and take strategic routes just so he wouldn't see those golden arches. "Mommy, I want a Big Mac – a REAL Big Mac!"

At home, I made him my substitute for a Big Mac. We called it the Mommy Mac. I thought they were just as good, but Jelani vehemently disagreed. (He anxiously awaited weekends with his grandma who would treat him to the real deal kids' meal!)

Still, every two weeks another check – *Funding my dream.*

My unopened bank statements grew and grew. I took a rubber band and secured five together. Then the stack grew to ten. Twenty. Before I knew it, it was thirty-six.

During this time, I was working at the LA Unified School District, and was truly unhappy with my stressful, unfriendly work environment. So to motivate myself to stay focused on the big picture, I had renamed it "my investor," as with this money, I was investing in myself. I then became grateful to work there. I knew it was just a moment in my life, and I wasn't going to put a period where God was putting a comma. I knew there were so many beautiful memories waiting on the other side of this temporary experience.

Even with that awareness, there were days when it felt unbearable. I felt as if I was losing time, losing momentum, and even losing my mind. I was now working two jobs (13 hours a day), had no social life, and was building a dream from a vision I wasn't even totally clear on. All I knew was that I had to give myself a chance.

Staring at the stack of unopened bank statements, now nearly forty high, I started to wonder if I had:

- *Saved enough*
- *Sacrificed enough*
- *Put away enough*
- *Prayed enough*
- *Worked hard enough*

Still not quite sure exactly what my dream was or how much it would cost, I was curious enough to at least go check my balance.

When I walked into that Wells Fargo in Los Angeles County on Hawthorne Boulevard, I held tightly onto Jelani's hand. He was five, almost six, now. When I started saving, he was two years old. My beautiful son was unrecognizable from that toddler. So much growth and change had happened for him in those three and a half years. Now it was time to see how much I had saved toward my dream.

I walked up to the teller. "Hi," I said. "I'm just here to check my balance. My name is Lisa Nichols." As soon as I said my name, I heard the mumblings in the bank start. A low, buzzy rumble. Several employees came running over. Then the manager came.

I was completely perplexed...and a little worried. With my history of low bank account balances and even nonsufficient fund checks, I couldn't imagine all this attention from executives and professionals meant anything good.

"Lisa Nichols," the teller blurted out. "You're the 'funding my dream' lady!" I exhaled. Then I listened closer to the growing chatter from all the gathered employees. I heard the surprise at how young I was... that I was African American...a mom. The buzz around me wasn't menacing. It held excitement. I just wasn't clear why yet.

"Well," she said, practically bouncing up and down on the balls of her feet. "You've written at the bottom of every single check you've ever sent here *'Funding my dream.'* We've all been wondering..." she paused for a moment, as if holding her breath in great anticipation for an answer that she'd been patiently waiting on for a long time... "What's your dream?"

That's when I realized why everyone was gathered around. They were there in anticipation of my answer. Apparently everyone in the branch had deposited one or two of the 91 checks of mine over the last 3½ years, and were dying to know.

I took a deep breath, as I hadn't ever been asked that question before. "Honestly, I don't know," I said. "But I know it involves inspiring people. And I know it's going to cost me something! And I'm willing to invest in me first." I went on to explain how I'd never opened any of my bank statements because I didn't want to become distracted or tempted as I built.

With great joy and anticipation, the teller excitedly wrote my balance on a sheet of paper and passed it under the thick plexiglass divider between us. I could feel all the other bank employees looking at me with great excitement too. I could feel them rooting for me with their eyes. I could feel their joy as they held their breath for me to discover the balance. It was as if this was everyone's win, and they were grateful to share this moment with me—especially now that they knew that my bank balance would be a surprise to me.

Silently I was praying that the number I saw would free me from my prison called my "J. O. B." A part of my prayer included wanting to feel like I had accomplished enough to treat my son to something special.

I took a deep breath, paused, and then opened the small piece of white paper with five digits written on it. I slightly gasped and, with widened eyes, said,

"No, ma'am. I'm Lisa S. Nichols. Can you please check that account again?"

At the time, I didn't know anybody with even five thousand dollars to their name...or ten thousand dollars. So, I knew this couldn't be mine. Then I saw all those bank tellers around me begin to get emotional. I was certain she had made an error, but everyone else was beaming with excitement as if they knew something different.

Not offended by my questioning, the teller graciously agreed to look again. She pushed a few buttons on her computer. Then she slid the same piece of paper under that plexiglass divider and spoke with the most calming, compassionate voice ever. "No, Ms. Nichols." She smiled. "That's correct. It's all yours. Whatever your dream is, you have enough to fund it now."

Everyone in the bank was now crying and/or laughing with joy. It felt like we all had won–that something had been made possible for everyone who was sharing the experience. I opened up the paper again, and staring back at me was $62,500 as my account balance. I worked to control my breathing as my heart was racing with query, and question, and purpose, and promise. (I did it!) With tears streaming down my face, I looked down at Jelani and made him a promise. "Baby, life is going to be different now for you and mommy."

Jelani, a bit confused and overwhelmed by all the emotion, looked up at me with big, pleading eyes. "Mommy, can we finally go to McDonald's now?" After the (real) Big Mac was enjoyed, we went back home. With great joy and a grateful heart, I gave my thirty-day notice to the LA Unified School District. With excitement and clarity, Jelani and I packed our bags and put everything we owned in the back of our old beat-up Ford Explorer.

We drove eighty-two miles south to land in San Diego. There I saw a big sign. New apartments. Bad credit welcome. Jelani and I needed both of those things. There, in apartment 102A, I set about transforming my walk-in closet into an office. (Actually, it was more like a "step-in" closet!) I fit a tiny desk into the crowded space. I hung manila folders on pants hangers and made the space feel bigger with six $2.99 mirrors stuck to the walls.

And that was where Motivating the Masses, Inc. was born.

For four years I worked in that closet, and as I worked, I sang to myself every day, **"I'm a hustler baby. I just want you to know. It ain't where I been.** *But where I'm 'bout to go."* ...with key emphasis on "where I'm 'bout to go."

Twenty-five years later, as CEO of Motivating the Masses, Inc. which has touched the lives of over 100 million people and become a global multimillion-dollar enterprise, I'm often asked to donate to someone's cause or business, and when I do, I often love to write in the memo line:

I'm honored to fund your dream.

About Lisa

Lisa Nichols is one of the world's most-requested speakers, as well as media personality and corporate CEO, whose global platform reaches over 170 countries and serves over 80 million people. Lisa's social media reach is over 2.4 million followers.

As Founder and Chief Executive Officer of Motivating the Masses, Inc., Lisa has helped develop workshops and programs that have transformed thousands of businesses, and the lives of entrepreneurs. As a result of her training, her students become unforgettable speakers, best-selling authors, and 6 and 7-figure entrepreneurs.

Lisa's extraordinary story of transforming her own life from public assistance to leading a multi-million-dollar enterprise is the inspiration behind her bold mission to teach others that it is possible to do the same. Today, fans worldwide revere Lisa for her mastery of teaching people how to accomplish unfathomable goals and tap into their limitless potential.

CHAPTER 2

THE WONDER OF POSSIBILITY

BY LAN J. SHAW

The ground shook, and the walls rattled. There was no time to think, only time to run. Amid the chaos, we fled for our lives. The building itself, once a sanctuary called home, now shuttered with an eerie symphony of cracking and trembling. In moments, our world had become a disorienting battleground. The walls now betrayed us with every groan and shiver.

The shaking violently woke us out of our sleep. It was 3:42 AM on July 28, 1976, when it hit. We lived in a three-story building composed of flats. Our flat was 500 square feet, and we shared it with two other families. Our home was confined to a 120-square-foot room for our family of four. Our unit shared a modest cooking space and toilet with the other families. There was no heat, no hot water, nor a shower. The narrow hallway, about three feet wide, served as a passage to the stairs and also housed our most prized possessions—our bicycles. Movement was restricted through the cramped space, but it was our only way out. I still recall the searing pain as my shin collided with the bike pedals and my neck with the handlebars as we ran amid the chaos.

We made it out, but some were struck and killed instantly by falling roof tiles all around us. It could have been us. Tiles crashed on the ground during our escape. Others were hit, but we were spared.

It all happened so fast. Over a quarter million people died that day.

A JOURNEY OF RESILIENCE
THROUGH ADVERSITY

I spent my early years in the outskirts of Tianjin, the third-largest city in China, in the mid-1970s. In the early 1900s, eight countries colonized different parts of the city, including Britain, France, and Germany, leaving their distinct marks. Tianjin, a bustling port city, shared similarities with Shanghai regarding business and trade.

The year 1976 brought a series of traumatic events to our country. An earthquake, the loss of Premier Zhou Enlai, our Chairman Mao Zedong, and the removal of the Gang of Four left our culture in shock for years.

Our living conditions were poor. The tiny room we narrowly escaped seemed like a luxury now. Since the earthquake, we lived outside with plastic sheets held by trees that divided each family. One sheet, a wall on either side, and one as a roof. These simple materials provided us with protection and a place to call home. The days became weeks, and weeks became months. For three years, we lived outside in our plastic shelter along with thousands of other families in the region.

Winters were severe, and we constructed makeshift shelters for tiny homes from available materials, like bricks and clay walls. We lacked hot water and a heater, relying on a coal-burning stove to endure the freezing temperatures. Seeking warmth sometimes led us back to the building we had evacuated, unsure if its crumbling walls would withstand the weight of our presence.

Food was rationed based on household size, and blackouts occurred several times per week. We relied on a single candle for light, even if it meant accidentally burning the tips of our hair while doing homework.

My parents instilled resilience in us, emphasizing the need to persevere and push through. Education was highly prized, as it promised a better life. Entrance exams, which were quite challenging, determined the quality of our education, making it our sole path to success. My parents, well-educated with college degrees, earned about $30 a month for our family, a significant amount compared to many others.

IT'S NOT WHAT WE SEE BUT HOW WE SEE IT

Even in the poorest conditions, I had a wonderful life, a loving family and received all the attention I needed growing up. At home, my parents were wonderful, and at school, the teachers loved me. I had great friends. What more could a girl wish for in a good life? I saw beauty in a broken world. I didn't realize my world was broken, which was beautiful in its naive way. I didn't know any better. It was a simple existence, with joy in life's simpler pleasures, despite the discipline needed to survive. Confined to the immediate reality surrounding me, I chose to see beauty in adversity, a perspective that continues to shape me today.

Eventually, the government secured our building with massive bars, preventing its collapse, and we returned home to a reinforced building full of cracks, grateful for the permanence and a true place to call our own.

Following the events of 1976, a new generation of leaders introduced new perspectives. Foreigners who visited our region dressed vibrantly, unlike us. Our clothing was limited to three basic shades: military green, deep blue, and dull grey. We dressed in these colors associated with military, farmers, or blue-collar workers, reflecting the communist values we held. Everyone wore the same colors, or so I thought.

It was shocking to realize there was a vast world beyond my own. In middle school, I began to understand we lived in a third-world country, leading me to question, "Why me? I'm smart, I work hard, so why do they have such a better life?" It was here that I began to be enlightened and began to explore the wonder and power of possibilities. Thankfully, I did not succumb to resentment or anger. Instead, I became resolute. I vowed not to raise my future children in this third-world setting, convinced a better life awaited beyond. I concluded the key to rising out of my circumstances rested within me.

THE POWER OF A MOMENT

In 1987, I was twenty-two years old. I remember it clearly. Stepping into a three-star Hyatt hotel in my city for the first time changed me. After years of living in such limited and modest conditions, the hotel was a revelation. The lobby was grand, with polished floors, carpet, and a warm, inviting glow from the chandelier. The furniture was plush and comfortable, a far cry from the reality at home. At the bar, I noticed a small candle quietly flickering. Wow, a candle meant ambiance for them. For me, it meant utility. It was a glimpse into a different life of abundance and luxury I had never experienced before. I knew there was more.

After college, I went to night school to study international business and learned American President Lines (APL), one of the world's largest shipping companies, was opening an office in Tianjin. I began working for them as a documentation clerk. The office was set up in that same hotel. I was determined to succeed. My attitude was: "I'll do whatever it takes."

The contrast between working in a luxurious hotel office and our conditions at home would be hard for most to believe. Witnessing the difference between my life and my American colleagues who enjoyed the fruit of their work in ways I never thought possible was eye-opening. They earned fifty times my salary. This inequality became a source of motivation for me. I knew it wasn't fair, but I also understood I had to choose to keep moving forward.

In just two years, I transitioned from a documentation clerk to customer service, then sales, and became the top performer in China for APL. I secured a spot in the prestigious President's Club, and what followed would change my life forever.

In March 1994, APL flew me business class from Tianjin to Maui for a one-week event at Sheraton Black Rock. I had the privilege of meeting the very best, the company's top performers and leaders from all around the world.

This trip marked my very first encounter with the first world and with the United States. I was 28 years old and earned my place here. I smiled because the changing world around me only confirmed what I had always believed in my heart since I sat in our family tent as a young pre-teen girl. I saw this moment many years earlier, and I reached it because I made a conscious decision to face adversity with resilience, to push through, and to optimize each moment.

OPTIMIZING MOMENTS LEADS TO OPPORTUNITIES (AND RISK)

Future opportunities would bring me to major cities around the mainland USA. In 1994, I came to New York and worked out of that office for three months to learn about management and operations throughout the United States.

In 1996, APL promoted and relocated me to Shanghai, and I joined the executive team. It was quite an accomplishment, considering I was the only Chinese employee on the executive team. While my compensation was probably only 20% of my American colleagues, I now earned in the top 0.1% of all of China in a prestigious executive management position.

Upon returning from a trip back to Shanghai, I went to my office on a Saturday and noticed balloons at the convention center nearby. Curious, I approached the entrance and noticed it was the British Education Fair. I was tired and jetlagged, but I walked in. Turns out, it was a recruiting fair. I wanted to earn my MBA, but I knew nothing about British business schools, so I started asking. Everyone kept recommending I visit the school called 'Lancaster.' They were the top one-year program in Europe. So I went there and said, "I would like to apply for your MBA program."

"Have you taken your ESL?"

"No, I have no English scores." I said.

"I'm sorry, you can't apply. Wait, you speak English."

"What do you mean?" I said in a confused pause.

"Typically, the Chinese students have great scores, but then they don't have a mastery of the language, but you can speak English."

"Ok, yes." I proceeded to explain what I did and why I wanted an MBA.

"Ok, walk around for thirty minutes, then come back." they told me with a positive disposition.

I explored the rest of the fair for a half-hour, then returned. They directed me to the back of the booth, gave me a stack of papers and a pen, and said, "You have two hours to write an essay about how a British entrepreneur can expand their business in China." I proceeded to write and then returned my completed essay. They asked me to return in one hour.

I don't remember what I wrote, but I returned one hour later to an application with my name already filled out, and it was signed by the Dean of the English Department and the head of admissions. What followed were a few formalities, but I learned at that moment I was accepted to pursue my MBA through Lancaster University Management School.

I was thirty years old, and my culture expected me to be married by twenty-five and conform to certain norms, but that path wasn't meant for me, which also meant no man would want to marry a successful woman like me. It was a bold and risky season, as failing in this unconventional path would signify a double failure for not adhering to cultural and family expectations. Self-pity and second-guessing were not options. There was only one way out. There was no "Plan B."

I completed my MBA within one year and accepted a job in supply chain management in California. I began a new life, getting married and having a son. I spent seven years consulting in supply chain management for Fortune 500 companies, including General Motors, Ford, Nike, and Kellogg.

REAL SUCCESS IS ABOUT HELPING OTHERS

In 2007, I had friends in California who started losing jobs. For the first time, I saw people cry over a job loss. I didn't know what it was like to be kicked out or unwanted. This broke my heart. I thought, "If I can help these major companies make big business decisions and improve their bottom line, I can help you as individuals." These dark moments among friends were the inspiration I needed to find an opportunity where I could apply my skillset to help others.

Soon after, with no clients, no license, and based solely on my experience, I was hired as a financial advisor for a large brokerage firm. They saw something in me. I began knocking on doors to gain new clients. One month after I began, The Great Recession was upon us. Some would say the timing was terrible, but three months into this high-risk journey someone wrote a $1.2 million check for me to manage. I didn't even have an office. I opened the account at their home on their kitchen counter, and I thought to myself, "Oh, my gosh, they trust me more than I even trust myself!"

"You have a brain. You have a heart. You have intuition and wisdom. You would do well for me." they said. My business grew as I continued to optimize each new opportunity.

EMBRACE YOUR STORY

Somehow, I continued to attract high-net-worth individuals, business owners, and entrepreneurs. I could see my clients' success increasing in complexity, which led to uncertainty, missed opportunities, and costly mistakes. However, I held back from sharing too much about my observations and opinions about their business. After all, I was concerned it might diminish my clients' interest in me because I didn't fit the typical mold for financial advisors, and what I saw was outside the typical scope.

A moment came when I could hold back no longer. I felt as if all the puzzle pieces had finally fallen into place in my mind. I could not resist connecting the dots. I stepped into the moment and, for the first time, openly shared how all the dots connected for my client. I helped them see how to maximize their business value, prepare them for future succession, and take care of their family while meaningfully growing their wealth.

"Lan, why didn't you tell me this before?"

I confessed, "Well, I thought perhaps it wasn't valuable to you. All the reputable financial advisors here have different backgrounds with a certain stereotype that are most desirable."

To my surprise, they emphatically stated, "No, people need *you*! What you offer goes way beyond investment products!"

This vulnerable moment profoundly impacted me, marked a turning point in my journey, and helped me reach where I am today. In 2017, ten years into my journey as a financial advisor, I decided to launch my own company, Vision Private Wealth[1], a multi-family office. We serve successful entrepreneurs and generational wealth builders with eight or nine figures in net worth. We help clients orchestrate and optimize their wealth, life, and legacy. The concept of optimization is engrained in all we do.

WHAT ELSE IS POSSIBLE?

I am grateful for the years spent in a tent with the comforting light of a candle. My story shaped me to help others, and one thing remains certain: I will always ask, "What else is possible?"

What have you overcome to get here? How has your story shaped you and helped those around you? More importantly, what's next?

Never stop dreaming, no matter how dark or seemingly impossible your situation is. Even when the world seems like it's collapsing and your ground is shaking, follow your heart and never stop searching for the wonder of possibility.

---

1. Vision Private Wealth, Inc. 2159 Central Avenue, Alameda, CA, 94501 (510) 358-8668. Lan J. Shaw (CA Insurance License #0F94440) is a Registered Representative and an Investment Adviser Representative with/and offers securities and advisory services through Commonwealth Financial Network®, Member FINRA/SIPC, a Registered Investment Adviser.

About Lan

Lan Shaw is the epitome of resilience, a visionary who rose from the aftermath of one of the deadliest earthquakes in history to become a prominent figure in international business and finance. Born into modest beginnings in Beijing, China, Lan's early life was marked by the trials of living through cultural upheavals and natural disasters, including the devastating 1976 earthquake that claimed over a quarter of a million lives.

Despite such hardships, Lan's indomitable spirit was fueled by her parents' emphasis on education and perseverance. Graduating with a degree that would set the stage for her future, she initially worked for American President Lines in Tianjin, where she quickly advanced to become a top performer. Her relentless work ethic and acute business acumen earned her recognition within the company, and soon she was mingling with the elite in international circles.

Lan's journey took a transformative turn when she attended a British Education Fair on a whim, leading to her acceptance into a top MBA program at Lancaster University Management School without the conventional prerequisites. This bold move reflected her determination to break free from the expectations of her culture and pursue a life of greater possibility.

Leveraging her MBA, Lan transitioned into supply chain management in California, consulting for Fortune 500 companies. In 2007, she took a leap into financial advising at a major brokerage firm, where she once again proved her ability by gaining the trust and managing substantial assets for high-net-worth individuals during one of the most challenging economic times.

Lan founded Vision Private Wealth in 2017 after recognizing a pervasive gap in the financial industry — the wealthy were consistently underserved, with a chasm between the potential of personalized, strategic advisory and the generic services often rendered. Vision Private Wealth, a multi-family office, was her response to this disparity. Lan's firm offers an exceptional level of service, dedicating itself to the comprehensive orchestration of wealth, life, and legacy planning. This enterprise stands as a testament to her integrity and commitment to optimal service, truly embodying the adage that there is always room for improvement and innovation.

Lan Shaw's life is a testament to the power of embracing one's story, of seeing beauty in brokenness, and of always asking, "What else is possible?" Her biography is not just a record of personal achievements but a beacon of hope, encouraging all to dream and to relentlessly pursue the wonder of possibility.

CHAPTER 3

SHATTERPROOF: A STORY OF RISING UP

BY SUSAN RUCKER

*One common belief among people everywhere is that life is hard. Each trial and tribulation can either make us or break us. Through my own roller-coaster journey, I've learned three keys through my own adversities and struggles that have enhanced my durability and impact resistance to become ... **shatterproof**!*

I. BELIEVE IT WILL GET BETTER

I wanted to crawl under a rock and hide. Or ... just crawl under a rock and die. Back then, I just wanted to go unnoticed.

Unfortunately, all the rocks were covered in snow, as were the trees and the wide-open fields. There was no place to hide ... no place to escape the hurtful bullying that had become part of my life as a young elementary school student in a frigid landscape.

I was a small, shy, yet observant Asian girl living in rural Minnesota, having been adopted out of a South Korean orphanage by a loving family at age two and having grown up in the middle of a small-town Midwest culture that was not yet ready for change.

It was the late 1970s in America, barely a decade removed from the civil rights era and barely two decades since the U.S. Supreme Court issued its landmark decision overturning segregation laws. It was the era of disco music and bell-bottom pants. It also was the era of tension and racial strife.

My parents taught me and my siblings gratitude, kindness and respect. They told us to love those who looked different, to treat others the way we wanted to be treated. They raised us with what we often dub 'good morals.' However, I learned quickly that not everyone else was raised that way, and others didn't practice them.

On this particular day in fourth grade, I was walking home alone from a long day at school, bundled up with my thick winter coat and gloves as I gingerly navigated a sidewalk littered with ice and snow. Each step on the one-mile journey was potentially treacherous.

I did my best to hide my face under my hat and scarf, my eyes barely exposed so as to navigate my surroundings. My goal was to sneak home without being noticed. My goal was to … *survive*.

"Hey, *Susan*," the girl shouted from just ahead, her high-pitched voice breaking the calm silence of the crisp, still air.

Gulp … I was caught.

It was Becky, a classmate who was twice my size and three times my strength, even though we were roughly the same age. She was the type of school bully you see on the big screen. She was the type of person who sneered at kindness, who mocked others for fun.

Unfortunately, she also lived in my neighborhood.

On this day, Becky was waiting for me on the sidewalk about 40 feet ahead, blocking my route home and wearing a proud smirk that screamed trouble. She brought friends this day – two girls, one boy – who always had her back.

I approached them, slowly, avoiding eye contact and daring not to speak. Maybe – just maybe – they would let me pass.

"You don't belong here," Becky shouted toward me with a taunting voice, her brow furrowed and her eyes staring straight into mine like a tiger eyeing its prey.

"You need to go back *home* – to your country," she added, laughing. The others chuckled, too. Out of the corner of my eye, I saw three of them making snowballs.

I walked a few steps to the left, hoping they would give up and go onto something else. Instead, they moved over too, blocking my path, and ensuring this tense confrontation would continue.

My heart pounded in my chest. My hands, though covered by gloves, quickly moistened. My breathing intensified.

"Just let me pass, please," I pleaded.

Yet, Becky's cruel smirk only grew wider, and it was clear that walking home this day would be far from simple.

One by one, they surrounded me. They were daring me to fight back as they hurled racial insults about my skin color, my small stature, and my homeland.

Suddenly, she pushed me into the snow, her friends pelted me with hard snowballs and fists, and yet I lived to tell the story. Regrettably, though, it wasn't my only confrontation with bullying. Scenes, just like that one, were played over and over in my childhood.

I never fought back. I never responded to their hate-filled words with even more hate. I was raised better than that. Even at that age, I was determined not to make a bad situation even worse. I was determined to lead with kindness.

Besides, I told myself over and over, "They just don't know better. They don't understand." Maybe, they … hadn't been taught to love.

Much like a 1970s-era record player that gets 'stuck,' my mind kept repeating a single phrase on a loop during such confrontations: *It will get better. It WILL get better. It will get BETTER.*

It always did.

Each time they pushed me down, I got up. Each time they tried to stop me, I kept going. Despite the odds stacked against me, I persevered.

That's what I've done my entire life. Each time anyone wanted to break me and shatter who I was, I'd tell myself I knew I was meant for something more and believed with all my might – *"It will get better!"*

II. BOOST SKILLS TO REACH NEXT GOAL TOWARD THE BIGGER GOAL

In fourth grade, my teacher predicted that Spanish would be an important language in the future world for business. Inspired, I went home and shared with my mom the first big goal I ever remember setting – "When I grow up, I'm going to Spain and learn Spanish."

In fifth grade, I felt, for the first time, the urge to be a leader of people after I successfully led a campaign to acquire the school's first playground equipment. But I had a major obstacle to overcome. I was afraid.

"How can I be a leader of people when I'm afraid of people?"

So, I focused on my talents: intelligence, high drive and a never-quit attitude as I created a plan to build the skills I lacked …

1) *Extracurricular Activities:* I forced myself to learn social skills by participating in school plays, gymnastics, music and even cheerleading. Over the next eight years, I tried numerous activities to reach the next goal of being more confident toward my bigger goal of becoming a leader.

2) *Work:* At ten years old, I decided to start working. My goals: help my family, start my college fund and learn more skills. From my first job delivering papers to owning my own company, Impactful Strategies, I've never stopped working, learning and building skills.

My philosophy was simple: To reach my next goal, I need to accomplish additional tasks, such as – *To become a leader, I need to overcome my shyness. To graduate from college, I need to earn money.*

3) ***High School:*** When my classmates were picking easy electives –
study hall, for example – I was choosing electives that would teach
me a new skill and that would help me reach my goals – accounting,
for instance.

While my classmates wanted fewer classes and the easy route, I was
wanting more. Was that a weird mindset for a high schooler? Of course!
However, building skills is like adding in layers of protection to be less
prone to shattering from an unforeseen impact – and becoming more
shatterproof.

During my junior year in college, I took an airplane ride – *my first ever*
– to participate in an international overseas program in Spain. Even
though I was excited, I was also terrified. There were times I let fear
win by secluding myself, but other times I stepped outside my comfort
zone to stretch and challenge myself, thus rising up toward my bigger
goals.

Once I graduated college, I decided to return to Spain so I could
improve my Spanish and eventually marry the special man I had met
there previously, who I thought was 'the one' who made me extremely
happy.

But life always has its unexpected twists.

"I've made the decision that I want my son to marry a Spaniard and
not you," my boyfriend's father told me. My heart stopped. My world
turned upside down with one sentence. "Just go back to your country."

Triggered. I had heard that too many other times in my life.

Once again, I wanted to crawl under a rock and hide. Or ... just crawl
under a rock and die.

I agonized over healing my wounded heart and returning back to the
USA or staying to work on my Spanish as originally planned, which
would take an incredible effort. I wanted the easy route. I wanted to
give up. Ready to book my return ticket, I realized my dream since
fourth grade was dying because I still didn't have the Spanish-speaking
skills I needed.

"No, Susan. It WILL get better," I tried to tell myself. I chose the harder route and stayed to keep my dream alive, despite feeling like I was shattering into a million pieces.

My mom still remembers me telling her as a 9-year-old, "When I grow up, I'm gonna go to Spain. I'm gonna study over there and use Spanish in my work" – *mission accomplished ... shatterproof!*

III. BUILD YOUR ADVOCATES ... *EVEN FROM DAY ONE*

In every job, I learned that building advocates around you makes all the difference in how quickly you can recover from a mistake. It also reinforces your own internal structure to incorporate impact-resistant strategies ... reinforcing yourself to be shatterproof.

On my first job as a store manager, my boss said he needed me to go into the store right away, even though I hadn't received any training. It was in bad shape, he added, and he didn't have the time to train me. He told me: *Trust yourself and your background. I've got your back. I'll be your advocate.*

Still, I was overwhelmed: *"How can I run this store when I haven't learned anything yet in this company?"*

I was given the unenviable task of firing an employee – she had stolen from the company – on my first day on the job.

She was twice my size and three times my strength, and she didn't take the news lightly. She got in my face, her eyes filled with anger, and her fists ready to fight as she told me through clenched teeth, "I'm going to beat the living s--t out of you! You'll regret this!" A supervisor, standing in the room and watching the events unfold, looked like she wanted to puke.

I stared back at this tall woman, calm as I could be, determined to stand my ground and determined to de-escalate the tension. After all, my childhood had prepared me for name-calling and taunting.

"I believe you," I said matter-of-factly, looking up at her. "I know you could totally beat me to a pulp." Suddenly, her look of anger turned to one of confusion.

I continued, "Right now, you've only lost your job. But if you hit me, you'll end up going to jail."

She no longer wanted to fight. "You're not worth my time," she huffed before walking out the door.

My life had come full circle. This time, I didn't get punched. This time, I had stood up to the bully ... and this time, I *had won ... shatterproof.*

People often ask me, "Why didn't you get help when you were bullied in school?" Truthfully, I believe I suffered from what many adoptees go through—not wanting to cause any 'issues' where adoptive parents would want to 'give them back.' Never mind that my parents displayed unconditional love. It's a deep-seated fear among a lot of adoptees, even if parents do nothing to make them feel that way.

I could have prevented so much more suffering if I had only reached out to someone. Do you reach out when you are suffering ... or, do you suffer in silence alone?

I have come a long way since my confrontation with Becky and her friends on that frigid day in Minnesota. Now, I actively seek out advocates and am an advocate for others. When I struggle, my inner circle of people helps me get back up faster and become even more resilient.

TYING IT ALL TOGETHER

Joan was an executive of a large organization. She was struggling with one of the teams below her that was dysfunctional and that often faced inner turmoil. Most employees were tenured but, despite their experience, didn't believe they made a difference. Employees were leaving. Others were putting in minimal effort.

Joan hired me to help turn the team around. After speaking with the key stakeholders and the team's employees, I realized a great place to start was utilizing the *Three Keys to Rising Up:*

1. **B**elieve it will get better

2. **B**oost skills to reach next goal toward the bigger goal

3. **B**uild your advocates

"Michael," I gently interjected as I listened to the director of a team speaking poorly of his employees and organization, "do you like the way you currently are leading this team?"

Silent then stammering, he replied defensively, "No, but …" and he proceeded to list excuse upon excuse.

I continued, "If you want to turn things around, it must start with you. Believing you can turn it around can only be decided by you first, so let me know when you decide that. Then, we can go from there."

Michael pondered deeply for a moment, nodded then asked tentatively, "How do I do that?"

Only now was Michael open to learning. Only now was he ready to turn things around. We discussed which skills and advocates were needed for him and the team. Through our partnership, Michael, Joan and the entire team were able to turn around their performance.

NOW WHAT?

Every chapter of life has a purpose. Every chapter has a lesson. Our experiences and trials shape us and refine us – much like the intense heat and pressure that transforms mysterious underground elements into a radiant diamond. Similar to that diamond, we can emerge from life's battles stronger than ever, with newfound resilience and purpose.

When I face life's hurdles, I remember the traditional gospel song: "This little light of mine, I'm gonna let it shine. Let it shine, let it shine, let it shine."

I *choose* to rise up and learn something to make me even stronger.

I *choose* to share my experiences and skills to help others.

I *choose* to crawl out – boldly – from under any rock that gets in my way.

I *choose* to shine my light – brightly – to light up the pathway for others.

Rising up and becoming shatterproof is not a one-time incident, but rather a continuous cycle of conscious choices. Each of us has choices, even when we think we don't. So, choose wisely, and you also can be on your way to become ... *shatterproof!*

About Susan

#1 Best-Selling Author Susan Rucker, Founder of Impactful Strategies LLC, elevates people, teams, and enterprises through motivational speaking, consulting and leadership coaching by building skills to make a real IMPACT. She is recognized as 'The People Whisperer' for her rare ability to connect with, and transform people and organizations, to achieve breakthrough results.

Susan was filmed by an Emmy® Award-winning crew for her interview on "Breaking Through with Lisa Nichols!" which aired on ABC, CBS, NBC, and FOX affiliates around the country. Her partnership with Jack Canfield on the #1 Best-Selling book *The Keys to Authenticity* helps the masses unlock the code to a fulfilling life and business.

Susan's decades of operational and HR experience in multiple industries includes overseeing 4500 employees and over $1 billion in revenue while increasing employee engagement and retention. Through her innovative programs and processes, she has saved firms tens of millions of dollars and helped them generate millions more.

Alongside developing strategies and optimizing processes, Susan has successfully coached and trained thousands of leaders on how to *Rise Up* and overcome the challenges in today's ever-changing and dynamic environments. As a Wiley Certified Authorized Partner for facilitating and providing solutions with DiSC® and The Five Behaviors®, Susan brings advanced tools and solutions to the table. Her Diversity, Equity & Inclusion (DE&I) work builds high-performing collaborative teams by cultivating inclusive workplace cultures that celebrate differences and ensure equity.

One client said of her: *"Susan is equally energetic and passionate, providing the light at the end of the tunnel for those seeking to experience a breakthrough and delivering eye-opening truths with a combination of authenticity and humor needed to embrace the impactful change necessary for transformation. She is lively, spirited, and approaches life with immense playfulness and abundant joy."*

Susan is fluent in Spanish and is learning Korean. Being adopted as a child by a loving family and being recently reunited with her biological family in South Korea are two miracles she is most grateful for in her life.

She has served many organizations throughout the U.S.A., including Stratas Foods, FirstService Residential, Dallas College, Alamo Colleges District, Michael Burt

Enterprises, and Vendilli Digital Group.

If you are a senior leader at a $10M+ company who wants to achieve results faster, improve employee retention, engagement, DE&I, and build high-performing impactful teams, contact Susan Rucker at:

- Impactfulstrategiesllc.com

CHAPTER 4

HEALING TO BE WHOLE
A WOMAN'S JOURNEY THROUGH TRAUMA AND GRIEF TO ACCEPTANCE

BY DEDE SHEPHERD, ND, PhD

As it is with so many people, my early life was not ideal. Battling the difficulties of shame from childhood sexual trauma, I was all alone. There was no one to confide in. The abusers were trusted friends and family, and I was afraid I would be blamed. Growing up I often didn't feel safe or loved, so I became distrustful of opening up.

I grew up in a harsh single-parent household, with a parent whose own parental relationship was also a struggle. Unknowingly, there were also generational challenges I had to bear. My grandmother didn't have the tools needed to nurture and love my mother. Her inability to create the right narrative for a healthy mother-child connection made my relationship with mom even more strenuous.

I spent all of my childhood living on pins and needles, worried about what would happen next. It was a daily stressful environment. My confidence diminished, and internally, my emotions were falling apart. This created a lot of self-doubt which was the perfect catalyst for self-hate, and as a result, I had problems trusting others and speaking up for myself.

Not realizing the impact of unresolved, suppressed trauma, I struggled academically in elementary and middle school; but in high school, life got even more difficult. What I didn't know was, I had become best friends with "depression." On the outside, I was the life of the party, but at home, depression was my security blanket.

But as Maya Angelou once said, "If you know better, you do better." Well, I believe the opposite is also true, "If you don't know better, you won't do better." I believe my mom did the best she could. She never learned any better, so she couldn't do any better. This is the brokenness of generational abuse. The facts are, hurt people…hurt people.

As a teen, I told myself I would not mistreat my future children. I was determined to break the cycle of generational trauma, and I did. But eventually, my trauma adversely affected my parenting style of over-protection. As you know, the life you live as a child has a significant impact on who you become as an adult. This reflects the power of learned behavior.

It even manifested in how I was pursuing relationships, making poor decisions, looking for love in the wrong places, all because I was searching for the love of a parent, rather than the love of a partner. I ended up in relationships with emotionally unavailable men or ones with low self-esteem who used domestic violence to control. I could no longer trust myself to make good decisions about anything. So, I suffered in silence, often too broken and embarrassed. I didn't want anyone to know about all my failings.

Life continued to bring its own challenges. I was angry, recently divorced, distrustful of others, and lived in isolation. This was the perfect recipe for disaster. When my son was about seven, I became emotionally overwhelmed and suicidal, so I had to seek help, because I needed to be here to protect him.

I didn't bond well with my therapist, but I was thankful for her advice that day, "Please hold on for your son. No one else can love him like his mother. You can't imagine what it would do to him. The statistics are horrible." She was right. Statistics show that kids whose parents die by suicide are three times more likely to do the same. I didn't want that for him, so I held on. It was my daily battle, but my son became my reason for living.

When he was about ten years old, we became a homeschool family. God had placed it on my heart to be more involved in his academic and spiritual growth. In addition, the school system wasn't giving him what he needed. He disliked sitting at a desk all day, he was more of an explorative learner. We did many field trips, experiments, and community service projects together. I taught every subject, including science, and I have the burn marks on the kitchen floor to prove it. (My eyelashes and a patch of hair were also burnt off while wearing goggles, but that's another story.)

It was now my son's senior year, and the challenges began – deadlines, college selection, graduation, and the emotional conflicts of life. Many of the high school homeschool moms were experiencing the same obstacles, and even though God had placed it on my heart to start a mother's prayer group, my life was too chaotic. I told Him, "God, I promise to start it if You can just get us through this school year," and He did. After graduation, we began the mother's prayer group in June. This group of homeschool moms needed the support of each other. My only regret was not starting it sooner. This group was divine intervention, but only God knew it at the time.

Shortly after, there was a sudden unexpected turn in my life. When my son turned 18, he decided he was moving out to live with his dad. I was devastated! This news threw me into another painful, emotional spiral. I felt rejected, like a nothing, and now, even my reason for living was gone. I remember thinking, "Dede, your purpose is done."

The day of departure came, I was numb and broken on the inside, but I held it all in as we drove, and gave only life advice – remain close to God, stay respectful, and keep the right influences around. I couldn't express my true feelings to him, I didn't want him feeling any level of guilt. As he grabbed his things and hugged me, I still remember the sound of the car door slamming for the last time, "WHAM!"

I waited a few minutes as they drove off, then I couldn't handle it anymore, I broke down in tears. It was too much for any mother to bear. My hope was completely gone, so that day, I began making plans to end my life. This is the danger of hopelessness. When people don't have hope, it's difficult to desire the joys of life. This is why no one should suffer in silence.

I then made a decision to not lead the prayer group. I didn't feel adequate to help other moms when my heart was so shattered, I had failed God. The next day I went to my "final" mom's prayer group. I was overwhelmed, I could no longer hold it together, the tears just poured. The feeling of failing as a parent was unbearable. But, then the Holy Spirit intervened.

Each mom encouraged and prayed with me. But what I didn't realize was, God had a specific mom from the group to be an added blessing to me. Erica was a soft-spoken, kind, thoughtful, and an encouraging woman of God who recognized my deep agony. She advised me to be faithful in prayer, that we were in spiritual battle. I don't know why these words impacted me so deeply, but they did. She pointed me to watch two messages online, and after watching, it became apparent that the enemy was trying desperately to take me out by using what I loved most – my son. I had to make a decision, to choose life. This was not an easy journey, as the dark thoughts continued daily and the low self-worth was a constant reminder, but I was just so grateful for the power of community.

Then randomly, the Holy Spirit nudged me, "Dede, why don't you look up the stages of grief?" I was certainly astonished. Immediately, I saw I had been suffering through the first four steps: denial, anger, bargaining, depression, with a big dose of guilt thrown into all of them. My last step was now to journey through acceptance. I learned that I had been grieving almost an entire year and had no idea, I was completely oblivious. I always thought grief was only related to death, but I now know grief takes many different forms. And my self-hate, the kind I'd been suffering with my entire life, only deepened the grief of losing my son's relationship.

However, reaching this understanding was incredibly liberating. For the first time in my life, I didn't feel like I was losing my mind, there was a reasonable explanation for my pain.

Throughout the years I became a business owner in a few different arenas, none of which had much success (at least in my eyes). Needless to say, I felt like I had become a professional failure. It's hard to be successful when you're not mentally healthy. What I didn't really understand, I was still hurting and ignoring my pains; this significantly hindered my growth. I began thinking, "Would I ever be able to positively influence others to overcome?"

Then about seven years ago, I wrote down that I wanted to become an author and public speaker. But, I was terrified, as this was my greatest fear —to speak onstage—so I absolutely did nothing. Then five years later, a complete stranger met me and told me to write a book. It wasn't until then I began writing my first devotional. A year later I remember another stranger telling me, "Dede you need to get on the stage, the thing you fear the most is what you need to do!" I was puzzled and terrified all at once. Does he not know I draw a blank onstage, my leg rattles, and I would rather hide in the audience? After a long three-hour conversation with him and my husband, I prayed about it and embraced the idea.

But I didn't know how to begin, so I began where we all begin: I searched online for 'Motivational Speakers' and found Millington. He's a keynote speaker, author, and resilience coach. I needed his unique approach, as it was going to be a delicate journey for me. He was able to walk me through each step of how to tell my story, and when I was emotional, he was patient. When I was stuck, I was encouraged to keep pushing through. He was a great support in my uncertain path of keynote speaking.

I began my keynote journey to help people with their financial challenges and major depression, like the one I suffered from. But I first had to make a decision to begin my healing process from guilt, shame, and the grief associated with it. Biblical Christian therapy helped me deal with the grief that was keeping me from living, and the community God built around me has been a source of light. Forgiveness has helped me to build a better relationship with my mom. She has also done her own work and now helps others through their grief. Unfortunately, her relationship with her mother is still a challenge, but we are still in prayer.

As for my son, I continue daily to pray for his heart and peace of mind. Does he know how much I love him?

I'm not sure he does. I wonder whether he remembers the good times we had: the family game nights, our slumber parties, and our road-trip car games. But I know God will give us that back someday. I claim this promise. (Romans 8:28)

There was also a dear couple that impacted me through this emotional therapeutic journey, Pastor Dan and Patsy Gabbert. They were just the sweetest, most gentle people you could talk to; I truly heard the love of God in their voices. I was able to understand the character of God and his deep love for me. This transformed my approach in life, and re-established my self-worth. I had a new sense of hope, and professionally, business began to take-off.

Today, I help individuals find the right financial strategies. However, the combination of making monetary decisions with negative emotions can create poor economic results for you. When you're broken emotionally, you can't deal with money in a healthy way. The emotional and financial guidance that my company – 'Inspire to Live Now' – offers, also employs financial strategies the wealthy have used for centuries to build their net worth and to create passive income, while maintaining control and access to their capital.

When one area of your life is not balanced, the rest of your life is also unstable. Recovering emotionally is key to overcoming holistically. This is why being a Doctor of Naturopathy became my aspiration, using natural methods to help others to overcome and flourish. When you rebuild mentally, spiritually, financially, and physically, it harmonizes the body and mind. Now I use my experience to bring those in pain along their restorative journey.

For example, we invite our clients to a five- to ten-day retreat, to give the body the proper environment needed to bring about restoration and removal of toxins. Remember, if your nutrition isn't balanced, if you don't get enough sunlight, exercise, etc., it's just a matter of time before your body begins to feel unhealthy, and illness or disease sets in.

Recently, my new inspiration has been Lisa Nichols. I love the way she brings together various women who are willing to be vulnerable and supportive of each other. I am constantly reminded that my story of childhood trauma that seeps into adulthood isn't uncommon. What isn't so common in success is, realizing you need to find "The Way" to restoration, to succeed.

After doing one of her virtual programs, many felt like it was better than therapy. Those comments inspired me to work more closely with her, and to become one of her certified transformational coaches. She has created a community of impact, designed to help people help people. God has truly given her a gift of deep connection. Now as a transformational speaker and coach, I educate on the topics of depression, trauma, shame, anger, forgiveness, self-worth, and financial literacy.

These days, I am focused on achieving my current goals:

- Running ten-day retreats in the mountains or the Caribbean on a quarterly basis.
- Help to build stronger marriage alliances.
- Empower more women to become emotionally healthy and financially savvy.
- Operate an orphanage in Jamaica, giving children who feel neglected or unsafe, a healthier environment to grow and thrive.

To get there, I will continue to live by these five principles:

1. I am not their opinion, I'm God's opinion.
2. I must learn from my past, but I shouldn't live there.
3. I can't give what I don't have, so mental balance is important.
4. Forgive, to be freed.
5. Healing is essential for greater community impact.

As I continue to grow, I look back over the past couple of years to see the path of healing and growth I've been journeying on.

Are you ready to join me on this journey?
(Contact information in bio on following page.)

About Dr. Dede Shepherd

Dr. Dede Shepherd is a Certified Mental Health Coach, Keynote Speaker, Financial Coach, and Professional Investor. She is a graduate of the International Institute of Original Medicine, where she has completed her degree as a Doctor of Naturopathy in Original Medicine.

She has also trained under world-renowned transformational speaker, Lisa Nichols, and is a co-author with Lisa in her new book, *RISE UP!*

Dr. Dede speaks at conferences, churches, and retreats, offering workshops on financial literacy, self-forgiveness, and resilience. Her focus and passion stems from helping clients break-free from the bondage of depression, financial slavery, and shame, to create a life of intentional, purpose-filled living.

Dr. Dede adds value to her audience by inspiring attendee involvement and providing impactful techniques that apply to their emotional and spiritual development. She also speaks to audiences on the topics of health, wealth, and mental wellness. She doesn't only teach strategies but focuses on community impact and transformation.

She is excited and committed to helping women hurt less and profit more, so they too can spend more time impacting the world, fulfilling their purpose, and connecting with those they love!

Additionally, Dr. Dede enjoys serving at her local church through musical sign language ministry and supporting the youth programs with her husband Rob and their two children, Ricky and Jaden ... and let's not forget about their two little kittens, Muffin and Chun-Chunk.

Learn more at:

- www.inspiretolivenow.com
- www.cashvaluesolution.com

CHAPTER 5

"WHAT I DIDN'T KNOW"

BY DR. FRED ROUSE

Not all stories end with, "...and they lived happily ever after."
Sometimes, the best we can hope for is the chance to say goodbye.

In 2018, my wife Teri and I checked our messages after being on vacation. I had a message from my younger brother, Chris. "Fred, I just want to let you know, Dad isn't doing well. Maybe you want to reach out to him. I know he'd really like to hear from you."

I hadn't talked to my dad in forty years.

———•••———

I grew up in the 60s in South Philadelphia, lower middle class, part of a large Italian family. My dad's family were Germans from Grand Rapids, Michigan. My mom was a local Italian girl. I was their firstborn. My parents had three more children, Diana Lynn, Renee, and Chris.

We got together at Grandmom's house, three blocks away, for Sunday dinners. Relatives were always around and provided a sense of community and belonging. But by the time I was a teenager, times were tough.

At home, Mom and Dad were divorcing, and it was not amicable. The state required they be separated for a year before the divorce could be finalized, so Dad lived in a room upstairs. At one point, homelife got so stressful, I left for a couple of weeks and lived on the street.

After Dad moved out, I moved back in. It didn't take long for my mom to find love again and she married a nice guy named Bob, who worked as an upholsterer.

It seemed like high school was just teachers telling me what I'd already read in the text books. I could read the books myself. What did I need them for? After two years, I quit and joined the Coast Guard.

My dad wasn't the most affectionate guy in the world. After he left, the general consensus (fostered by my mom) was that Dad was a 'controlling asshole'. Since I didn't have a tight relationship with him anyway, that wasn't too difficult for me to believe.

In my five years in the Coast Guard, at the tail end of the Vietnam war, while I was running Search and Rescue missions out of Cape May, NJ, I saw Dad for an occasional Sunday breakfast. But basically, I went my way; he went his.

The rest of the family still met for Sunday dinners. When Grandpa died, we started having Tuesday or Thursday dinners at my mom's because that's when everybody could make it.

My younger sister Diana Lynn was a good-looking girl and ended up getting pregnant. Nobody in the family knew who the father was. She left home and eventually moved in with a lesbian. She changed her last name, and my father pretty much disowned her. My mom raised Diana Lynn's daughter and after grade school, Tanya went to live with my other sister, Renee.

Renee was into the latest fashions and social things. She worked at the Navy Yard and married Pete, who worked for the postal office. They live in an upper middle-class section twenty minutes away in New Jersey.

Then there's my younger brother Chris. Chris was always a kind person. He's a big guy with a big heart. In high school, Chris took a mechanical drawing class. My uncle, who worked for Scott paper, designed the machines that made the paper at the plant in Chester. He said, "Chris is really good." Chris ended up making this his profession.

Life was coasting along with a few bumps in the road. I got married, had a son – Matthew. Then got divorced. A couple years later I met my second wife, Teri, and she's the love of my life. With her daughter, Kristen, and my son, Matthew, we became a new family. On one of our family dinner nights, after the rest of the family left, Mom let me know she and Bob didn't have a lot of money. Retirement (forced) was coming up fast. Here's where my story goes off the rails.

When Mom and Bob both retired, they couldn't afford to stay in their house. At one of the family dinners, I said to my siblings, "Look, everybody chip in a couple hundred dollars a month, then Mom and Bob can stay in the house." But nobody could afford that. It was frustrating because, of all of us, I was the only one without a salary coming in or a company/government pension and benefits.

By that time, I had 20 years in business doing real estate, investment management, and financial advising. I gave my mom $900 a month in a sort of reverse mortgage-life annuity situation. Being a 'proud' person, my mom didn't want any charity. She insisted that we do this through my business. From a business perspective, I was taking an extreme risk. I paid off their existing credit card debt and the remaining first mortgage and agreed to provide monthly payments that would increase as they needed for the rest of both of their lives. In exchange, I would get back all the money advanced plus interest after the house was sold and the remainder would be split with the remaining three siblings.

For years I had advised my clients to always have the paperwork drawn up and signed or else, when the money comes in, there will be problems. I also warned them against doing business with family members, which usually ended in disaster. I recalled this advice when I was making the offer to Mom. *But this is my mom*, I reasoned.

For the next ten years, I cut a check every month. Some months it was tough, but Mom and Bob got that money no matter what was happening in my life or business. Then Mom got sick. I hadn't drawn up the paperwork yet (why didn't I listen to my own advice?) so I hustled to get it prepared. Mom got sicker and was hospitalized.

While in the hospital, she signed the paperwork. She was of sound mind and had no hesitations about making official the agreement we'd been living under for a decade. Then my siblings got word. They'd all known I was giving Mom and Bob money and acknowledged on several occasions how, if I hadn't, they would've been forced into an apartment long ago. It would've been the final indecency, publicly acknowledging that they were broke.

Now, my siblings were accusing me of stealing money from them. "Wait a minute," I argued. "No one was willing to help out. I had to do this on my own to keep them in the house."

Originally, the plan was to sell the house when Mom died and split the proceeds four ways. The siblings knew this. But Renee accused me of brainwashing Mom in the agreement. Everyone was in an uproar.

And then, my family stopped talking to me. Even my teenaged son Matthew, who had dropped out of high school and left home a couple years prior, wouldn't acknowledge me after hearing from his Aunt Renee what "I was doing to the family."

Then Mom died.

We only heard of her death because Kristen saw it on Facebook and called Teri. I didn't attend the funeral because I didn't know about it. A few days later, I was served papers. My siblings were suing me.

I was asked to provide twelve years of bank records because the attorney didn't believe I'd actually written all those checks. The animosity was so intense, I ended up settling the case. I still held the mortgage but now the interest was cut to near nothing. I was angry for years at both the loss of the interest, which would have been my 'pension' and the way the family turned on me for doing what none of them was willing to do: help Mom and Bob financially.

Bob lived in the house until his death in 2019. One day I got a notice the bank was looking for a payoff figure; I still had a mortgage on the house. The offer was greatly reduced and I lost $250,000 in equity on the deal. I got my base money back and very little interest. When the house sold, the siblings split the money three ways.

Prior to Bob's death and selling the house, I didn't hear from anyone in my family until the summer of 2018 when my brother Chris called to tell me about Dad. Teri and I made arrangements to fly down to South Carolina where my dad had been hospitalized.

Teri shared how nervous she was to finally meet him because all she'd ever heard at family dinners was what a cold, unloving father he'd been. But we went, and we actually had a really nice visit. Dad was kind, soft-spoken, and polite. For the first time in my life, I was able to have several long, face-to-face conversations with him, man-to-man.

My dad reminded me of the time we dug out the basement, which was clay, so we could turn it into a gym. He had completed some bodybuilding correspondence course. He never won anything, but he got opportunities to compete.

I hold that side of him up again a softer side, which he also talked about during our visit. He experimented with different kinds of art. Dad tinkered with painting for a while; he tried doing sculpture, chipping away at stone. This was a side of him he didn't share with many people.

When we left, I told Teri I wanted to come back and see him in a month or so to continue rebuilding our relationship.

A few weeks later, while I was away on a business trip, Teri got a call saying Dad's condition had worsened. This was on Wednesday. I flew home from Seattle on Thursday and Friday we took the first flight to South Carolina.

When we walked in the hospital room, Dad asked, "What are you guys doing here?" We told him we'd come to see him and bring him some homemade pizzelles (he loved pizzelles). We spent the day with him and I got to speak with him privately for a couple of hours.

I knew Dad had a half-brother who'd visited us one year. I have a memory of him driving me around on his motorcycle. Later, that same brother got sent to Vietnam and died over there. That was the first time I ever saw my father cry.

Growing up, I knew Dad had been in the Navy. What I didn't know... what he hadn't revealed to any of his children, was that he'd been in the Korean War. Embedded in a Marine combat unit. Upon hearing that, the puzzle pieces began to drop into place. The things he saw...the things he had to do...

War changes a person. But my father's detachment from his children, his anger, wasn't because he didn't love us, it was because something inside him changed while he was over there. He came back different. I don't know how to put into words all my feelings, but my eyes are not dry while I type this.

Friday night, we went to dinner and Saturday morning, we flew back to Philadelphia. We got home, unpacked our bags, and the phone rang. And it was Helen, my dad's second wife. "Your dad just passed away." We were the last people to be with him. I was the last person in his family to see and talk with him.

Teri tells me she thinks Dad did that on purpose. That he was at peace enough because he'd told his oldest son the truth of his story, and could finally let go.

After Dad died, I called to let my siblings know. One of the things Dad shared was his concern for the family. He knew it was in shambles since Mom died. He never said anything nasty about my mother. Never. At any point. But he knew problems existed. He knew Renee was a problem. But he wanted everybody to come back together.

My brother Chris arranged to have a funeral ceremony on the U.S.S. New Jersey, anchored in Camden. Renee came. Tanya and her husband Joey were there. The kids were there. It was a nice ceremony. Afterward, we invited everybody back to our house. Having them come to our home felt like the right thing and could be a beginning.

The family agreed to come. Hours later, Chris was the only one who showed up. But it gave us time to tell our side of the story, and Chris started to understand what actually had happened. He apologized for getting sucked into the situation with Renee. This was the beginning of a new relationship that has since continued to grow and flourish. The rest of the family, however, has not reunited. To this day, nobody wants to upset Rene. She is skilled in the art of steamrolling. Renee and Pete, Tanya and Joey are out there somewhere. And Matthew, who has a story of his own.

———————◆●●———————

Life will knock you down; there's no avoiding it. The question is how we respond. When all this went down with my siblings, especially for the 18 months it took for the case to flush through the legal system, I was pissed. All the attorney's fees, all for nothing. I was holding on to so much anger ... for years! Then I reached a point where I had to let it go. Because when you're angry, you're stuck in that moment in time. I wanted to move forward. So I did. And life got better. I have my wonderful wife, we have Kristen, who recently got married, and we have a place in Delaware on the water that I love going to.

In 2019, I gave my tax practice away (literally, I didn't sell it, I gave it away). After forty years in financial services, the last twenty-eight as a Certified Financial Planner, it was time to shift my business model. Years before, I'd created a small program that showed people how to make money by trading just two commodities. Now, teaching others this program is my purpose in retirement. I have a big impact on the few people I let in every month. Some of my students are making $30,000 a month using the program. I'm happy and doing what I love with people I love.

There's a silver lining in all this heartbreak. In one phone call, the wounds from my father began to mend. When somebody is at the end of their life and they call for you, you go. No matter what they've done, you just go.

The hope, though, is that people won't wait until the end of their life to reach out and begin the healing process.

About Dr. Fred

Dr. Fred Rouse, aka 'The REAL Money Doctor', is an award-winning and best-selling author of multiple books. He is a retired Certified Financial Planner (CFP®) and the nation's leading authority on short-window retirement planning.

Near the end of the Vietnam War, he served five years in the US Coast Guard running small boats for search-and-rescue. He spent ten years as a Registered Respiratory Therapist (RRT), starting in a small community hospital and ending up at a large inner-city university teaching hospital working the ICU, CCU, Pediatric ICU, Level 1 Trauma, and Level 1 NICU. On the side, he founded a business in financial services, eventually earning his credentials as a Certified Financial Planner™—which he held for the last 28 of his 40 years in financial services before he retired.

In his early days, Dr. Rouse turned a $5,000 account into $2 million dollars in two years. Attempting to double that, he lost it all in six months. To pay the bills, he went back to nights and weekends as an RRT, while weekdays building his tax and business advisory service by serving individuals and small businesses with 0-6 employees.

Ten years and $350,000 later, he had researched, developed, tested, and retested a financial system freeing him to retire. The stock market crash in 2008 failed to dent his system's predictable cash flow results, which consistently outperformed the markets. Two years more and the system was a course for his clients—men and women desperately needing predictable cash flow for the option to retire sooner—or at all. Short Window Retirement Planning is the only system exclusively for the unique needs of people ages 50 and older. Younger people use it to get a jump start on their retirement.

Now in his retirement, Dr. Rouse wants to help others get, protect, and enjoy their money, life, and retirement. His small program shows others how to enjoy retirement sooner regardless of world events, independent of stock market ups and downs.

Dr. Rouse has been quoted in *The Wall Street Journal, FORBES, Newsweek, Inc Magazine*, and more. His work has been seen on ABC, NBC, CBS, Fox, CNBC networks and on other TV and cable outlets.

Dr Fred, his wife Dr Teri, and their dog Gus-Gus split their time between their home in the Philadelphia suburbs and their shore house on the bay in southern Delaware.

Learn more at:

- https://DrRouseNow.com/
- https://DrFredRouse.com/

CHAPTER 6

IT'S TIME TO TAKE FLIGHT

BY RACQUEL BERRY-BENJAMIN

I come from a family of fishermen in the U.S. Virgin Islands, which is where I grew up. We would catch what we could, sell what we could, and what was left would come home with us.

While we were poor financially, we were rich in love and laughter. This is the case with many poor families—they struggle and live paycheck-to-paycheck, never getting ahead financially—but nothing could compare to the bond they share.

One of the most crippling effects of poverty is that it causes people to remain stagnant and be fearful to even think they deserve more. The popular trap of 'getting a good government job' permeated my community and I fell into it for two decades.

On its face, there is nothing wrong with serving in local government and I've lived long enough to see that it was part of God's plan for my life to have had that experience. However, I grew up hearing everyone around me push the idea of getting a 'good government job' to get 'good government benefits.' At that time, a government job was viewed as 'the job to get' because it was believed to be stable, safe, and secure. While it was not a belief I subscribed to, I still fell into the trap because I had one young child and was pregnant with a second. Still, I knew there was more for me out there.

When I was in elementary school, *The Oprah Show* had just started, and we all came home to watch Oprah. I admired Oprah and the businessmen and women I saw wearing suits on her show and in my community. I knew from that young age that I wanted to be a businesswoman. Back then, I had no way of knowing what being a businesswoman was all about, but it looked like these people had money, and I wanted what they had so I could provide for myself and my family.

As I grew into adulthood and began thinking about my life and career, I quickly fell in love with teaching. I was caught between a head and a heart space because I wanted to be as far away from poverty as possible, but a teacher's salary would not help me get there, at least not in the timeframe I wanted. Plus, I had other teachers telling me, "You're still young, you can make more money doing something else because teachers don't make any money." Although I understood that teaching would not fully change my financial story, it was the *'little Racquels'* I saw every day at the school where I worked, who were also growing up in poverty that caused my heart to win over my head, and my 20-year journey in education began.

As someone who enjoys travel, I spend a lot of time on airplanes thinking about life and how the world works. One of the things I often think about is how airplanes themselves get off the ground and safely remain in the air. Some years ago, I learned about the four forces of flight: drag, gravity, lift and thrust. Drag and gravity are considered negative forces; while lift and thrust are considered positive ones. However, both forces are necessary for an airplane to rise and take flight. Through this research, I found many important parallels between flying and life itself.

Drag is the air resistance that slows the forward movement of an airplane—the force that pulls it backward. The drag in your life can be patterns of behavior that keep pulling you back into the same cycles that are stopping you from rising and growing at the speed and levels you want. It also involves having false beliefs about the things that keep you comfortable in life.

It was never my plan to work 30 years as a government employee and then retire; I'm even surprised I stayed for 20 years. I wanted to do more and knew that starting my own business was a goal I would achieve. Over the course of my career in education, I would set dates to transition into full-time business, but there would always be setbacks—drags—to keep me comfortable where I was.

Drags, for me, came in many forms—from my children getting sick to remind me of how valuable my government-issued health insurance was to my facing financial challenges of every kind—that reminded me of how safe it felt to get a steady paycheck every two weeks. Situations like these always pulled me back into the cycle of being an employee and not launching out into full-time entrepreneurship.

There are times when we all feel stuck and unable to move ahead in life. When it comes to flying, this is likened to **gravity**—the force that pulls objects downward. If you take two steps forward, something inevitably happens that causes you to take three steps backward. These could be falsehoods you were conditioned to believe or the strongholds of bad decisions you made in the past that keep resurfacing.

Becoming a mother at sixteen was a form of gravity that could have held me down. However, I was determined not to live a life of poverty that I had experienced early in life. I wouldn't allow being a teenage mother to stop me. In fact, this experience taught me how to remain focused in the face of obstacles. I had to exercise mind control, determination, and say a whole lot of prayers to remain positive and motivated. At this point, I was even more determined to finish school because I was now seeing the world through a different lens, one with greater responsibility, and it was up to me to strive for better or settle for the life I lived as a child. I was determined to achieve the former.

Throughout my career, I have had my share of gravitational or 'crabs in a barrel' experiences while climbing the career ladder. I have always challenged the status quo and taken the path less traveled. This has caused negative reactions in some who could not stand to see me progressing. I never took any of these experiences personally because I learned early that opposition would come with the rise. Once you decide to take action toward your goals and dreams, you will be talked about and targeted. Your actions will activate the critic in others and if you are fearful of being judged, you will remain on the sidelines in the game of life.

Despite the many gravitational pulls I've experienced in my personal and professional life, yet 'still I rise.' And so can you. Here's the thing—I did nothing extraordinary to move ahead. I simply had the courage to make up my mind, put action to my thoughts, and not settle for the status quo.

When my heart won over my head and I decided to embark on a career in education, it was because I wanted to make an impact on the lives of those *'little Racquels'*—a decision that afforded me many opportunities, culminating in my leading the USVI's public education system as the commissioner of education, the highest-ranking position in the field. However, this was not without taking risks and courageous steps that others who were playing it safe would not take. For example, I heavily invested in continuing education by way of conferences, mentorships, and specialized training that would enhance my knowledge and skills in education, leadership, finance, and business. Furthermore, during my education career, I chose not to work in unionized positions to ensure a level of freedom and autonomy in my work and salary.

The **Lift** in flight is the upward force created by the movement of air above and below the wings of an airplane. It is the force that directly opposes the weight of an airplane and holds the aircraft in the air.

The lift force in our lives are the people, places, things, ideas, etc., that inspire us to do and be more. It is our network of mentors, coaches, and supporters. Their collective shoulders are the rock upon which we stand. The lift force in my life has steadily evolved, as there is a season for everything under the sun. Some people are constant, like my parents, who have always been a source of encouragement and support.

As I entered the field of education, there were persons who inspired and mentored me, and were always there to offer advice on everything from teaching to leadership. When I eventually transitioned to the world of business, my network expanded, and I gained new mentors. Having mentors in both fields served as the lift force that upheld me, especially in my most difficult times. These are people who never give up on you and want to see you succeed.

Thrust is the final force that comes into play that makes air travel possible. It is what moves the plane forward through the air and is produced by a jet engine or propeller. Similarly in life, thrust is that internal force that fuels and lights a fire within you, causing you to take action. It can be referred to as your 'WHY.' It keeps you moving forward, despite the hurdles life throws your way.

At the end of my commissionership, I decided not to return to the field of traditional education, but well-meaning peers and colleagues from across the country kept offering employment opportunities that paid twice the salary I made as commissioner. However, I knew it was time for me to dedicate my time and talent to fulfilling my life's work and building generational wealth in my family at the pace and level I desired. Taking another government job in the same fragmented education system in another part of the country would not allow me to make the level of impact I wanted to make, nor the income I desired.

I declined the offers and dedicated myself to fully realizing my childhood dream of elevating from poverty, building my empire, and helping others to do the same. Although I had achieved financial success by this point in my life, I still had my empire to build and much work to do helping others to do the same. I decided the next phase of my life would be dedicated to doing just that.

As a little girl, I always knew I did not want to live in poverty. Depending on government assistance, not having enough money to meet basic needs, and being subjected to behaviors and mindsets borne of poverty, were things I knew all too well and desperately I wanted out. Furthermore, I did not want my children and future generations of my family to have those same experiences with poverty.

This is and has always been my 'WHY'. It has thrust me into striving to be the best me possible and to break the cycle of generational poverty within my family. Most importantly, it gave me the resilience to keep getting up from each punch life threw at me (and there have been many).

You don't know how to make money and leave a legacy if you don't know how to do that for your family and I wanted to change that. Now, through writing, speaking, advocacy, and developing educational products, I am helping families by drawing on my past experiences and introducing them to the tools I used to find my way out.

Champions for Financial Literacy, Inc., and Pathway to Prosperity are organizations I created to bring financial and economic education to others. I know from decades of experience that the traditional education system is long overdue in bringing these very important topics to the classroom. I believe financial and economic literacy are the missing links that would give children the insight, knowledge, and skills they need to make, manage, and multiply money to escape the shackles of poverty. But financial education is not just for young people, it's for everyone.

In public housing communities, like the one I grew up in, children are raised in homes where neither they nor their parents understand money and how it works. It is my personal belief that financial and economic education must be valued and taught at home, in schools, and within the community. Champions for Financial Literacy and Pathway to Prosperity will help bridge the gap.

The way I see it is that our best approach to weathering the negative forces of life is to accept them as vital and necessary parts of the design of our lives. The key is to figure out how to respond to them and create balance.

Did you know that the opposing forces of the airplane balance each other out? It's true. The lift equals gravity and the thrust equals drag. If there is any imbalance between the thrust and the drag, the plane will fall. The same is true for you. It might be difficult to accept, but not having enough bad experiences can stop you from taking flight. When you've been tugged and pulled hard enough from negative experiences, something inside lifts and thrusts you forward into your destiny. In the words of the great Frederick Douglass, "If there is no struggle, there is no progress."

Negative forces come in the form of people's thoughts, words, and actions. It might not be possible to distance yourself from some of these people because they may be family or close friends of your family. But the key is to decide how you will create balance when facing such opposition and still be able to fly. Remember, the airplane needs both negative and positive forces to remain airborne, and you need both to keep rising in life. The negativity of poverty while growing up and the negativity of people I have experienced as an adult were the catalysts that pushed me to keep striving for what I knew was mine to have. It was my inner determination that allowed me to be triumphant each time. Negative forces give us perspective and help us to strive for more. In the words of our wise and fearless First Lady Michelle Obama, "When they go low, we go high."

Positive forces are more powerful than negative forces. Darkness cannot overshadow light, but light can brighten darkness. *"The light shines in the darkness, and the darkness has not overcome it."* – John 1:5 NIV. Turn on your bulb and be a light for others.

Are you ready to Rise Up? Spread your wings. It's time to take flight.

See you at the top!

About Racquel

Racquel Berry-Benjamin is an accomplished education professional, transformational speaker, astute businesswoman in real estate investing and business finance. She is the founder of Pathway to Prosperity and Champions for Financial Literacy, Inc., organizations created to navigate families and communities toward a brighter economic future.

But more importantly, Racquel is a luminary. She is a change agent on a powerful mission to turn impoverished pasts into wealth-sustaining legacies for generations to come. Driven by a relentless commitment to shift the mindsets of families around wealth, Racquel's personal and professional journey is a narrative of resilience and a testament to the transformative power of education.

While serving as Commissioner of Education in the United States Virgin Islands, Racquel's vision of transformation, which earned the Virgin Islands Department of Education national recognition, included a five-year strategic plan and *A Portrait of a Virgin Islands' Graduate* – a framework that stipulated the integration of financial and economic education into the local public education system.

Racquel's childhood in poverty, two decades of trailblazing in the field of education, and her studies in personal finance, all inform her authority and advocacy on financial education for individuals and families. The two-time bestselling author is committed to redefining the narrative for underserved communities by using her "Pathways to Prosperity Generational Wealth Framework" to start and change conversations about money.

Now using the world as her classroom to continue her mission of empowerment through education, Racquel's work in this next phase of her career is to lead a financial awakening to break the chains of economic hardship, and light the way to generational wealth for those bold and brave enough to answer the call.

Known for her uplifting messages, Racquel brings her wisdom and signature style to stages across the globe. A captivating and powerful speaker, Racquel is guaranteed to leave audiences educated and empowered to reimagine their family's legacy and financial destiny. Racquel honors God in all she does, values family and takes great pride in her Caribbean roots and culture in the United States Virgin Islands, where she lives with her husband, children and close-knit community of extended family and friends.

Connect with Racquel on her YouTube channel, @RacquelSpeaks, where she continues her mission of empowering families and entrepreneurs with relevant and relatable information to help them make, manage, and multiply their money.

For more information,

- email: racquel@racquelspeaks.com.

CHAPTER 7

BEYOND THE ODDS

BY FRANK BRESE

It was a cold day in the Northwest when they dropped the bomb on me. After twelve years with the Japanese, building their American business in kitchen ventilation from the ground up to five million dollars, they decided to ditch the U.S./Canadian market.

"Thanks a lot, but we're going to go chase China. It's a bigger market," they said.

And just like that, at 61 years old, I was out of a job with only eleven months to figure out what the heck I was going to do. Panic mode set in real quick. I had a home and roots in the city, and I sure wasn't looking to relocate. They were ready to dump $550,000 worth of inventory we had in Cincinnati to some liquidator. You know how that goes – five or ten cents on the dollar. But I'm not one to back down easily.

So, I went to them and said, "Listen, instead of selling it off for peanuts, why don't we work out a deal? I'll buy that inventory from you at a higher price." That caught their interest, but dealing with this Japanese company after working for them for twelve years was like talking to a brick wall. To them, I was suddenly an outsider.

Negotiations ensued for eleven intense months. They wanted over a million dollars for the company name, which I didn't even like because Americans couldn't pronounce it right. The company was Fuji Industrial USA, and the product name was "FUJIOH," which I was not interested in. So, I told them I'd form my own company, buy the inventory, and pay them a better price. For months, we fought over how much, what product I would take, some product that was dead, some that wasn't moving, etc. The banks weren't any help either after the market crash. They'd only lend if you had two years of profitability, and even then, they would only lend a small portion of my cash profit, which was no help.

I had to get creative.

"Look, I tried my best. I have my home, but I can't afford the deal we agreed on."

After rounds of negotiation and 56-page contracts, they agreed to carry a contract for me. But here's the kicker – a personal guarantee for everything I owned: House, cars, my half-interest in a rental property, motorcycles, and the business. If I missed one payment...it was all gone.

"Are you out of your mind? Is this the best deal you could get?" my CPA asked in disbelief. It was the best deal I could get. I believed if I lost 50% of the customers I had, I would still be profitable based on the changes I would make, reducing cost and overhead. I wouldn't be anywhere near as profitable as I am today, but at least I felt I had a 50% chance.

The one big factor in my decision was this–if it didn't go my way, if I did lose 50% of my customers, was I willing to stay dedicated enough to the cause and to the end goal to do whatever I needed to do to make it happen? Yes, I was, and I signed that contract with the weight of the world on my shoulders. Everyone thought I was nuts, and if I'm honest, I probably believed them.

The first payment of $50,000 was due in forty-five days. I had enough equity in my home to make that first payment. From there, all calendars work the same. You make a payment on the first of the month, you better hope you're in a month with thirty-one days because you only have thirty more days before you make another $50,000 payment.

Meanwhile, I had to struggle with redesigning the product, finding

U.S. manufacturers, and surviving without income. I had sales but no money coming in. I was all in–no safety nets or trust funds, just a stubborn belief in myself. If I failed, I'd lose everything.

For seven months, I worked tirelessly, selling invoices to a factoring company that helped me float the days and weeks I needed between invoices and payments. I lost sleep and didn't eat. I shed 29 pounds from the stress and sheer anxiety of it all, but I made it. *I paid off the Japanese in seven months, in December 2012.* Since then, I've had a line of credit with the bank but never used a penny of it, never had to.

That's my story – an Italian guy from the inner city of Cleveland taking on the Japanese, the banks, and a ticking clock. Against all odds, I came out on top – with VMI as a thriving manufacturer and distributor of kitchen ventilation and related products. Our customer base includes major kitchen cabinet manufacturers throughout the U.S. and Canada. In addition to our large O.E.M. customers, we have more than 250 dealers, including small custom-cabinet shops, kitchen and bath dealers, designers, and contractors.

Some ask me, "Frank. How'd you do it?" It was hard, but it wasn't that complicated. Besides taking on a wild risk at the right time, it is all about the customer. Do what your competitors won't. If you want to win in business, do your due diligence. Find out everything that your competition does for their customers. Do every one of those at a minimum. But more importantly, if you want to ensure your success, and this is based on my history, find out all the things that they don't do for their customers or refuse to do for their customers. Do as many of those things as possible, and you won't have to advertise. Believe me, the word of mouth will come.

My personal cell phone is on my business card. If a question comes up, usually technical or something, because of my experience exclusively in kitchen ventilation for over twenty years, my dealers give my number to their customers. They can call me, or I will call them. I take cell phone calls until 7:30 in the evening (my time on the West Coast), seven days a week.

Kraftmaid, one of the largest cabinet manufacturers in the United States, is my largest customer. They are in every Home Depot and

Lowe's store throughout the United States and Canada. For the last 21 years, I've been the exclusive supplier for every liner and blower that Kraftmaid has sold in a Home Depot and Lowe's store.

I take calls for 50% of the people who buy at Home Depot and Lowe's and tell their wives, "Hey, honey, we don't need a contractor. I can do this." And then they get into it and don't know the difference between a phillips-head screwdriver and a flat blade. If they call, customer service will not walk them through an installation because they've never installed it. Instead, they give them my number, and I spend hours and don't charge for that consultation.

I hear it all the time, "Frank! You could make thousands of dollars by charging a simple $100 fee to talk with me!" Sure. But I don't, and it seems to be working just fine. Why? Because my competitors would never do this. It sets us apart. Instead, my competitors put the demand back on their dealers to try and fix the problems.

I tell my dealers, "If you've got a problem with my product, you just need to call or email me. Or you can have your customer call me, or I will call your customer. When I'm done solving the problem, I will follow up, and get back to you to let you know that it's been taken care of, and how it's been taken care of."

If you are willing to do what your competitors won't do,
it will set your business above the rest.

In closing, here are a few points of perspective and encouragement from my story for you to consider that can help you in your journey to success:

1. **Empathy leads to trust, which builds relationships.** I think a little unconventionally, but with my customers, my dealers, and everyone else, I try to put myself in their place. That's why I've been so successful in sales over the years. I jump onto the other side of the desk and say, "Okay, if I was listening to a salesperson, does he know his product? Is he trying to help me solve my problem? He realizes my biggest concerns, and he's trying to address those." And, if I can't address the problem, I'll even recommend a customer to somebody else, even a competitor, if necessary! My customers

believe I care. They understand, and it leads to success. It's pretty simple, really.

2. **Believe in yourself.** Stay on the positive side of what you believe you can accomplish yourself. Avoid listening to the negative naysayers, including family and friends. I mean, had I told people what I would do and sign that contract and what I was willing to risk, I assure you, nobody would have told me, "Yeah, that's a good idea. Go ahead." I felt if I'm going to lose everything I have, I'm not going to do it on a $5,000 bet. I will bet on the one thing I know for sure: that's me. Sometimes, it takes believing in yourself, which may be all you have. Do it anyway.

3. **Life isn't always fair, and things can change in a heartbeat.** It's amazing. A guy I did business with years ago once told me, "Frank, I'm going to tell you. It doesn't take very long to go from the penthouse to the doghouse." Things can change very quickly. If you understand this early, it will help you to be prepared and overcome what might otherwise be too difficult to face.

4. **Out-work and out-hustle the competition.** Be willing to put in the time and the sacrifice. I didn't go on vacations for 15 to 18 years. Of course, that was my choice, but it was what I decided to do to succeed in my business.

5. **When battling self-doubt, don't give up!** I took a lot of hits. I've had self-doubts. Was I scared? At times, I thought, "You've never done this before. Can you really pull this off? I mean, what if it doesn't work?" Remember that just because everything tends to fall down around you and you think that you've got no way out, you do. You really do.

The way I looked at my situation was, "If it doesn't work out, what's the worst thing that can happen? If I lose everything? I'm not dead. I'm still alive. I can start over. It's not going to be easy. But I can do this."

I knew the risk would be worth the reward. Some people say without risk, the reward isn't there. My other philosophy in life would be that if you're not living on the edge, you're taking up too much room in this world, but you don't want to live on the edge 100% of the time. Timing matters.

6. **Sometimes, the worst thing that can happen is the best thing**. When I look back, the Japanese company pulling the plug on me is one of the best things that could have happened to me, though I couldn't see it then. I would have stayed as a national sales manager. Sure, I would have made good money, but I would still be under their thumb, and I never would have been able to reach the income levels, the philanthropy, and everything else that I can do now to make the world a better place.

We never see the horizon during the storm, but
it doesn't change the fact that it's there.

Don't give up and do whatever it takes to RISE UP!

About Frank

Frank Brese has more than 24 years' experience in Kitchen Ventilation products and installation. He offers his vast knowledge of information to both individuals and companies – before, during and after purchase. Most of his customers have been with him for more than 15 years.

Frank is the President of VMI Inc which is sold under the Air-Pro brand name. In addition to the standard products offered, which include blowers, liners, and wood hoods, VMI offers modified standard and full custom products based on customers' needs and requests.

VMI, Inc is a manufacturer and supplier of Kitchen Ventilation products to some of the largest kitchen cabinet manufacturers in the United States and Canada. VMI's customer base includes Cabinet Companies both large and small, Kitchen and Bath dealers, Distributors, Wholesalers, Designers and Contractors.

VMI is a long-lime member of the National Kitchen and Bath Association (NKBA) and participates in the annual KBIS show to support the Kitchen and Bath Industry.

VMI's corporate office is located in Redmond, Washington and maintains a warehouse in Cincinnati, Ohio with more than $500,000 in inventory.

You can contact Frank at:

- sales@vmi-inc.net

Or visit the website at:

- www.vmi-inc.net

CHAPTER 8

HARRIET AND ME

BY KAROL V. BROWN

It wasn't the first time James hit me, but it was the time I remember the most. There were other times, but this is the memory I keep going back to.

James and I were high school sweethearts in Dayton, Ohio where we grew up. We dated, fell in love, and got married in 1974. I began my career as a dietitian, James was a barber at a military base, and we started to build a life together. We liked Ohio, and probably would have spent the rest of our lives there, but it seemed as if everyone James met in the Officers club barber shop, would talk about the beauty of the pacific northwest. "You've got to see Washington State," everyone said. "You've just got to." So, we vacationed in Seattle, and agreed we would move our family there. It was three years later, but without knowing anyone there, James and I packed up our three small children and headed west.

We moved to Washington State in September, and I had my job by June working as a dietitian at the VA hospital. I loved that job and stayed there thirty years. The position was challenging but it allowed me to help people and serve on various committees. I became the African American Employee Equal Opportunity coordinator, which included planning black history month. I was the Federal Women's Program coordinator for a period of time and planned Women's History month events. I was on the employee stress management team and I managed MOVE! – a Veterans Weight Management program. And, at our church in Tacoma, I spent ten years coordinating events for breast cancer awareness.

Around 1998, I became fascinated with Harriet Tubman. I think I was drawn to her willingness to help others and I admired her courage, determination, and ongoing faith. She never stopped trying to help people. Her story is of a woman, who was unlikely as a little girl growing up in slavery, to be remembered 200 years later, but she is. And changed the lives of so many.

I started researching her life and began portraying Harriet Tubman at events. Harriet lived to be 93 years old and did a lot more than the Underground Railroad, so I portrayed her as an elderly woman as I learned and perfected the art of storytelling. James would go with me. We traveled all over Washington State and James would sing Negro Spirituals during these events—James had a great singing voice.

After I had studied all the books I could find on Harriet Tubman, and shared her stories, I felt I had a new perspective on her. So. I thought about making my on-stage program one aspect of my offerings and also have a book and an in-classroom curriculum. It was written on the 5th-grade reading level and has a glossary in the back.

My first book was, *30 Lessons in Love, Leadership, and Legacy from Harriet Tubman.* This book has 30 short chapters, each lesson includes a quote by a well-known leader, a first-person story as I portray Harriet Tubman, and discussion questions and prompts to write in the workbook/journal. The end of the book talks about Harriet Tubman providing a home for homeless people and one of the tips always stuck with me; be grateful. I wrote a second book that has become the launching pad to my new focus on my life, *The Harriet Tubman Way, An Inspirational Guide to Self-Love, Empowerment and Legendary Leadership for Girls.*

Life moved on for James and me; the kids were growing up and before we knew it they were out on their own which brings us to the moment that I was telling you about...that time when James hit me.

James and I moved back to Ohio, we were in our 60s and this is where I would retire. We were driving when it happened. Through a neighborhood we used to live in decades before and something just came over James. We were talking and he suddenly was accusing me of things from forty years ago; infidelities, unfaithfulness, things that never happened but to him it not only did happen but occurred yesterday.

This anger came over him and he kept asking me specifics about allegations from decades before, *where did you go that morning, where the mud on the tires come from, what road did you use, what was the traffic like that time of day?*

And as I'm trying to figure out where all of this was coming from, that's when he hit me. And what's interesting is that in the movies, when the man hits the woman, the argument stops. But with James, it did not. He kept screaming at me, getting more angry even after the hit. *Tell me the truth—tell me the truth! Then he would call me all sorts of names as well as—why did you marry me?* and *you don't love me!*

From that moment on, I never knew when it would happen again. Everything would be fine, we'd be sitting at dinner and then something would snap and he would try to get me to admit that I was with someone—*I saw you trying to talk to the guy who moved us in the house, who were you talking to on the phone?* It became a constant battle.

It got to the point where I wouldn't ride in the car with him. Because if we were home, I could escape because my home office had a futon and a door that locked. It was just us alone in that big house, I hadn't retired yet but James' health wasn't the greatest and he stopped working years before this. And since James never took responsibility for our problems, so he said, *"Well, maybe we should have an exchange student come stay with us or something, that way I won't be so upset."*

So at this time, my sister was raising her grandchildren and my mother was living with her. Mom was 99 years old at the time and since we had this big house we decided to have mom move in with us. And for the most part, we all seemed to all get along fine for a while. My mother, well, she and James were never warm to each other, but it didn't take long for things to become cold.

I was getting close to retirement, and James had always talked about going to China. James had not been working for a while, I was the breadwinner, so I took some of my retirement money and we planned a trip to China. Before we went, I bought security cameras for the house, that way I could check them from my phone no matter where we were. When we got back from China, James began using those cameras to keep an eye on me.

We still had our arguments. We could be watching TV and then he'd suddenly be screaming, accusing me of something. I could feel the stress on my mother and as soon as James would begin to yell, I would take my mother to the other room and lock the door.

I checked myself into hotels at least six times before my mother moved in, and moved my mother into hotels another two times. And James would always convince me that it was going to be okay, and I'd come back. I hadn't talked to anyone about what was going on, we didn't go to church, we were very isolated at that time. I never went out the back door in case the neighbor was out there because James would accuse me of having an affair with him—I didn't even know the man's name.

One particular night we were in bed watching a movie. When the movie was over, James went to the bathroom and when he came back he was angry as can be. I got in the habit of picking up on the mood changes early and when I saw them, I would grab my pillow and head for the other room and lock the door. He would call me all kinds of names through the door. I would cry and I remember thinking—*I prayed for help; I need to figure this out; I don't feel safe anymore.*

I could just actually feel that I was slipping away…that I had lost my joy. And then I heard a voice that said—*Get Out!* I heard it a second time, *Get Out!* So the next morning I told James that I was moving out and wanted a divorce.

I started looking for an apartment for my mother and myself. We needed one with a walk-in shower for her. There was a brand new senior housing apartment across town and I liked it. I went back and forth, delaying accepting the apartment, trying to see if things would get better. They didn't.

So I moved my mother and myself out of the house, and while driving away, I felt like I was just being lifted up. I recalled how I tell Harriet Tubman's story of being free for the first time, and I felt that transformation in my life.

We had moved out in August and on December 16th, 2021, it was going to be my mother's 100th birthday. We planned a big party for her and the kids were coming back and it made sense for us all to stay in the big house together so my mother and I temporarily moved back in. The kids were all home, the party was great and then James talked us into staying for Christmas. After Christmas, I gave up my apartment and we moved back in.

Before two weeks were over I had to move back out. My apartment was gone by then so we had to find another one. I would block James from my phone. And then I would unblock him. It was after this second move that I discovered Lisa Nichols and enrolled in her Certified Transformational Training Program. I invested in my future. At age 69, I found my joy again, and things opened up a lot for me.

Our oldest daughter, Adia had been in remission from cancer, but it had come back. And when I found out she was sick I began to research on alternative healing—so she didn't have to go through chemo again. I discovered that emotions are energy and once we understand that we are all energy we can look at these trapped emotions in the body. Adia lost her fight with cancer in February (2023). She was 48 years old.

James health was deteriorating, He didn't look the same and even his handwriting was changing. We knew he had leukemia for about 8 years, but he didn't want anyone to know.

There are a lot of emotions as I write this, many I'm not able to share without tears. I loved my husband and I know he loved me. We did so much together. We enjoyed each other and I have a deep sadness for losing James. James and I spent some time together after the divorce which was final in March 2023. We actually had a date planned, he was going to cook for me and we would go to the movies and I expected to continue to see him during family events. So, even though I knew our marriage was over, I thought we would continue to be in each other's lives for years to come. I know that death is expected at some time, but losing the relationship before his death was the hardest.

James died in June 2023. The night he died, I was at his apartment and had planned to stay the night because he wasn't feeling well. Around 7 p.m. he said he felt worse than he ever had so I called 9-1-1. *He was taken to the hospital and I drove about 10 minutes behind the ambulance.* While I was driving, I was praying and asking God, *"Who is going to take care of James when I leave?"* I had announced to everyone that I was planning to move back to Washington. Well, God solved that problem when James passed on. My mother passed away at age 101 in October 2023.

Three of the closest people to my heart are now gone – my husband, my firstborn child and my mother. If it was not for me now believing that we are spirits in a body and that we never really die, along with grief support, I would not have been able to continue. But I have a deep belief that we all come to live in the body and personality here on earth by choice. We have other souls that come with us to help us remember who we are, God, experiencing life as each of us. I know that James, Adia and my mother were all part of my group of spirits who came with me to help me move toward my purpose.

My life's purpose has become clearer to me during the last two years. I am a healer, and I have been told that I am a medium. I have these gifts to share with the world. The time away from James had allowed me to find myself. The quest to find answers for healing my daughter led me to seek to learn healing techniques. I am now certified in the Emotion Code – an energy healing technique. I am grateful to James and Adia for being in my life and I will be with them again.

My life is now full of new and exciting experiences. I drove 3,000 miles across the country with just my dog with me, and I have traveled more this year than any other year in my life. I find every day is a new opportunity to find something new about myself and I no longer feel that there are any accidents or coincidences. I have learned not to judge others and that everyone is living their lives as they come to experience it. And if they want to express themselves in a certain way, then there is no reason for me to have any judgment toward them.

I have goals that I am still working towards. I want to launch a movement of *Girls United By Love*, which is all about teaching girls of all ages self-love. The time and investments I have put into being trained as a transformational trainer with Lisa Nichols, the interview on her TV program and this book are all leading me along the path to realize my goals. I know that if I do what my purpose in life is, that all my needs will be met. I just have to trust and surrender to my life's journey.

Everything is there for me to notice and learn from. Everything. And I look forward to what I am going to receive, and the messages I get, from each new person I meet.

About Karol

Karol V. Brown, a dedicated professional with a Bachelor of Science degree and a Master of Public Health, certified as a Lisa Nichols Transformational Trainer, and skilled in Emotion Code Energy Medicine. Based in Washington State, Karol is a seasoned health educator, accomplished author, and captivating storytelling artist. With over 23 years of experience, she has passionately shared the inspiring stories and wisdom of Harriet Tubman.

Karol is the author of two impactful books, *30 Lessons in Love, Leadership, and Legacy from Harriet Tubman* and *The Harriet Tubman Way: An Inspirational Guide to Self-Love, Empowerment, and Legendary Leadership for Girls.* Additionally, she has co-authored three other books, namely *Rise Up* with Lisa Nichols, *LIVE. LOVE. PROSPER.* with Authors Who Care, and together with professional storytellers, *How to be a Storyteller.*

Specializing in interactive storytelling workshops and compelling speaking engagements, Karol focuses on empowering young girls and women to discover their inner strength and potential, drawing inspiration from the remarkable life of Harriet Tubman. Her presentations center around essential themes such as self-love, peace, joy, gratitude, determination, and imagination.

Learn more at:

- karolvbrown.com

CHAPTER 9

CREATIVE RESTLESSNESS

BY NICK NANTON

I put my pencil down and looked up at the clock. I'd just completed my first exam in law school. I popped up, grabbed my bag, and made for the front of the classroom. The guy next to me looked up from his page. "Dude, what are you doing?" he whispered. "Giving up?" We'd been told the first day to look to the right and left because those students wouldn't make it to graduation. "Not giving up. I'm done." The guy's mouth fell open. I scooted past him, dropped the test on the professor's desk, and walked out. We'd been given three hours to take the test. I'd just finished it in 37 minutes.

Many thoughts probably come to mind when you read the above, but I can assure you I'm not some super-genius – actually, far from it. I have quite the opposite problem than you might expect...I can literally only focus on something for 15 to 30 minutes in one sitting. I'd been advised for the entirety of my school years to double check my work, but when I did that, I'd often undo the answers I had right. My best grades were made when I quickly pushed my way through assignments. Probably not a technique to add to the parenting books, but all I can share is what worked for me.

This chapter may not seem like the other ones you've read so far. I don't have any massive adversities that I overcame, like losing a parent or a child. I've had regular challenges like everyone; I don't minimize those. And like everyone, I've had monumental moments that shifted the trajectory of my life.

One of those moments came the day I graduated from law school because it marked the end of the years I'd spent being educated—from kindergarten through law school—20-plus years. That's a long time for anyone, but especially for someone like me. Let's just say as a kid, we took many trips to the pediatrician to have me stitched up (yes, one time he had us meet him at his office where he kindly paused his card game with some other local docs to stitch me up). I was definitely all boy, super-hyper, adventurous, with loads of energy to burn. I had a few teachers along the way, who probably had boys of their own, who understood me. But for the most part, I felt like the narrative, at least what I heard in my head, was, "Can't you just sit down in that chair and be normal?" But I didn't learn that way.

My coping mechanism was to finish whatever I had to in order to get to recess or lunch or circle time. I loved the social aspects of school, making friends came easily. But I was bored out of my mind with the work. When I finished the assignment, I'd go to centers where I'd get a stamp for each one I finished. At the end of the day, I'd leave school with tattooed sleeves from all the stamps I'd gotten.

Fast-forward to college. My parents ingrained in me and my brother the belief that education would set us up in life. They'd say, "I don't care what you do for a living, just get a profession." My family are immigrants from Barbados who moved to America when I was ten months old and my brother was nearly three. Education would ensure we had the freedom to live the life they dreamt of and sacrificed to give us. There was never an option of how well we'd do in school. My brother went to Tulane Medical School, completed his Psychiatry residency at Duke University, his Child Psychiatry fellowship at Duke, his Forensic Psychiatry Fellowship at UC Davis, and is now a Child Forensic Psychiatrist, boarded in five specialties. At the time, my dream was to be the president of a record label. I knew a lot of CEOs were lawyers, so I applied to law school.

For someone with my energy level, law school was grueling. I'd gotten used to undergrad where full time is 12 hours and I could fill in all the extra hours with creative ventures. I managed bands and ran a recording studio in Gainesville. I started a T-shirt company that printed all the fraternity and sorority T-shirts. (Let's just say it was fun AND profitable!) But law school was a whole different gig.

In most law schools, first-year students aren't allowed to work due to the workload. That was a problem because I had two growing businesses. I petitioned the law school and was granted permission to continue.

During my first year of law school, I hit the jackpot, the University of Florida installed wireless internet in the classrooms. While sitting in class, I built the first independent site that sold MP3s legally. I hired a web designer in London and a programmer in India who I'd group message using AOL Instant Messenger. I had no way of knowing Apple was about to launch iTunes...but we released our site within a couple of weeks of their launch. Then I sold it to move on to other ventures.

I went to law school with no intention of setting foot in a courtroom. I chose law because I knew part of owning a record label, or running any kind of business for that matter, involved negotiating contracts. Over the years, it's funny the respect I've gotten, by default, for not practicing law, because I'm usually the only lawyer in the room.

My last year of law school, I got offered a job to be the CEO of a music company. My business partner was friends with the owner of Cinemark Theaters and convinced him to start a division called Cinemark Music. They hired me as CEO. My job would be to produce bands and their music videos. The plan was to play their videos during the movie trailers, and then tour the bands through the theaters on the nights of the week they weren't busy. Pretty brilliant plan, right?! (Spoiler alert...not for long!)

This meant my moving to Orlando to be near my business partner and the closest Cinemark Theater. I applied to a private law school in the area (you can visit at any accredited institution for your third year of law school and still graduate at your home institution). At this point, I had one more year, and I was seriously tempted to quit. I remember having a conversation with my mom. She said, "I guarantee, if you quit right now, you'll regret it the rest of your life." I called my business partner and filled him in. "She's right, you should finish. Look, you got in. You're there. It's not like you have to get straight A's. You're not trying to get a big firm job, just stay in the middle." Law school is truly on a bell curve. For every A, there's an F; for every B, there's a D; and most everyone just gets C's. So to graduate, I just had to outwork four or five classmates. No problem.

I headed into my final year of law school with the added expense of $50K tuition and the stress of having to take night classes, as I would be working during the day. I showed up for work the first day, ready to go. My business partner met me at the office. "Hey, I got bad news. Over the weekend, Cinemark sold to private equity. There's no longer any plan for Cinemark Music."

The Cinemark Music fall-out was painful. I finished my final year, graduated from law school, and stood on a point where behind me were all those years of being educated, and ahead of me were endless opportunities. All those years of sitting at a desk, my potential growing, while simultaneously moving along a parallel track of learning from opportunities that popped up, that I then jumped at because I had creative energy to burn. Sure, I wasn't the CEO of a music company, but the whole wide world was in my view now and nothing would slow me down.

———◆◆◆———

Growing up, I was repeatedly told to relax, not to rush, give things time, not to take on too much at once. This is common advice, but I learned that part of overcoming the obstacles we meet comes from knowing our unique giftings. Mine is being restless—creatively restless—so I was constantly bringing a creative restlessness to every position I had. We all have to come to terms with who we are and where we fit. I eventually realized that energy is what makes me different. It makes me stand out. As a result of following my instincts, I started having success.

What made me not fit in at school, or law school, or in the corporate environment, is what makes people call me today. It's not something I would say at a dinner party, but I'm really proud to be ranked in the top 10% of songwriters in the world today, and I've been blessed to win 22 Emmys. I try to bring energy to every situation. I got through what I knew I had to do in school so I could do what I wanted to do, which was spend time with people, hear their stories, produce music and films. Mom, Dad, I found my profession! Today, I don't have to do the work I don't want to do. I'm doing what I was put on earth to do, which is have meaningful conversations that lead to produced outcomes.

There are times in life when, in order to progress, you have to play by someone else's rules. I could have been lazy and produced sloppy work when I was rushing through my assignments, but my parents had expectations, healthy expectations. I figured, if I had to do it, I might as well do it to the best of my abilities. I still believe that today.

Are there parts of my story that you can relate to? Here's the thing: we all face absolutes. But instead of playing the game the way everyone else is playing it, what if you asked yourself, *"What can I do not only to make it bearable, but to make it fun, and have it be a win? How do I play a different game than everyone else is playing?"* By the time the others figure it out, you'll be so far ahead they won't be able to hold you back. Finishing school was an absolute, but I made sure to keep honing my instincts for opportunities, and I grew despite feeling the weight of slogging through coursework.

As a kid, lunchtime was my favorite time of the school day because I didn't have to be on someone else's agenda. I could just hang out with my friends. Today, being on my own schedule and talking to friends (including clients, film crews, songwriting collaborators, and business partners) is how I fill most of every day. My job is to have meaningful conversations that produce desired outcomes. I used to think I hated learning, but that's not true. I'm actually addicted to it, but not the way it's done in school—sitting still in a chair for eight hours and writing papers. Now I get to learn from the best in the world in an immersive way. The people I interview for documentaries aren't just people who are pretty good at something. They're being interviewed for a documentary because they're spectacular at something.

This comes back to learning how to play the game. If you're going to play, you might as well win. I want the greatest adventure life has to offer. Winners get invited to do the most awesome things because people like hanging around high achievers. But it is more than that. I'd been raised in a home that valued service to others, so achievement is never the end goal. I want to perform well so I can be valuable to other people. I'm a highly social person; and my greatest wealth is my family and my closest relationships.

I once hosted a mastermind group where people came in and shared their business successes and problems. A woman got up in front the room and went on for 30 minutes about how she was changing everything because nothing in her company was going right. People had let her down, employees weren't performing to her standard, and on and on. It hit me; this person is never going to be happy because she's too self-focused. Everything was about her. She hadn't yet figured out that serving others is actually what makes a person happy.

During the pandemic when the world came to a screeching halt, I had a lot of nervous energy. Dr. Nido Qubein had once told me, "Nick, a life well-lived is a life lived in thirds. 1/3 earning, 1/3 learning, 1/3 serving." When I shifted my focus away from myself and served other people, my restlessness settled. That doesn't mean you have to go hop on a plane bound for a mission field. At that time, the nation was still in lock-down, so my serving took the form of things that weren't at all exotic, like helping my parents figure out how to get on Zoom because they wanted to see their grandkids. Small things done with great love is service.

Maybe you don't have creative restlessness. Maybe your restlessness is intellectual or physical – you may want more than anything to write a book or travel and explore the world. We have all been gifted with an undeniable skill that other people in the room likely don't have. I believe these gifts are given to us by God. Have you had the experience of telling someone your dreams and they say, "Oh, you probably shouldn't do that." People respond this way because God didn't give *them* that dream, He gave *you* that dream. Now you have to sell it to everybody else. Ask yourself: *What do I love doing more than anything else?* Now, how could you combine that with something you're already doing? Don't wait for someone to give you permission to use your greatest skill-set.

What if you combine your unique gifts with something you currently do that's already providing value in the world – and see if anyone notices. Test it out. The more you do it, the more people will start celebrating you for that gift, and the more you'll be invited to do it. No one ever asked me to make a documentary. I decided to try it and it worked. I walk through the doors God opens for me.

I'm motivated to bring value to God because I may be in charge of the business, but He's in charge of me and everything else. When we bring our talent and gifts to our work, it provides extra value to whoever is around us. You don't have to wait for approval or permission from people to go be who you are. Chase anything you want. Your chances of success are higher if what you're chasing includes serving or helping other people. If what you're chasing is self-serving, you might have financial success or celebrity status, but there's a reason we hear so many stories of suicides and depression. Self-centeredness is a hole that never gets filled. The definition of true success is how many lives you can positively affect.

God gave me so many gifts – I had great parents who still love me and come to every one of all three of my kids' events; I have a loving wife of more than 20 years; I have my health... So, if I don't wake up every day and give God as much as I can with the gifts He's given me, I see that as a failure. None of this is about achievement. It's about rising to the level of expectation that I feel I owe Him and those around me because of what I've been given...because of how a loving God has *served me.*

Not everyone has the same interior motivation. Whatever energizes you, makes time seem to fall away, and adds value to the world, go do that thing. Whether it's in your current occupation or a new adventure you've always dreamed of taking.

What will your next bold move be?

When you do that, well, you'll be rewarded with whatever currency it is you desire.

About Nick

From the slums of Port au Prince Haiti with special forces raiding a sex trafficking ring and freeing children to the Virgin Galactic Space Port in Mojave with Sir Richard Branson, 22-Time Emmy Award Winning Director/Producer, Nick Nanton, has become known for telling stories that connect. Why? Because he focuses on the most fascinating subject in the world: PEOPLE. As an award winning songwriter, storyteller and Best-Selling Author, Nick has shared his message with millions of people through his documentaries, speeches, blogs, lectures, songs and best-selling books. Nick's book *StorySelling* hit *The Wall Street Journal* Best-Seller list and is available on Audible as an audio book. Nick has directed more than 60 documentaries and a sold out Broadway Show (garnering 43 Emmy nominations in multiple regions and 22 wins), including:

DICKIE V (ESPN/Disney+)

Rudy Ruettiger: The Walk On (Amazon Prime)

The Rebound (Netflix)

Operation Toussaint (Amazon Prime)

Nick has shared the stage, co-authored books, and made films featuring:

Larry King
Kathie Lee Gifford
Hoda Kotb
Dick Vitale
Kenny Chesney
Magic Johnson
Coach Mike Krzyzewksi
Jack Nicklaus
Tony Robbins
Lisa Nichols
Peter Diamandis

And many more

Nick specializes in bringing the element of human connection to every viewer, no matter the subject. He is currently directing and hosting the series "In Case You Didn't Know" (Season 1 Executive produced by Larry King), featuring legends in the worlds or business, entrepreneurship, personal development, technology, and sports.

Nick's first love has always been music and has been writing songs for more than 2 decades and his songs have been aired on radio across the United States and in Canada. Currently ranked in the top 10% of songwriters in the world, his songs have been recorded by Lee Brice, Darius Rucker, RaeLynn, Joe Bryson, and many more, and has amassed more than 3 million streams on Spotify, Apple Music, Pandora, and SoundCloud. He received 3 Gold records in 2018 for his work with the global touring band A Day to Remember.

Nick has written and/or produced songs that have appeared on the following shows or in promotional commercials for:

- Fox primetime series *Glee, New Girl, House, Hell's Kitchen*
- The MLB All-Star Game
- ABC Family's hit series *Falcon Beach*
- CBS primetime series *The Ghost Whisperer* starring Jennifer Love Hewitt

CHAPTER 10

"BRAVER THAN I BELIEVED! ...AND SO ARE YOU!"

BY DR. TERI ROUSE

"Fred, I'm not smart enough to do that."

We were standing in the kitchen, me situated in the corner between the sink and the stove. I'd just shared with my husband that a colleague had recommended I get my doctorate, and he reminded me he'd been telling me to do that for a long time. But years before, someone had planted the seed that I wasn't bright enough to do much simpler things and self-doubt had taken root.

After confessing my deepest fear, that I didn't have the smarts to get an advanced degree, Fred gave me a look that bordered on anger. I had spent too many times in a corner with an angry man staring at me. When he saw my eyes fill with tears, his expression instantly shifted.

"Of course you're smart enough, Teri!"

That wasn't what I was expecting to hear. For so many years, my first husband emotionally and verbally abused me, controlling where I went and when, what I could do, and what I wasn't capable of doing on my own. Those false beliefs were deeply ingrained in me even all these years later. Fred wasn't angry with me; he was angry that I still believed this about myself and so assumed he'd failed to convince me of my true worth. Now we both had tears in our eyes.

This memory is so vivid in my mind because, in that moment, two things got very clear: One, I felt a solidarity with my husband; and two, I started to actually believe I could earn that degree. Fred was confirming something I believed deep down about myself but was too afraid to bring to the surface.

I enrolled in the doctoral program. I studied hard. And I graduated. The degree gave me the confidence and tools I needed to better help families improve their relationships, and it allowed my daughter to see that her mom was capable of accepting a degree as a doctor. I'd be lying if there wasn't also a small part of me that did it to spite my ex-husband. There's only one person in this world that, when they meet me, must call me Dr. Teri. That's him.

ESCAPING TRAUMA

"The moment that you start to wonder if you deserve better, you do."

I grew up in a loving, healthy family, first in New Jersey, then in Pennsylvania. My sister, parents, and I have always been close. I was the kid who took on the bully who lived down the street because he wouldn't let my sister roller skate down the block. I was fearless. I think back on that time and what an unexpected and gradual progression it was to become a shell of my former self.

As a young woman, I dreamed of living on my little green acre with my husband, children, and dogs, enjoying life. When I was 23, I got married and that dream slowly and methodically came to a halt. My first husband never hurt me physically, but then again, he never had to. His threatening words and his physical presence struck terror in me.

Fear gripped me so deeply that I stayed, frozen, afraid to move, like a deer in the headlights. He controlled every situation, which included not having people over and not leaving the house unless necessary. My life with him was small and getting smaller.

The last straw came when he threatened to take our daughter and disappear into the mountains of West Virginia. "You'll never lay eyes on her again." When our daughter Kristen was 7, I finally grasped the reality that if we were going to make it out of this, we needed to escape, and so we ran.

While I'm grateful for the solid upbringing my parents provided, which modeled for me what a healthy, mutually-respecting marriage looked like, abusive relationships peel away a person's self-confidence. The abused will second-guess themselves because they no longer trust they can make good decisions. My daughter and I needed to leave, for our safety and so I could shield her from expecting this to be how the man who loves her will treat her. I've heard it said a woman should never invest in a relationship she wouldn't want for her own daughter.

After we left, I had an arsenal of anger for how he'd separated me from my family, told me I was not a good mother, and convinced me I wasn't smart enough to make anything of myself. Deep inside, I knew what he was telling me about myself wasn't true, yet other parts of me became convinced. The internal battle of claiming my true identity was ongoing.

Once Kristen and I were settled in a safe location, I began the slow work of healing. I took responsibility for my part in this situation— allowing him to treat me that way for so long. I was fortunate enough to get away when so many women aren't so lucky.

I've had an unwavering source of support and healing around me, including my parents, sister, brother-in-law, and eventually, my future-husband Fred.

STARTING OVER

"The scars you can't see are the hardest to heal."

Fred and I married two years after I left my first marriage. I'd told Fred some things about my first husband, but he didn't truly comprehend the emotional damage the trauma had not only on me, but on my daughter. Once, one of our dogs had gotten sick and I started to give her medication. Kristen said, in front of Fred, "Mommy, you can't do that. You don't know how." She'd witnessed years of my ex-husband dispensing the dog's medicine because he said I wouldn't do it right. That's all Kristen had ever heard. When she said that to me, Fred looked at me, and he looked at her, and before he spoke, I put my hand up to signal 'stop.' I leaned down in front of Kristen and said, "Kristen, Mommy can do this. I promise. Come and watch me." Afterward, I had to explain what was going on so Fred would understand, that was all she knew.

I was not the person my ex-husband told me I was. I didn't know who I was just yet, but I knew who I wasn't. It was essential that Kristen see the truth of who her mom was. I felt some of those negative core beliefs dissolve as I settled into a new life where I was no longer barraged with my ineptitude.

Over time, with Fred, I began to exert my personal preferences—something as small as saying, "Hey, I don't feel like cooking tonight. Let's go out" was a brand-new behavior for me. I'd been told for years that if I made any decisions, I'd mess things up, or worse, something terrible would happen. All my decisions were fear-based. I wouldn't drive after the sun set because accidents and crime and other bad things happened at night. Fred helped me to build my decision-making muscles.

I was healing every time I did something that in the back of my mind was a little bit brave. It started with baby steps like, "We're going to the mall Friday night." To drive to the mall, in the dark...on a weekend! That was huge. I had all kinds of encouragement as I took each courageous step and saw that, in fact, I could trust myself.

FAMILY CRISIS

"You can't change someone who doesn't see an issue in their actions."

Meanwhile, Matthew, Fred's son from his first marriage, had significant behavioral issues. I was aware of this before we married and didn't hesitate to walk into that situation. At the time I was a special-ed teacher whose job it was to give kids emotional and behavioral support.

At first, I was the buffer between Matthew and the rest of the family. I would stay up late talking with him, trying to understand and help him. What became clear pretty quickly was that I'd underestimated the scope of Matthew's disorder and overestimated my own ability to help improve the family environment. As a young teenager, Matthew's behavior had become routine at that point and Fred didn't have the context to know Matthew's actions were far from normal.

The presence of one behaviorally-challenging teen in a household can up-end the entire family structure. Others were quick to criticize the methods we used to create a stable, healthy home environment. We were told we were bad parents because none of the traditional solutions worked. We tried a variety of medications with no luck; individual counseling didn't help, nor did family therapy or punishment. In hindsight I see we did several things wrong, but we simply didn't know what else to do.

Over time, I became resentful of Matthew. I was tired of all the times he'd say he'd do something and not do it. Once, it had snowed and Fred, Kristen, and I were outside shoveling – mind you, I have a bad back – and the phone rang. Matthew answered and my dad asked to speak with me. "Grandpa, hi. She's outside shoveling snow." My dad's gruff response was, "What the hell are you doing inside then? Get outside and help!"

Then three months before graduation, Matthew dropped out of high school and moved away. That was hard to accept because the kid is brilliant. When he left, the family system didn't just boomerang back into normalcy. We were so used to living in chaos, we didn't know how to do 'family' any other way, so we continued living in chaos, until we figured out we didn't need to. We were and still are a work in progress.

Not having a favorable relationship with Matthew within the family intensified some of those doubts about myself and my effectiveness as a teacher, coach/consultant, and parent. I came to see that Matthew leaving wasn't a reflection on me and my professional/mothering skills. His leaving had to do with him. I was sad because I knew things could be better, I just didn't know how to make them better.

One of the reasons I was driven to get my EdD. was to figure out how to help others in family situations like ours. Those years with Matthew certainly helped me experience firsthand what so many struggling families go through when one or more members are dealing with mental health issues. I became adamant that parents should not ever feel they are all alone in their crisis. I wanted them to have the tools at their fingertips that I wished I'd had. Tools that we craved and pleaded for!

HELPING OTHER FAMILIES IN CRISIS

"You're not broken. You're just being rebuilt. Believe that this time of change is for the better."

I began teaching in higher ed and had much more freedom to view the world from a different lens. I traveled and started writing. I began speaking at conferences and working one-on-one with families. I worked to construct two programs: the R*E*A*L* Peaceful Parenting Framework and Braver Than You Believe Program. The programs aren't fancy or complicated; they're mostly common sense. But when you're in the middle of chaos, it's hard to stay grounded in what's reasonable. By having these skills become habits, family members are able to apply them automatically in times of crisis.

Forming these roadmaps for other parents became a means to forgive myself after Matthew left…and to forgive myself for being in an abusive marriage. Helping families learn how to improve their communication, calmly resolve conflicts, and restore peace in their homes and in their hearts will help others learn to forgive themselves as well.

In the years after I remarried, I watched Kristen go from the child who hid behind my skirt whenever she met a new person, to being an independent, outspoken young woman. I laugh because now Fred doesn't drive anywhere – I'm the driver because in my first marriage, I didn't drive anywhere except work. I wasn't *allowed* to drive! I was a basket-case and heard regularly that my driving was unsafe. I still remember the first time I drove at night and nothing bad happened. Those memories are transformational for me. These triumphs are what happens when we move out of dysfunctional family structures and claim the lives we were meant to have all along.

I looked over my shoulder for years. I don't anymore, because I figure, at this point, if my ex was going to do something, he probably would have already. I am braver than I ever believed. And I believe you are too. When we find ourselves on the ground, knocked down by the circumstances of life, we get back up, no matter what. We can't let other people or situations keep us down. We all have a light to shine into the world that someone else needs to see.

———◆◆◆———

As someone who helps parents and caregivers in challenging family systems, I sometimes imagine my younger self coming in to seek help. What advice would I give her? One thing we don't realize when we're young is that all our life experiences – the good ones and the hard ones – are lessons. Some can cause us anger and resentment, but others come along and bring us joy and tranquility. This is life. We take these experiences and learn from them so we can become better versions of ourselves.

I'd want my younger self to know that I see her and what she's living through, and it's a low point. But it isn't where our story ends, in the grand plan of our life. What she has inside her is beautiful and unique and the world needs to see it. I'd tell her to keep getting up, not for the purpose of making someone else proud, or to make lots of money, or even to leave a legacy. She must get up and do the brave thing because someone else needs to know it's possible and then decide they can get up too.

I'd tell her, "We are not survivors, we are thrivers...we were braver than we ever believed we could be, and it all worked out for us." It's the same thing I'd tell you, dear reader, you are braver than you believe. And you're not alone.

References
The quotes after each subhead come from:
Ngan, Calvin. "30 Quotes on Leaving Abusive Toxic Relationships and Be Yourself Again."
https://www.geckoandfly.com/25156/quotes-abusive-toxic-relationships/
Accessed 10/31/23.

About Dr. Teri

Early & Behavior Interventionist, Reading and Autism Specialist, educational coach and consultant, six time best-selling author, Quilly Award recipient, member of the National Academy of best-selling authors, International speaker, mother and wife — all describe Dr. Teri Rouse.

Dr. Teri has been recognized for her varied areas of expertise in education, positive behavior support and behavior management, autism, literacy, writing and speaking.

She is a member of the Division of International Special Education Services and Hawaii University. International Conferences, where not only, for the past several years she has spoken internationally, on topics of literacy, People First Language, and addressing challenging behavior in children, but she is also a proposal reviewer.

As the founder of KIDS: Interventions & Direct Services, creator of the Real Peaceful Parenting Framework, Braver Than You Believe empowerment program and Snuggle Bunny story time and book club, she is dedicated to helping families improve communication, calmly resolve conflicts, and restore peace in their home with a variety of easy to implement, tried and true tips, tools and techniques.

Dr. Teri has been seen on ABC, NBC, CBS, Fox, Bravo, Yahoo News.

She is an executive producer and producer with Abundance Studios, working with their multiple Emmy award winning directors, producers and videographers. Most recently she was an Executive Producer with for the documentary *The Truth About Reading*, highlighting the extreme level on illiteracy among adults in the US. She also was a producer for the *Dickie V Story* which was shown on ESPN and Disney+. And she received a Telly Award for the documentary *It's Happening Right Here*, stories of human trafficking happening here in the United States.

Dr. Teri enjoys writing, reading, visiting schools, making wine in the basement, time in her yard with her daughter, son-in-law, three grand puppies, and evenings watching the sunset from her porch on Rehoboth Bay with her husband, Dr. Fred and their dog GusGus.

To learn more about Dr. Teri, her programs and how you can work with her, go to:

- Drterirouse.com

Follow her on:

- Facebook: Dr Teri Rouse
- Instagram: dr_teri_rouse
- LinkedIn: Teri Rouse EdD.
- drterirousefearless@gmail.com

CHAPTER 11

OVERCOMING CHALLENGES WITH FORETHOUGHT, FLEXIBILITY, AND FAITH

BY FRANCIS X. ASTORINO
– PRESIDENT, THE ASTORINO FINANCIAL GROUP

As an experienced financial adviser now, I wouldn't recommend setting out to build a career the way I did. With just a few years' experience and not fully qualified, I struck out on my own with high hopes and a $25,000 credit card limit.

Forty years later, I lead a successful wealth management company for affluent, High Net Worth, and Ultra High Net Worth Families. It is fulfilling to assist clients in stewarding their money well for themselves and for their families and guiding them in their philanthropic giving. But there have been many challenges along the way.

In overcoming them there has been a central thread—the belief that it is never wrong to do the right thing. Smart practices will get you so far, but only solid principles will sustain you there. For example, in the financial world there are things you can do with your money to protect and grow it that are legal but, in my opinion, not ethical. In building my business, I have determined only to offer advice that is both honest and congruent with my clients' most deeply-held values.

Ultimately, for me it's about a commitment to justice—'rightfulness' as the dictionary defines it—that can be traced back to some significant adversities I have faced. Partial poetic justice was being a walk-on at a Division One University yet with no financial assistance.

While in high school, the singles position I had earned via playoffs on the tennis team was usurped by the actions of a wealthy parent with a legal background who used his influence to get his lower-ranked twin sons placed ahead of me. With that position went the opportunity for any scholarships, requiring me to work my way through college as a tennis pro.

This experience fueled a desire to protect others from being taken advantage of by becoming an attorney. But while I thrived in pre-law classes, I struggled when it came to the timed multiple-choice exams I had to take, so I ended up diverting into the financial world. Here was a place where I could make a positive difference, I believed, by helping provide people with some concrete measure of protection and security.

Once again, I discovered that not everyone chooses to act rightly. When I found myself shortchanged by tens of thousands of dollars of commission in an assigned planning case while employed at the financial company I had joined, I decided to go independent.

Looking back, it was almost suicidal, but I was left with no other option than to persevere. It took fifteen years of slow and steady work before I considered I had reached a level of stability and success. It was a time of great professional and personal challenges. With my exam-taking difficulties, it took longer to achieve all my financial certifications. I did all that I knew to master the volume of topics, from trying medication to hypnosis. (Today, my twenty-something self would be diagnosed with ADHD!) I delegated what I needed to while I persevered, ultimately earning my master's in financial planning and the many attendant certifications and licenses needed to offer a wide range of financial advice along with complex problem solving.

Meanwhile, I was also navigating some serious stretching at home. After years trying for a baby without success, my wife, Debbie, and I were overjoyed to be able to adopt a little girl from Romania, with all the complications that brought. Then, when she was still a toddler, we were amazed and thrilled to learn we were expecting triplets. They came prematurely, and I spent many hours working from the hospital. Once they were home, we had the delight and demands of four children in diapers, while I continued to plug away at building my business, one client at a time. I moved my office to within a mile of my home so I could be sure to attend all the kids' sports meets and events.

Though life was full, I felt it was important to be involved in the wider community. In addition to helping with different organizations, for many years I served on the local council—where I was disappointed to find that political expediency and personal benefit sometimes trumps a true commitment to public service. Subsequently, I put more energy into philanthropy.

PLANNING AND LETTING GO

Through all of these experiences, I learned that to achieve enduring success takes time. You can read a lot about life hacks and shortcuts these days, but my experience has been that some things cannot be hurried.

That has been the hallmark of the financial advice we have offered to a growing roster of clients. My team and I endeavor to protect and prosper them, putting their interests first. Our approach is not to try to beat the market or make a quick killing, but to determine what is the appropriate level of risk and attainable reward for each client.

In facing any challenge—from managing money to health crises—it is important to understand what you can control and what you can't. That requires forethought – looking at the facts. When you have identified the things that you can impact, you should do everything in your power to meet those responsibilities and opportunities. There is no substitute for hard work. But then, you also need to recognize that you can't control or know everything.

You can do all your due diligence, but you can't guarantee the way things are going to turn out, whether that's in the market or in the most personal areas of your life. Anyone who tells you they know how things are going to go isn't being honest. The best you can do is make well-researched, intelligent assumptions. But life is uncertain in many ways, so I always advise people to have a 'Plan B' in mind. That requires being willing to be adaptable, to change the way you approach something depending on the new circumstances.

Indeed, even the best plans need to be reexamined and reevaluated as time goes by and situations change. In my business, I identify sixty-two life transitions—from remarriage to retirement—that require assessing whether what has brought you to where you are will get you to where you now want to go.

All this means being open to new information and new insights. It's one thing to be confident, it's another to be certain. While we should develop our skills and expertise, I believe it's also important to stay humble and teachable. None of us knows everything; we can all learn something from others if we are willing to listen and consider.

We also make a mistake when we try to compartmentalize our lives, because there is inevitably bleed between those different areas. We are not watertight beings. When I look at someone's financial records, I don't only see a story of numbers; I also see a number of stories. The way they have used it tells me how my clients feel about money and what is important to them. With that in mind, I have incorporated an emotional dimension into my practice, which I call financial life-planning—financial planning that recognizes it's all about individual lives, with their own unique histories, hopes, and dreams. There is no cookie-cutter plan that works for everyone.

I have a psychologist on my team whom I consult when trying to determine how best to work with some of my clients and their concerns. On occasions, I recommend they consider meeting with a therapist to address some of their issues which might be clouding their ability to see clearly when it comes to money. One time, I plainly told a medical professional he needed to sort his personal life out before I could ever begin to sort his finances out. Thanking me later, he said that advice saved his life.

Then there are the hidden power dynamics that can play out between couples, and which need to be recognized and understood. Especially sensitive issues can arise when working on financial planning with blended families—which account for forty-three percent of families today.

CHOOSING TO BE THE CHANGE

While some of my youthful experiences first awakened in me a heart for injustice, I have to credit my father with setting me on the path I have pursued by giving me the belief that I could actually do something about it.

A kind, smart man, he instilled in me some of the faith that has been an important thread in my life. When we were getting ready to play tennis one day, when I was about fourteen or fifteen, he asked me casually what I wanted to be when I grew up.

Having held some different leadership positions at school, I told him with the naiveté of a typical teenager that I thought maybe I'd like to be president one day. He noticed a measure of uncertainty in my answer, though, and asked what that was about.

"What's the problem?"

"Well," I said, reflecting on what I'd read about some of those who had held that office, "some of them don't seem to have been very good people."

"So, change it," my father said, matter-of-factly. The simplicity of his response has never left me—his surety that things could be different, and his conviction that I could be part of making that happen. It deposited in me a sense that I could help make a difference if I was determined to do so.

Another great influence in my life was Father Francis Murphy, one of my history professors at Boston College. In addition to teaching, he pastored The House of Nazareth, an orphanage caring for children from difficult backgrounds. The stories he told of some of the children's experiences resonated with me, as did his final words to our student body – that our education was a responsibility, and we should use it wisely. Much of my community and charitable involvement has been a reflection of Father Murphy's selfless example.

Though I never became an attorney, I have had an opportunity to help ensure justice. One of my clients lost her husband in the terrible

9/11 attack on the Twin Towers. That event had a profound impact on our country and became a defining moment for me. Being their financial advisor was humbling as I prepared them with calculations and professional relationships to facilitate their financial future amidst incalculable loss and devastation. Their story and journey alongside mine have been inspirational in my own pursuit of justice.

It has also been immensely rewarding to be able to help clients steward their money well, providing for loved ones, ensuring a legacy, and enabling them to make a difference in the world through their philanthropic giving. That has meant not just offering the best financial advice but taking their whole life into consideration—such as babysitting one client's beloved dog when she was in the hospital. With her having no family to help, taking care of her closest companion while she was unable to—and needing to get our Persian rugs cleaned as a result!...was a small price to pay for providing the peace of mind my client enjoyed. More significantly, we were able to create a charitable foundation that ensures her love for animals lives on after her death.

LIVING IN GRATITUDE

Overcoming adversity isn't just about dealing with external factors. It also requires facing internal issues. While I had resolved a lot of the pain of past injustices through the years, I became aware recently that some of it was still there beneath the surface, affecting the way I related to others.

I met with a coach who explained it was like standing on a beach ball in a swimming pool. I was having to expend a lot of energy in stopping the ball from bobbing to the surface where everyone could see it—energy that I could be using to swim freely and enjoy being with everyone, if I just stepped off my place of control. That insight has been so liberating.

My faith has also been an important element in coming to terms with being treated unfairly by others. I know that we are all imperfect people, and that individuals can make bad choices that hurt others. But we don't have to be held captive by them. So, I have chosen to forgive. Rather than focus on the wrongdoers and their actions, I want to look for ways that I might be able to offer support and encouragement to others who may have experienced some similar kind of mistreatment, and help them pursue and realize their dreams.

My faith also helps me not lose sight of all that I have to be thankful for. Regardless of all the challenges, I have experienced so much more goodness in this life—most importantly, a faithful wife with whom I've shared the joy of raising four remarkable children. Gratitude makes me want to serve my clients well so I can help them experience their fullest life too.

It's never wrong to do the right thing. And it's never too late to start doing the right thing.

Francis X. Astorino is President of The Astorino Financial Group (www. astorinofinancialgroup.com) in Fairfield, N.J., serving entrepreneurs, corporate executives, and individuals with proven tax, estate planning, retirement, and planned giving strategies.

About Francis

Francis X. Astorino, MS, CFP®, CPWA®, is the founder and CEO of The Astorino Financial Group, Inc., a successful financial services company serving clients since 1986. As a CERTIFIED FINANCIAL PLANNER™ Professional with extensive experience in risk management, tax and retirement planning, and investment counseling, he has also established a reputation for delivering specialized financial guidance to a broad range of clients.

Prior to founding The Astorino Financial Group, Frank worked as a registered financial advisor with The Financial Network from 1983 to 1986, where he provided fee-based planning and acted as chief case writer. He is a frequent public speaker and advocate for sound wealth management and was a member of the International Association of Financial Planning leading to a board position.

Frank holds several licenses and certifications, including Series 6, Series 7, Series 24, Series 63, and Life, Accident & Health Insurance. He earned a master's degree in financial planning (Master Planner of Advanced Studies) and is a Certified Financial Planner (CFP®) and a Certified Private Wealth Advisor (CPWA®).

With a commitment to helping clients achieve financial goals and improve financial well-being, Frank built The Astorino Financial Group into a professional financial services company. His extensive experience and in-depth knowledge of financial planning enables him to provide specialized guidance to individuals and families at every critical life transition.

Frank was recognized as among the Best-in-State Wealth Advisors by *Forbes Magazine* (2018).* Frank has appeared in several publications, both as an author and subject. He has been featured in *Forbes, LPL Financial, The Wall Street Journal*, and appeared on CNBC, among others. He is an active member of the Financial Planning Association, NJ Board (2016-2017), and he remains committed to helping individuals and families achieve their financial independence while enjoying a life of significance.

Frank is also an active philanthropist and serves as a board member for the non-profit charity, Write on Sports/Write on Arts. His dedication to helping others is evident in both his professional and personal life.

---

* The Forbes Best-In-State Wealth Advisor ranking, developed by SHOOK Research, is based on in-person and telephone due diligence meetings and a ranking algorithm that includes client retention, industry experience, review of compliance records, firm nominations; and quantitative

criteria, including assets under management and revenue generated for their firms. Portfolio performance is not a criterion due to varying client objectives and lack of audited data.

CHAPTER 12

ADOPTED ON PURPOSE

BY ELIZABETH GIBSON DUNN

I was born into poverty, somewhere in or around Mexico City. My parents, younger brother, and I lived in a one room shack without electricity or running water.

My relationship with my dad was warm and loving. As a child, I hungered for my mother's love and approval but sadly, never received it. Instead, she would scorn my existence with a constant barrage of verbal insults and physical abuse, a pattern that intensified whenever my dad was not around. I learned, from a young age, not to ask my mom questions. Questions only brought on her rage and I would do anything to keep her from getting angry at me.

When I was just three years old, my mom expected me to do the caregiving for my little brother. If I could not get him to quiet down, or fall asleep, she would explode at me. Caring for a child was especially challenging because I was just a child myself.

I was also given responsibility for fetching pails of water from the local river for drinking and cooking the little bit of food that we had. My mother strictly forbade me from talking to anyone that I might cross paths with, but I remember there was an elderly woman who lived in a shack similar to ours. One day, she approached me and kindly whispered in my ear that if I ever needed anything to just come and find her. It was almost as though she sensed the trauma I experienced on a daily basis.

I never knew what my dad did for a job. My only guess is that it was some type of physical labor. I remember that my dad sustained an injury leaving him handicapped and no longer able to provide for our family. Suddenly thrust into the role of having to figure out how to earn enough money to sustain the four of us, my mother spiraled into a cycle of anger and desperation the likes of which I had never seen before. As a result, I became hyper-vigilant.

My mom began prostituting herself and drank heavily. One night she returned home so drunk and angry, she yelled at my dad for no longer being able to provide for our family. In a fit of rage I won't ever forget, she grabbed my dad's belt and strangled him to death with it right before our eyes.

Instinct took over. I rushed to shield my little brother's eyes from the awful sight and held him tight. Fearing for our lives, I did my best to keep him from screaming. It seemed that my mom had planned this act as two men came into our shack shortly afterward to remove my dad's lifeless body.

Then my mother announced that it was about time that I started doing something to contribute to the family. Still just four years old, frightened and traumatized, my mom started inviting strange men into our shack to molest me in exchange for food or money.

Then the warrior in me rose up!

One day, when my mom was gone, I grabbed my little brother and took him across the street to that old woman's shack. Summoning all my courage, I knocked on her door.

"Help," I said. "My brother and I need help."

FIRST RAYS OF LIGHT

The old woman was able to deliver us to safety. This meant, however, that I would be separated from my little brother. He was taken to a boys' orphanage while I went to one for girls.

I arrived at the girls' orphanage feeling ashamed that everyone there had heard my terrible story. For the first time in my life I had regular meals as I arrived terribly malnourished. The orphanage was run by Catholic nuns who were not the least bit shy about hitting us with a ruler when they thought we were not following their strict code of conduct.

During the years living there, I was taught a strong work ethic through chores the nuns assigned. This was also my introduction to education. I loved learning the subjects they taught in school. I also loved playing on the playground with other girls since I had not yet experienced the simple joys of just being a child.

Every girl in the orphanage had big dreams. We all hoped that someday we would be adopted by a family who would want us. Whenever an American couple would arrive on the premises, we would all run for the window to see which direction they would go.

Were they interested in adopting a younger child? Or maybe someone a little older like myself?

For many years, I watched prospective families go to the side of the orphanage where the younger children lived. My friends and I on the older side, would commiserate, feeling like nobody wanted an older girl. Especially, I felt, one with such a troubled past.

I remember one of the nuns overheard us whining that no family wanted us. She quickly got our attention by slapping her ruler on a nearby table. I remember she said that we must learn to have faith, behave, do our chores and homework. For some reason, I chose to believe her and started behaving accordingly.

Then the magical day finally came. I was seven years old when an American couple arrived with their older son in tow. I heard they were looking to adopt an older girl. That nun kept her promise and she presented the family with three well-behaved girls.

Brought in to meet this American family and an interpreter, we all froze with nervousness. We hung our heads in silence, not daring to look up or speak.

The nun said, "Don't you girls have anything to say to this nice family that has come all the way from New Jersey to give one of you a home and family?"

I remember sitting between my two friends when I felt something rise up in me that said: "This might be your only opportunity at a better life".

I looked at the interpreter and said, "Can you please tell them that if they choose me that I promise to do my homework, my chores, and will make them proud of me."

FINALLY, A HOME

Two weeks later, I was out playing on the playground when one of the nuns grabbed me.

"They chose you," she said.

I was stunned. I had been waiting for this moment for what felt like forever and yet, for some reason, I didn't quite know what to say.

"Come on," the nun continued. "They're here to take you, let's go."

What followed was a whirlwind. I went to a foster care home and took lessons in English. Those transitions finally ended six months later when my new family and I flew to NYC and then drove to my home in New Jersey. For the first time in my life, I had a stable place. Here was finally somewhere I could feel safe.

But the shadow of my past proved difficult to escape. Coming out of the orphanage, my adoptive parents took me for my first medical examination. In addition to being severely malnourished, my growth was stunted, and my eyesight was poor, requiring me to wear very thick glasses. I also looked different from my peers in the private Catholic school where my parents placed me for a couple of years, but there was enough diversity that I was generally accepted.

However, the summer prior to starting 5th grade, my parents decided to move us to the suburbs in northern New Jersey. There I was enrolled in my first public school where I was a Mexican girl in a student body that was mostly white.

Every day on the school bus I endured relentless bullying. They picked on my skin color and the way my hair looked and called me four eyes because of my thick glasses that made my eyes look tiny.

Kids would say things like, "Why don't you go back where you came from?"

But I was resilient and not about to allow them to get the best of me. I remember one bully in particular, a boy who I discovered was struggling with schoolwork. I saw this as my opportunity.

One day, I approached him and said, "I'll help you with your math."

The bully agreed. For a while, that was how I managed to keep the kids off of me. That did not last long though. A local family adopted a Puerto Rican girl whose hair and skin was much darker than me. They made fun of her the same way they had me. I remember how they used to trip her in the cafeteria and made monkey noises as she walked by.

Helping the bully with his homework didn't earn me respect. It bought temporary protection. Seeing the way they abused her made me angry. One day out on the playground, I reached my limit of their abuse. I pounced on that bully and beat him up. Blinded by rage, I kept hitting him, over and over, until the teachers pulled me off.

STRUGGLES IN SILENCE

I never talked about these struggles to my parents. Years of abuse and neglect had made me something of a people-pleaser. I was afraid that by having my own problems, I would let them down. I suffered the only way I knew how: in silence.

My parents were considerably older when they adopted me. They were already in their fifties, coming from a very different generation, one that was not open to therapy. My father used to refer to therapy as one wacko talking to another.

I taught myself to keep on going, pushing through as though nothing had ever happened. I told myself that if I could just get myself through to the point where I can earn my own money and be independent, everything would be fine. Getting to the point where I could be self-sustaining, not having to count on anybody else, became my constant drive.

My first professional career was in nutrition. I worked with adults in hospital and clinic settings before focusing on children. Working in healthcare was good for me, but I discovered that privately I was constantly on edge. All those years where I avoided seeking help were slowly wearing me down. But it was not until an experience with my own daughter that I found the courage to continue my rise and make real change.

For my whole life, doctors told me I could not have children. They said because of my damaged reproductive system, I would not be able to have a child.

I accepted this. When I met my future husband, I told him straight out that if he wanted to have a family, he needed to find someone else. We planned a life that did not include children.

Whether I should call it a miracle or not, I don't know, but I ended up getting pregnant. We were going to have a little girl, a blessing to our lives.

Raising a small child was hard. It is for most parents. But when my daughter got older, I found myself becoming highly agitated with her actions. For what I call typical misbehavior, I would yell and scream at her.

I finally had a moment of clarity and realized something profound. My volatile behavior was scaring her. When I saw it for what it was, it frightened me, too. Although I had not seen my mother in years, I felt her coming out of me.

I didn't want that.

I knew right then that I had to talk to someone. Continuing down the road I was on would only jeopardize what I needed from a relationship with my beloved daughter. I scheduled an appointment with a therapist. It took time to find the right person but eventually I found the right fit.

We tend to under-celebrate ourselves for all of the small things we accomplish. Everyday victories can be seen as triumphs though. I celebrate that decision, after many years, to finally engage in therapy and start talking about my experiences.

I didn't stop with simple therapy though. I took an on-line course with a psychologist named Terri Cole, who had written a book called *Boundary Boss*. I recognized that, as a lifelong people-pleaser, I was continually burning out. By now I had moved onto real estate, a career which can be demanding on boundaries. People had constant access to me whenever they wanted. I would tell my clients that they could call me anytime, which led to calls and texts at all hours.

Once I learned to start putting healthy boundaries into place with new clients, something amazing happened: I started to attract the right clients who were respectful of my time and my energy. I no longer had to answer the phone at unreasonable hours. I could assert my boundaries with conviction, without concern that people wouldn't want to work with me.

I felt like I was telling the world, for the first time ever, here I am, take me or leave me as I am.

RISE INTO PURPOSE:

What I know about my biological family, all these years later, remains incomplete. I understand that my mother served time for murdering my father, but I don't really know the details.

The same is true for my brother. He went to the boy's orphanage where our paths forever diverged. I hold onto faith that he was eventually adopted and is living a good life. I also have to believe that I did the best I could for him in that terrible situation. I got him to safety.

Despite the broken connection to my biological family, my childhood experience continues to inform my life journey. It fuels my rise. Years ago, I learned that adoptees are four times more likely to attempt suicide than non-adoptees. That number shocked me. But it also stirred something.

Most adoptees suffer in silence. I identify with this because I did and I resolved not to go to my deathbed knowing I could have done more.

Through painstaking therapy, I learned that my trauma does not define me. Because I was powerless as a young child, I now empower others to take back the reins of their own lives. I'm proud to share that I graduated from one of the most rigorous certification programs led by Lisa Nichols and Sean Smith, which has provided me with additional skills necessary to transition to become a transformational life coach. My focus is helping other women who have suffered trauma, particularly if they were adopted from other countries. It is my hope that as I continue to rise, I can be instrumental in helping others transform and rise as well.

I'm grateful for my adoptive parents, who I will forever love!

About Elizabeth

As a transformational life coach and facilitator, Elizabeth Gibson Dunn is on a mission to empower women to transcend their past trauma by first adopting their authentic selves. She has been undergoing her own transformation to heal from her early childhood trauma prior to being adopted from an orphanage in Mexico City. She has earned a dual certification as a life coach and transformational facilitator from Martha Beck's Wayfinder Life Coach Certification Program and Lisa Nichols Certified Transformational Trainer Program.

Prior to embarking on her calling, Elizabeth had been guiding families and individuals in both the buying and selling of their dream homes and/or investment properties in her role as a bilingual Realtor for 8+yrs. In her 23+ years as a bilingual Registered Dietitian, Elizabeth was honored and humbled to have served numerous adult and pediatric patients in her clinical roles, as well as provided leadership to her staff in her various management roles.

She's most proud of the loving family she has created alongside her husband of 20+ yrs. This includes their college-aged daughter and two rescue dogs. In her 'me' time, Elizabeth enjoys meditating daily, walking her dogs, spending time alone, w/her husband, w/her family and friends, as well as volunteering, traveling, dancing for fun and listening to her favorite podcasts and books on audible.

CHAPTER 13

SURVIVING IN BALTIMORE

BY PATRICIA CARPENTER

He was a sweet man, the maintenance man in our building, but I knew something was wrong just by the way he stood at the door.

"What is it?" I asked, while shifting the baby to my other arm.

"Well," he said, uncomfortably. "My wife said that I should tell you, because we're pretty sure that you don't know."

"Tell me?" I asked. "Tell me what?"

He looked around to make sure neighbors weren't nearby and then answered softly. "Well, they're going to evict you on Monday morning, around 8:00 o clock."

And the words just hung there. Because they were words that didn't make any sense. Evict me? How? I've been giving the money every month to my husband to pay the rent.

"Evict me?"

"I knew you didn't know," he said. "We both knew that you didn't know."

This was 1979. I was twenty-five and my husband and I had been married for about three years. We had a baby daughter to take care of.

Well — I had a baby daughter to take care of because my husband was rarely around and I was the only one working.

I had fallen in love with the first person that came along because that meant getting away from my mother who was not a very nice person and we had a…what's the word? Tumultuous? Yes, we had a tumultuous relationship and it's bad to this day. So I fell in love with the first person that showed me kindness and when you're young, kindness is love. But I never looked any deeper than that, because all I wanted was to get out of my mother's house. So I got married to the first man I met.

"Well, how much do we owe?" I asked.

"$600," the maintenance man answered. "But they usually start evicting Monday morning around eight o'clock, so if you can have the money ready for them when they come, you should be okay."

I could have killed my husband if he was around. But he wasn't. So as hard as it was, I had to reach out to my mother. And she went to my aunt who came up with the money. And on Monday morning, my mother, my aunt and I waited for the manager to come, and we put $600 in his hand and I was able to stay in the apartment. And the greatest day was months later when I had saved up that $600 and gave it to my mother to give back to my aunt.

A few months later I was coming home and saw flashing lights. I thought, *What the heck is going on?* We get to the apartment and the police explain to us that there was a break in. And I'm thinking, *we're a young couple, we don't have much to steal.* The police finish up but a detective comes later that afternoon, which was strange because why would a detective be at a simple break in?

So the detective walked me over to the window. "See, how there is no glass on the rug or the floor? That means the window was broken from the inside."

My husband had faked the break in to collect the insurance money. It worked. But worse off, it gave him a taste for it. And from then on, my husband branched out to lawsuits. He became a lawsuit person. If you looked at him the wrong way, he would sue you.

I thought, okay I have insurance on the car and when the insurance company pays me I'll replace that old raggedy car with a less raggedy one. What I didn't know was he had sued the lady that hit him. He sued her on my behalf and on my daughter's behalf because she was in the car. My husband claimed that he suffered neck issues and because of those injuries (and I'm laughing as I'm writing this) he couldn't perform his husbandly duties.

I was pregnant with our second daughter at the time and I didn't know he sued until the lawyer that represented him called and said that they can't issue the check unless both our signatures were on it. I found out that the settlement was for $10,000. Now $10,000 would go a long way. My husband refused to work and winter was coming, we had no winter coats, we needed food, and we were behind on the rent.

So we go to downtown Baltimore and we get the $10,000 and the lawyer must have sensed something about my husband because he says, "Well, I don't feel right letting you leave my office with this $10,000 check." So he walks us across Calvert Street to the bank to open an account. And I feel good knowing the money is now in the bank. I got to work the next day at my job at the Social Security office and that's when it hit me. *Oh, my God, I just put $10,000 in the bank, and his name is on that bank account. Oh, my God, how could I be so stupid?*

I knew in my heart that I needed to get to that bank. So I tell me boss that I won't be in the next day as something came up, and the next morning my husband asks, "Aren't you going to work?"

And I said, "No, I'm going to get the money out the bank."

So he comes with me, I put the baby in the backseat and we drive to the bank. When we get there, he doesn't get out of the car.

"Aren't you coming in?" I asked.

"No, I'll wait here."

And yes, I thought that was strange, but all I could think about was getting that money out of that bank and away from him.

I walk in and show the lady my bank book and tell her that I want to withdraw this money. And she looks at me kind of strange and says, "Let me get my manager."

The manager comes over and he asks to see my driver's license and then he says. "Well, I'm sorry to tell you, there's only $200 in the account."

"What?" I said. "How? Just yesterday we put $10,000 in it. It's only been in there one day."

And that's when he told me that a man and a woman came in yesterday and took the money out.

Have you ever been so angry that you see red? That was me. I couldn't believe that man drove me to the bank knowing what I was going to find out. If my hands were big enough I would have strangled him when I got back in the car.

"Where is the money?" I screamed as I got back in the car.

We had gotten a Pinto because the lawyer was able to work out a way for us to get a car on credit because we knew the money was coming in. We were going to pay that loan off but he went and spent $5,000 to customize the Pinto. A car we didn't even own yet.

"Where's the rest of it?"

And he told me that he gave his mother a few thousand and was handing out hundred dollar bills to his friends.

I couldn't believe it. I just couldn't believe it.

By that Thursday, I was able to get $2,000 of the $10,000 back. And with that little bit of money I went right out and bought my baby shoes that she needed, bought myself a coat, groceries, paid the electric and then we were broke again.

After that, I'm not sure why I agreed to it, but my husband said, "Okay, since you are working all the time, I'll take care of the bills. You give me the money and I'll pay them."

And at the time, yeah, it seemed like a good idea. Until one day he picks me up from work

"Well, I got something to tell you before you get home. The gas and electric is off even though I paid it."

And again, he let me drive to the gas and electric office with him, argue with the woman, knowing full well that he hadn't paid it in months.

I was so angry that when we got back in the car I started pounding on the steering wheel. Just pounding until I heard a crack in my hand.

And I remember screaming, "I broke my hand because I can't kill you."

After that I didn't really care because I had my second daughter, I was working, I was paying the rent and I was making sure there was food on the table, that's all that mattered. I didn't care about him. And I was preparing to leave him.

So I had stockpiled food in my mother's freezer and I had hidden canned goods in the apartment and dry goods and noodles and things. I knew I would need an escape plan.

Then I went to rental office to tell them, that I was leaving, and that I was the one paying the rent for the past year. So I had asked if they had something I could rent, just in my name on the lease and I'd leave him in that apartment. So I took another apartment in another building down the street up on the third floor. I called my uncle and his son and asked if they help move me on Friday. Then I called my girlfriend; she could watch the kids and her husband would drive the U-Haul. It was all set.

So here is the best part, I never told my husband I was leaving. But come Friday he could see I was starting to pack. So he jumps in and starts throwing my things in a box.

"Since your gonna leave." he announces loudly. "Then I took the liberty of finishing packing your crap. Get out."

And I thought, *thank you, thank you, God!*

I smiled. "Okay," I said, and ten minutes later the U-Haul was there. And then my uncle and his son show up and start carrying boxes to the U-Haul. And the kids weren't with me because they were already at my girlfriend's house and we were on the bottom floor. So all the truck had to do was go around to the big glass sliding door. And the two guys jumped out, and I slid the glass sliding door back.

And he's just standing in the living room, like – *What the hell is going on?*

And I just started pointing, "Take that, take that, that one is mine..." So they just start loading up the truck. When it's packed, we leave and he walks outside in disbelief and watches the truck pull around the corner to our new apartment. I look back and he was just standing in the middle of the driveway with his hands on his hips, still fussing and cussing. Not believing what just happened.

Oh my god, I was so relieved...I was so relieved...I was so relieved.

A few days later my aunt came to see where I had moved. And she saw that my two girls had bunk beds. But I just had a little twin bed I found in a thrift store.

"Where's your bed?" she asked.

"Well, it's only me. I don't need a big bed."

"No, no, no," she said. "I'll get you a bed.

So we went out and she bought me a bed.

We get it set up and she says. "And you don't even have to add this on to the $600 that you owe me."

And that's how I found out that my mother had never given my aunt the money I had saved. She had kept it.

But we moved on. I paid my aunt back—again—and I began working as a nursing assistant, but then had the opportunity to begin the nursing program. I started the class and I was terrified just because I hadn't been in a classroom in years and everyone was much younger than me.

I had a routine where I would get up to see the kids off to school. I would study from 8:00 to 12:00 and take a half-hour lunch, and then I'd go back and study from 12:30 to 3:30. My girls would come home from school. I'd feed them, my sister would come watch the girls at 4:00 and I'd take classes from 5:00 to 9:00. Then I'd come home.

Forty hours/week of study for thirty months while working forty hours and I was able to accumulate six months of college credits. Then it was time to take my state boards.

So, I'm working at the hospital as a graduate nurse – just haven't gotten my license yet, but I'm a graduate nurse. So I call home and asked my daughter if the envelope came yet about the test results.

"Yes," she said. "It's here.

And before I could tell her to set it on the table, she opened it up.

"Mommy, it says you passed."

"What?" I said in disbelief. "Are you sure, Stacey?"

"Mommy I know how to read. It says *pass*."

I passed it on the first try.

I started that day as a graduate nurse making ten dollars an hour. And I walked in the very next day with my license in hand and my income just tripled.

My strong faith, conviction, determination, focus and especially my two girls kept me going. It kept me studying for thirty months—a total of 28,795 hours—long days and a lot of hard work. And as I look back on it all I know is that having such a terrible *starting line*—made getting to my personal *finish line* so important.

About Patricia

Patricia Carpenter is a retired nurse with a specialty in Dialysis. She spent 38 years in the medical field, 11 years as a nursing assistant, 32 years as a Registered Nurse. She returned to nursing school and with great determination and focus completed the thirty-six-month program in thirty months. She worked at the local hospital 40 hours per week, and an additional 36 to 38 hours in the evening-weekend nursing school program, while raising two young girls ages ten and seven. At that time, she was divorced, living on minimum wage, and barely meeting any of her financial obligations.

After graduation in 1991, she did very well and her finances tripled overnight. The doctors were quick to offer her jobs in the local dialysis units. She enjoyed her nursing career, working many avenues of dialysis, and did very well. Patricia retired as Area Manager for five dialysis units throughout northeast Baltimore and Frederick, Maryland.

Her two adult daughters are doing well for themselves. They were her rocks of support during those extremely hard times in nursing school. She would open her books to study on the table with them when they were younger, and they checked on each other's homework. They laugh at it now, but at that time they lived on a tight budget for food, housing, and transportation.

Patricia got married a second time to a wonderful man, a retired military officer and physician assistant. They became good friends but had their own agendas. He left for medical school, and she continued raising her two girls, later entering nursing school. Five years later, he returned to Baltimore as a medical doctor. They were married in May of 2000 and enjoyed traveling: riding the rails across the U.S., and cruising the Caribbean and the Rhine River in Europe to mention a few. His health began to decline in 2018, requiring intense medical attention. Each episode was worse than the last and he never made a full recovery. She retired in 2018 to take care of him. Those five years were very stressful, demanding and heart-breaking. She buried her handsome soldier in March 2023.

In the past five years, Patricia found outside interests such as the Red Hat Society-Baltimore Belles; as an entrepreneur with Mary Kay Cosmetics, and she has studied extensively with Lisa Nichols: Motivating the Masses: Speak for Ultimate Impact 1 & 2; Speakers Mastermind 2022 & 2023, Ignite 2022 & 2023, Breakthrough Retreat 2023, and Certified Transformation Training Program 2023.

CHAPTER 14

MY PATH TO *LA DOLCE VITA*

BY DAWN MATTERA CORSI

As an Italian American, I had spent much of my life wanting to travel to the home of my ancestors with my dad and his older brother, Johnny. Their parents had immigrated from Italy, and I was dying to see where they came from, and to meet the family members who were still there.

For years, I asked. For years, Uncle Johnny said someday—and for years, my dad told me he couldn't take that much time away from work. When he finally agreed to make the trip with me and Uncle Johnny, in 2001, I was ecstatic and immediately started making plans. I wanted to believe that it would happen. My dad's staff, on the other hand, took up a pool. How many days before we were supposed to leave would he cancel? They knew, as we all did, that my dad had allowed the work ethic bestowed upon him by my grandparents to turn into workaholism. Would he really go? I prayed every night that he would.

Fortunately, and somewhat surprisingly, every bet in the office pool was a loser. My dad boarded the plane, and the three of us took off for the trip I had been dreaming about for decades. It was truly a once-in-a-lifetime experience.

I was thankful I had persisted through years of wanting that trip to happen. Because if I hadn't, then it would've been too late. Just under a year after we returned home, my dad passed away at the age of seventy. He had been forced to retire on a Thursday, went into the hospital that Sunday, and never came home.

DESTINED TO BE DETERMINED

Perhaps I was destined to have a strong resolve. My grandparents had come to the United States as legal immigrants from Ischia (EE-skee-uh), an island in the bay of Naples, back when it was a rough time to be Italian in the United States. My grandfather came first, looking to make a better life for himself and his soon-to-be family.

My grandfather courted his future bride by sending romantic letters across the ocean. They obviously worked, because my grandmother soon followed, and they were married in New York City. My father and Uncle Johnny were both born in Providence, Rhode Island.

None of them spoke English until my dad and his brother were forced to learn it in school. My grandparents worked hard to speak 'American' too. They were proud of their new country and did their best to honor it. In fact, the only time they spoke their Italian dialect was when they argued, or they didn't want us to know what they were talking about.

The truth is, they jumped in the deep end when they crossed the Atlantic Ocean. They made every effort to build a better life for themselves. They lived fully, with great courage and determination. My grandfather had a quiet strength and a fierce work ethic. My grandmother did the absolute best with what she had to take care of her family. They taught me an important life lesson: When it's time to sink or swim, swim hard and with purpose.

DOING WHAT IT TAKES

After high school, I paid my own way through the University of Rhode Island with grit and grace, working full time and going to school full time. (I don't recommend that if you want a good GPA!) I studied electrical engineering, which helped me earn minority scholarships because there weren't many women in the field at the time. Rather than be offended by that, I used it to my advantage both during school and afterward.

After graduation, I went to work for a defense contractor, earning a secret security clearance, and doing projects for nuclear submarines and the B2 Stealth Bomber. Though the work was interesting, I left engineering after a decade because the corporate environment was too cutthroat for me. I felt that people would pat you on the back just to look for a soft place to stick the knife.

When I had the chance, I jumped into sales for a health and wellness company. Most people thought I was crazy to leave a steady income as an engineer for an unpredictable paycheck in sales. Yet I knew I needed the change—and if you want something badly enough, you'll do what it takes.

I'll admit that the ebb and flow of the money in sales took some getting used to. Some months I made close to what I earned as an engineer. But some months I made almost nothing. At the very least, it forced me to learn how to budget. I worked for the same company for seventeen years—five in sales, the rest in training, marketing, and public relations.

WE ARE STRONGER THAN WE THINK

In 1985, I married another engineer I met at the company I worked for in Minnesota. We moved often, including to Colorado, Kansas, and New Hampshire, as he changed jobs. Whenever layoffs at his office were looming, he didn't seem to have any determination and appeared to give up rather than strive to keep his job. He didn't fight to keep what's important—including me.

In 2008, after twenty-three years of marriage, he asked for a divorce. This was devastating and brought to the surface feelings of not being good enough. That destructive thought of not being enough started in my childhood. I was the only one of my siblings born out of wedlock, and I was made fun of because I was overweight. The divorce only reinforced those feelings of worthlessness.

We hadn't been happy for a long time, but where I come from, you don't get divorced. You endure. You make the best of what life hands you. I was prepared to be the dutiful wife and live that way for the rest of my life. I was shocked, but more than that, I was horribly embarrassed. And worst of all, many of the people I thought loved and supported me wanted to know what I had done to make him want to leave. Even some people in my church turned on me, gossiped about me, left me to deal with this life-altering event on my own. It was a lonely, scary time. I felt so betrayed, and I wondered whether I'd ever find love.

I was also devastated financially. We had paid off debt with an inheritance I'd received later in our marriage. Also, moving several times is never net-positive financially. Our last move hit especially hard. We lost a substantial amount of equity when we sold the home because of the divorce. Emotionally, spiritually, financially, I was left to fend for myself.

So, I did.

Of course, I did have support from a few friends and family. Mostly, though, I prayed and I made a deep commitment to myself to make my own way through.

So, I did.

I realize now that if all of that hadn't happened, I wouldn't be the woman I am today. I'd be living in Idaho, trapped in a loveless marriage, unaware of my own strength and courage. I now know what I'm capable of handling because I've lived through it. And if I did it, so can you.

THE LOVE OF MY LIFE

To get back on my feet, I moved back to Rhode Island and reconnected with the strength and perseverance that I learned in my childhood. I reached out to old friends and made new ones. I eventually bought my grandparents' hundred-year-old home, complete with Grandpa's grape arbors and Grandma's hydrangeas.

Getting back into dating was hard. Heck, I'd been out of the game for more than twenty years! Most singles meet people who have some connection to their jobs. My office was in my home, so that wasn't much of an option unless I had a crush on the mailman. Eventually, I did what most people do these days: I turned to the internet for help, signing up on Match.com.

My first dates ranged from meh to fine. The first man I dated exclusively was a South American director at MIT. Since he was eleven years younger, the relationship was fresh and exciting. However, as time passed, I found him to be a controlling narcissist. When I realized I was falling back into old patterns, the relationship was over.

Putting myself out there again was scary. But the desire to find love was greater than the fear of rejection. I did meet some nice people, but not *the one*. I decided to take myself off the site until I returned home from a trip to Italy. Two days after I got back and reactivated my profile, I got a 'wink' from a guy named Bob, who, I'd since learned, was just about to abandon online dating for good.

I winked back. A day later, we met for dinner in Providence's Little Italy. That was a Thursday. We had our second date that Saturday, and except for work travel, we've been together every day since.

Today, I am married to the love of my life. We share the same interests. We have common values. Our lives are rich, and they're richer because we are together. More importantly, everything about our relationship is real; it's authentic. Good, bad, or indifferent, we know exactly who and where we are.

This process of getting back on my feet proved that old patterns get old results. Courage and conviction help create new, healthier patterns.

LA DOLCE VITA (THE SWEET LIFE)

Today, I have a thriving career helping people live *la dolce vita*, the sweet life. I have learned that you do that by focusing on four things: faith, family, friends, and, well, food. (I mean, I am Italian American, after all.)

Faith is a belief in something greater than you, a higher power, if you will. My faith is in the God of the Bible. Yours might be in nature, or logic and science, or The Force. Wherever your faith comes from, be sure you honor it intentionally and often. Faith is a critical piece of being fulfilled.

Family is important, no matter how you define it. I'm fortunate to have family I'm related to by blood and family I choose. Some people have only one or the other. No matter the makeup of your family, be sure you are intentional in deepening those relationships. They are who will support you through rough times.

Friends are the people who increase your capacity for joy and broaden your life experiences. Building and tending to a network of friends from all the walks of your life is not only important for a rich social life, it's the key to lifelong learning. When you surround yourself with people you like and respect, who also know things you don't, you can't help but grow. And growth is important to *la dolce vita*.

Food was the common bond that held my family together when I was growing up. We gathered around my grandmother's table for Sunday dinners and holidays. And while the food was delicious, of course, the joy we found in being together and celebrating the relationships we had with one another was the most valuable part of the day.

Food is a powerful way to stay connected with the people in your life who matter. There's just something about breaking bread together that deepens a relationship. A good piece of dark chocolate doesn't hurt, either.

Whatever trials you have gone through, or currently are facing, I recommend you focus on finding your *dolce vita*. It doesn't just happen; you have to create it with intention and purpose. And the results will be well worth it.

My father's death could easily have thrown my life into a tailspin. Instead, it lit a fire in me. What could I do, what can I do, to make the rest of my life the best of my life? I strive to answer that question every day.

Since 2001, I've been to Italy twenty-six times. I go at least once a year, and it has changed the trajectory of my life. At age forty-two, I moved there for a couple of months to immerse myself in the culture and learn the language. From there, I continued to take lessons and even taught for several years. Today, I am fluent, and I participate in Italian conversation and cultural groups to stay in practice between visits.

All this has allowed me to connect with my heritage in a way that makes me want that for everyone. I do it to honor my family and everything they did to make me who I am today. I have made a serious commitment that the connection with our heritage will not end with my generation. I will pass it on to my nieces and nephews, and I help others carry the torch for their families. We'll do our part and hope that the next generation will do the same.

Today, I am a woman filled with passion, peace, and purpose. It wasn't easy to get here, Lord knows. But now that I've arrived, my goal is to help everyone I meet take a few more steps toward their own *dolce vita*.

Through the years, I haven't endured abuse, battled addiction, or had the heartbreak of losing a child, but, like many people, my story has had more than its fair share of life's twists, turns, surprises, and difficulties. Yet I have overcome them with determination and perseverance.. Regardless of what life throws your way, you can too. Life has taught me that you don't disregard your past—rather, your past shapes you; it's part of you. This is mine—and it's an important part of who I am today.

I feel peace knowing everything I have experienced and endured in my sixty-plus years has shaped me. It is me. And most importantly, I know now that whatever I face, I am enough. And, my friend, so are you.

About Dawn

For over twenty-five years, Dawn Mattera Corsi has helped people create a *dolce vita* by connecting to their purpose and by continuing their legacy. A former engineer, Dawn is also a best-selling author, a certified coach, and a motivational speaker. Her coaching style offers proven techniques, heartfelt empathy, and a dash of tough love!

Within the span of a few years, she was divorced, laid off twice, moved three times, and faced her most challenging emotional and financial difficulties of her life. Rather than sink into old patterns of depression, Dawn overcame despair to design a life of passion, peace, and purpose.

She has spoken for the American Cancer Society, March of Dimes, WeightWatchers, and a defense industry contractor. A regular guest on CBS and Fox News, she has been featured in numerous media outlets.

Dawn, along with her husband Bob, have taken gladiator lessons in Rome and driven vintage Vespas through Tuscany. Her search for the best gelato continues.

- Website: www.DawnMattera.com
- LinkedIn: Dawn Mattera Corsi - Author and Speaker - Self-employed | LinkedIn
- Instagram: https://www.instagram.com/dawnmatteraauthor/
- Facebook: Dawn Mattera Author & Speaker - Home | Facebook

CHAPTER 15

SURROUNDED BY OCEANS OF GRACE

BY DR. COLLETTE WAYNE

As he pulled the giant refrigerator away from the wall, water suddenly flooded the dark wooden floor. Just then his phone rang, and he muttered something about a work emergency. He backed away from the chaos and escaped out the front door. I couldn't believe it. I had no idea how to stop the flooding, and I knew the guy who'd created this mess wouldn't return.

My leg throbbed. I'd fallen off a ladder the week before trying to take down my beloved fairy lights. They hung in a tree overlooking the beautiful yard of a home I'd grown to love. I'd broken my femur and badly damaged the same knee that ended my military career some twenty years earlier. My ankle was the size of a softball.

Less than thirty days before, my landlord had told me they were selling the house. Unexpectedly, my children and I had to pack our belongings and go. Somewhere.

We were deep in COVID. While my children navigated distance learning, I had to pack twenty years of belongings (alone) and vacate our rental. Donation centers were closed, but days of haggling over fifty cents at yard sales left me exhausted. With little capacity left, I dragged everything onto the lawn and put up a sign. "If you need it, take it. If you can leave money, put it in the mailbox."

People combed through and took away a lifetime of belongings, from practical to sentimental. Some gave generously. Others strapped so much to their cars the police came knocking, suspecting we were being robbed.

As I packed, sold, trashed, and gave away everything possible, I also had *thirteen* dogs zooming around my ankles. Before that fateful call from the landlord, we had taken on fostering a pregnant dog as our COVID project, and she ended up having a large litter of puppies. The mayhem was complete, but their soft ears, puppy kisses, and buoyant mischief brought moments of solace, laughter, and distraction.

This refrigerator was the last possession standing between me and my security deposit and avoiding another month's rent.

I was supposed to be out of the house the day before, and when my buyer left, the weight of managing this move alone became too much. Sitting in that empty house and flooded kitchen, I crumpled against the wall and cried. My eleven-year-old son, the 'man' of the house, came and sat next to me, uttering a simple, powerful sentiment.

"Mom, can I pray with you?" As we prayed through the tears, that moment's beauty and light illuminated everything. My son had faith, and I could too.

After the water was mopped and the fridge found another buyer, I was loading a small storage pod with the last of our stuff. A woman arrived, asking if we had a desk. Snarky and stressed, I told her to look around. She inspected me intently, including my swollen leg. "Are you doing this alone?" Tears once again filled my eyes.

"I'll be back," she said. Yeah, right, I thought as I silently counted all the times I had been let down by broken promises. But this complete stranger, true to her word, soon returned with her son—and food and water for everyone. She stayed until 3:00 a.m. and worked alongside me for the next three days.

That woman, now family, is a constant reminder that even in heartache, grace gifts abound. They can even show up as a 5'1" spitfire with an angel's heart, a sailor's mouth, and a seasoned warrior's work ethic, tirelessly fighting to make a difference in people's lives.

SEEKING HOME, STABILITY, AND SAFETY

Raised in an unstable home, I was living on my own by sixteen. Despite these challenges, I graduated near the top of my class. Three days later, at seventeen, I left for the US Air Force. An on-the-job knee injury and a botched military surgery left my knee permanently damaged, and by twenty, I was a disabled veteran.

Undeterred, I used my military benefits to put myself through a bachelor's degree in animal biology. I'd always had a passion for science and a deep connection with animals. They were my refuge as a child, one of the few things that brought me joy and connection. They made my world a better place, and it fostered a deep desire to repay the favor by making the world a better place for them too. Committed to my mission, but torn because I wanted a family, I had three children while earning my master's and doctorate degrees in animal behavior and welfare.

I soon secured my dream job, a high-level government position regulating the Endangered Species Act. In 2015, after a four-year stint in the nation's capital, I transferred to another amazing role protecting our nation's natural resources. We moved the family to Ventura, California, and bought a beautiful home overlooking the picturesque seaside town. Despite chronic pain, including serious flare-ups that left me without the use of my hands, from the outside, I was living the middle-class suburban dream.

THE DREAM DISSOLVES

In 2016, a complete and devastating upheaval in my personal life, coupled with years of unresolved trauma, erupted into severe health issues. This included adrenal failure, which almost killed me. Hospital stays and near-constant medical appointments forced me to medically retire from the career I had spent decades working toward.

I was soon in financial ruin. I lost my picture-perfect family and home, my mental and physical health, the façade of my suburban bliss. I'd been broke, in pain, and depressed before, but this time was different.

During past hardships, my mission always kept me going—my commitment to making the world a better place for those I deeply loved and the critters that had always been my safe space. I could always count on my competence. I was a high achiever who placed my worth and value on external accomplishments. This time, when all my accomplishments disintegrated and I lost my career, I also lost my carefully-constructed identity. Feeling like a failure at everything that mattered to me, I lost my ability to trust myself, my instincts, and my intuition.

Now, just a few years later, here I was again, having to uproot my children from another home. I knew one thing for certain. No one would ever again tell me and my children to leave another home before we were ready.

FINDING A WAY FORWARD

When I made that declaration, I was single, on disability, in debt, and living in one of the nation's most expensive places. I didn't see a path forward, but the 'how' didn't matter. I knew I had to do better for my children. With unshakeable resolve, I used all my savings to buy a janky old RV. "Give me six months," I told my children, "and I'll buy us a house."

I knew spending time in nature would be healing for our souls and driving the California coast sounded like a great way to save on rent and have a fun adventure with the kids...or so I thought. Turns out, teenage daughters need space and privacy from their little brothers and mothers, making my brilliant idea a hard sell. Adding to the difficulty was the fact I'm not the best driver. I'd never driven anything like an RV before, and the prospect terrified me. But I didn't see another way, and one line kept reverberating in my head.

If you can't, then you must.

I couldn't let fear sit in the driver's seat. I had to take control of the wheel, steering my life toward a new and hopeful direction. At first, it was an adventure. We stayed at stunning beaches and beautiful national parks and forests. Then reality descended.

While going downhill late at night in the dark Los Padres mountains, the hydraulic brake system failed. I ended up pulling the e-brake and throwing the RV into park. The horrific sound of grating metal filled the air. Grace once again filled my heart as we miraculously inched into the RV park. Terrified. Shaking. But alive.

Then COVID shut down all the parks.

Suddenly we had nowhere to stay. We could street park, but homeowners weren't bringing out their welcome mats. We were constantly moving. Police were always knocking on our door, telling us we had to leave or that where we'd parked wasn't safe. The stress of being unhoused weighed heavily on our shoulders.

My days were spent in survival mode, but I thought, I'm resourceful. There has to be a solution. I was a veteran with money still coming in, but I grossly underestimated the COVID housing crisis. Nothing was available to rent or to buy! I called every conceivable center, church, and organization. We weren't destitute enough to qualify for any assistance. I logged hours on the phone, growing more and more hopeless with every mounting response.

"Sorry. We can't help you."

I made offers on houses, but people were overbidding by tens of thousands. And paying cash. My offer, a VA loan at asking price, couldn't compete.

THE POWER OF PRAYER

After several rejected offers, my Realtor said, "I know the perfect house is out there for you. We'll find the right fit, but you need to write a letter. A really compelling letter." I sat down and wrote about my struggles, aspirations, and my 'why'—my beautiful children and my vision for connecting people, animals, and nature. I prayed those words would find us the right house. Not long after, my prayer was answered. Somebody finally accepted my offer.

The news coincided with my youngest son's tenth birthday. After celebrating in a park, we stopped in front of a seemingly random house. I handed my son one last present. He pulled the assorted letters from the bag, eventually realizing the jumble could be rearranged into his name.

"They're to hang on your wall," I said. He looked at me with complete confusion, knowing he had no wall to hang them. Pointing to our new house, I said, "In your new room." Confusion and disbelief turned to excitement as realization dawned. Everyone started shouting as joy-filled tears streamed down our faces.

When we opened the door to our new house, the woman who'd answered our prayer was waiting with a candle-filled birthday cake. She wanted us to celebrate his birthday right in our new home. Then she gave us another gift. This was her second home, and she donated everything in the house to us. Furniture. Appliances. Dishes. We went from having nothing to everything in one day.

I was overwhelmed with gratitude, joy, and relief. The realization hit me. Letting go of what no longer serves you opens you up to something so much more beautiful. A few days later, my daughter made a comment that took my breath away. As the oldest and a teenager, the last five years of hardship had been particularly hard on her.

"Do you know what you just did, Mom?" she said. "You bought your kids a house. With their own rooms! You did that. For us." Her acknowledgement of my sacrifice and work brought tears to my eyes. I had asked my kids to give me six months. We closed on the house after five months and twenty-seven days.

MY BIGGEST TAKEAWAYS

When we moved into that RV, I didn't know how or if anything would work. I just knew I needed to find a way forward for my family, and I was determined to triumph over our hardships. Conquering the fear of the unknown and following through on my commitment to my kids taught me some powerful lessons.

- **Everything happens for a reason.** Even the most incomprehensible experiences are part of the tapestry of our lives. We tend to live stuck in fear, but everything is intertwined, even when we don't see it. Our Creator is looking out for us.

Being unhoused and enduring all the physical, mental, and financial trauma illuminated my true mission in life and led me to launch Oceans of Grace Consulting, where I get to create wellness solutions to help people, animals, and the Earth. I couldn't see it then, but pain can lead us to our purpose.

- **Matthew 7:7.** "Ask and it will be given to you; seek and you will find." When we look for the bad, we find it, but when we look for the good, we find that too. By choosing to seek the grace gift in everything, those tender, heartfelt silver linings become easier to find. A son's prayer when you have nothing left to give. A stranger to help you pack and then forever forward have your back. A surprise birthday cake and love-filled house that's just the right fit. A resilient, beautiful daughter expressing her gratitude.

- **"I'll be happy when" isn't the path to joy.** My entire adult life, I'd suffered from depression and chronic pain. With a baseline of apathy, I wasn't ever really happy. Although well accomplished, it was never enough. It took losing everything I thought would make me happy to find what brought me true joy and fulfillment. Triumph over hardship allowed me to emerge knowing the essence of my soul and who I was created to be.

I once thought finding peace and joy in any situation was an impossible prayer. On the other side of this journey, I learned our souls hold the answers to our deepest prayers. We just need to listen.

- **Self-love is the first step**. My capacity to love anyone else, even my children, is only as great as my capacity to love myself. *Putting our oxygen mask on first is necessary before we can help others.*

- **Understanding your telos is essential.** Telos is a concept that means ultimate purpose or aim. In animal welfare, it's an objective way of determining whether or not an animal is suffering or thriving. It's an eagle's *eagleness*. A tiger's *tigerness*. Your 'you'ness. Only when we're living in our telos can we truly thrive.

Recently, I visited a beach we had frequented while in our RV. It was sunset. I'd just presented a draft proposal to a team of high-level government officials that had the potential to help people and animals all across the country. The idea was well received as novel and innovative. A huge victory for me. This idea to help our nation thrive had only come to me following my greatest adversity.

As I watched the orange flames of the campfire dance against the brilliance of the purple, pink, and crimson sky, I soaked in a profound sense of peace. My telos was unequivocally clear. I'm a victorious warrior. An ecosystem wellness scientist fighting for those without a voice. A model of resilience and determination.

Every step in my journey, every challenge and triumph, every ebb and flow, has been and will forever be beautifully cradled in the vast, serene oceans of endless grace.

About Dr. Collette Wayne

Dr. Collette Wayne, CEO and visionary behind Oceans of Grace Consulting, LLC stands at the forefront of 'ecosystem wellness,' a field that interweaves the well-being of humans, animals, and the environment. Her early-life journey was marked with trauma, overcoming a tumultuous upbringing and an injury that left her a disabled Air Force veteran with lifelong chronic pain by age 20. These experiences shaped her remarkable ability to transform adversity into strength.

Pivoting from the military, Dr. Wayne's lifelong passion for protecting animals and desire for understanding the natural world, led her to pursue academic success, culminating in a bachelor's degree in Animal Biology from the University of California, Davis, and a Master's and Doctorate in Animal Well-being and Behavior from Purdue University.

Over a 25-year career, Dr. Wayne has significantly contributed to animal and environmental wellness, including a notable public service career regulating the Endangered Species Act. Her experience spans academia, government, private, and non-profit sectors. Now based in Ventura, California, her diverse perspective shapes her innovative approach to addressing intertwined challenges in human, animal, and environmental health. Dr. Wayne's work, pivotal in aligning human rights and wellness with ecosystem health, has greatly impacted social and environmental justice, and conservation.

At the heart of Dr. Wayne's commitment to creating a better world is her role as a mother to three accomplished teenagers. Watching them flourish as they realize their "telos" or ultimate purpose, she finds a constant source of inspiration and motivation. This personal experience deeply influences her professional ethos, reinforcing her belief that with 'wholistic' wellness, every living being can achieve its inherent potential and create a meaningful contribution towards the collective wellness of our ecosystem.

Beyond her professional pursuits, Dr. Wayne is passionately involved in nature and animal-related activities. She finds solace and inspiration outdoors and rejuvenates her soul by participating in wildlife rescue and rehabilitation, training service dogs for disabled veterans, and supporting equine therapy for veterans and at-risk youth. These endeavors provide her with the strength and clarity to continue her crucial work towards a thriving planet.

Dr. Wayne's life and career, embodying resilience and compassion, highlight the impact of dedication to ecosystem wellness. Her story demonstrates how individual commitment can effect significant change, emphasizing the importance of passion, resilience, and a holistic perspective in creating a healthier and more sustainable future.

Learn more about Dr. Wayne:

- www.OceansofGrace.Earth
- Social media: @DrColletteWayne
- Social media: @oceansofgrace805

CHAPTER 16

DEFY THE "NO!" – MAKE ROOM FOR THE MIRACLE

BY JENAE JOHNSON

I planted my feet on the linoleum floor and steadied myself in the cushion-less chair, my three-month-old daughter cuddled in my arms. "I hear what you're saying, Dean Woods, but I'm not leaving until I have the courses I need to graduate in May."

Eight months later, I'd be in this Howard University Dean's office— again. Explaining that I was pregnant—again. Explaining that my babies' father (also a Howard student) had abandoned us because I refused to abort our second child. Explaining that I had been in a deep depression and missed weeks of class. I was there again to defy the 'no'—and press forward until it was a 'yes.' And yes, I did graduate in May 2004—with my sleeping eleven-month-old daughter in my arms, and my son in my womb.

This idea of defying the 'no' has been a constant theme in my life. I wish I could tell you a double pregnancy in college was the only major obstacle in my adult life. Far from it. But before you shed any tears for me, here's a spoiler alert—my life worked out. Like *really* worked out. Those two babies are now college students. I'm married to a wonderful, God-fearing man with whom I had two more babies. I'm the founder and CEO of a multi-million-dollar consulting firm. My life is not without obstacles and trials, but it's *full* of blessings beyond what I imagined possible.

Before this became my reality, I had many other struggles and losses. I lost a house and a car in 2009 because I couldn't keep up with rising costs on a teacher's salary. I received very little help from my kids' father, as he would occasionally try, but was never consistent in his financial support or physical presence. He'd go years not seeing his kids and months without sending money for their care.

My relationship with God, while sometimes fractured, was the only constant during those years. But no matter how many 'no's' were in my path, that faith-fueled defiance made space for countless miracles. During this time of financial strain, a friend introduced me to *The Secret*. I remember seeing one Black woman on the back cover. My friend also introduced me to other thought leaders who taught The Law of Attraction. That idea resonated with me deeply. It aligned with what I knew intuitively about how God and faith *actually* works but was very different from what I'd been taught growing up in church.

I resigned from my teaching position (before I had another full-time job lined up, because of, well, the whole 'defy the no for the miracle' thing) and then got hired as a corporate trainer for a Fortune 500 company. I was so grateful for the salary, and my great boss, but it was only temporary because I knew, one day I would have my own business.

Very temporary, as it turned out. Eighteen months into the role, a major oil and gas company recruited me to work for them for a lot more money, but with a catch. It was a contract role, which meant at any point, the company could end my tenure. Most people would never leave a secure job for something with no guarantees, especially as a single mom with no significant savings. But my faith wouldn't let me rest on the easy answer, and I defied the 'no.' I left that secure corporate job and started down a path of uncertainty. It was one of the best decisions I've ever made.

Over the next few years, I defied many more 'no's,' making way for many miracles. By 2015, I had created 'a business on paper,' meaning I was a company of one, with no real infrastructure other than an LLC and a business bank account. I liked the flexibility of contracting and eventually started taking on two contracts at a time. I was dating my now husband David, and making over $100K. I'd come a long way from struggling on a teacher's salary, but I felt restless...lost. So, in the summer of 2015, I booked a solo trip to Santa Monica with one purpose—to hear from God what I was really supposed to be doing with my life.

In August of that same summer, a friend sent me a link to register for a live series Lisa Nichols was broadcasting on Periscope (remember Twitter's first attempt at livestreaming?) about speaking, writing, abundance, and building successful businesses. It looked interesting (and free), so I registered. I didn't recognize Lisa at first, but eventually I remembered her as one of the co-authors from *The Secret*.

On day one of Lisa's broadcast, she extended her time and did some 'behind the scenes' filming after dropping juicy nuggets on business and abundance. She took us into her home, shoe closet, and beautifully landscaped backyard and pool. I couldn't stop staring at the screen. I knew her, somehow – not from *The Secret*, but some other way. I ran through a list of my 15+ aunties in my head, trying to figure out if she looked like one of them, but that wasn't it. *My spirit knew her.*

She talked about her upcoming conference and invited us to enroll. Every day, no matter how drawn to her, I would exit out of the broadcast, thinking, *I don't even understand what her business is. I've never paid that much for any conference. This isn't for me.* But God wouldn't leave me alone about registering, so with one eye open, I typed in my credit card info on the last day of the registration period.

September rolled around and I left my laptop, boyfriend, and kids back in Houston because I wanted to hear from God about my life with no distractions. I took an early flight to LA and as I sat eating my breakfast, I googled events around the city. I caught sight of a jazz and poetry concert that night. *Oh yeah, I'm going to this.* But the website said it was sold out. No problem. At this point, I was used to defying the 'no.'

I found contact info on the website and sent an email. "Hey, I just got here from Houston. I understand the show is sold out, but I'd like to attend." Then I closed my tablet, finished breakfast, and headed for a massage. Later, I checked my phone. The organizer had left me a message: "We have one VIP ticket left. If you'd like it, call me back." Crazy, right? Oh, it gets crazier.

That night at the theater, I flagged down an attendant to help me find my seat. He ushered me over to Lisa Nichols and her team, who were also waiting for the show to start. Read that again slowly. It was Lisa… in person…at the same show that had been sold out. I'd defied the 'no' and I was seeing the miracle unfold before my eyes.

I was a mess. Stuttering, crying, sweating. I could barely get the words out. "Lisa! I'm coming to your conference. I can't believe I'm standing here in front of you!" She smiled, hugged me, and explained she normally stays at home with her family when she's not traveling or speaking, but one of her coaching clients had invited her, so she obliged. We took a picture together, and, needless to say, I look crazy in the picture.

The next morning, and every morning during my stay, I walked to the beach and prayed. Every morning, God gave me a vision for my life that was way outside of what made sense. But He had already confirmed so much for me with my encounter with Lisa that first night, I was open.

At the time, I wasn't sure my boyfriend, David, would ever marry again after being hurt in his first marriage. But God's vision showed me our future marriage and family, which included an abundance of purpose, wealth, children, and world impact—none of which we had at the time. I kept praying, listening, and writing what I heard—even though it all seemed impossible.

I flew back to California in November for the conference. It didn't take long to realize why I'd needed to attend. Beyond the brilliance Lisa shared from the stage, I connected with so many angelic strangers who spoke into my life, as if they could see the better version of me… the future me. One lady told me, "I don't know what it is, but you have power in you. You will be very successful."

Attending these conferences emboldens a person to believe in miracles, and I was ready. As I sat absorbing the content from the stage, I kept thinking the material for participants didn't reflect the value of what the speakers were offering in the room. I had an idea.

As Lisa closed out the conference from the stage, I tiptoed out the back door to catch someone in the hallway. I found myself face to face with Susie, the then-COO of Lisa's company Motivating the Masses. I steadied my gaze and quieted my pounding heart. "Susie, I'm coming to you because I believe Motivating the Masses is my next client." I explained what my business did for companies, and what I'd observed about the content.

She took my card. "Actually, our director of content just resigned." And in an unforgettable, hilarious moment, she leaned over and told me, "I'm gonna put your card in my bra because I want to remember you."

Lisa had just released *The New York Times* bestseller *Abundance Now* and planned to develop online products. Back at home, I created a proposal for building self-paced videos that aligned with the book, pinching myself at this surreal opportunity.

Susie and I met in December to review the proposal. "Listen, we can't afford to pay that amount. Could we do a trade? Are you interested in attending the Global Leadership Program?" The program was Lisa's signature and most exclusive offering, worth $40,000. Easy decision. The miracle was rapidly unfolding, but my miracle, and my life, would soon be hanging in the balance.

A week later, I discovered I was pregnant. Three days later, David rushed me to our local ER, doubled over in pain. After a frantic ultrasound and blood work, I braced myself against the gurney as EMTs hoisted me into the back of an ambulance. In an effort to save my life, they transferred me to the Houston Medical Center for emergency surgery. My fallopian tube had ruptured, causing extensive inflammation and internal bleeding; some of my organs were shutting down.

I awoke from surgery, my head spinning from all the sobering realities. I'd lost the baby, a fallopian tube, and too much blood. In those early recovery days, I'd also lost my faith. A week later, the doctor called to check on me. "I didn't want to alarm you, but I'm glad you came in when you did. If you had waited until morning, you may not be alive today." His words shook me and I mustered a shaky "thank you" before hanging up. After all the miraculous moments in 2015, this was how my year ended.

The emergency surgery and subsequent recovery halted my momentum.

I'd just signed onto Lisa's company as a client and the GLP started in February. January came and I remained weak, anemic, and grieving the miscarriage. But I could sit up in bed, so I asked David to move my office items to the bedroom. I was determined not to miss an upcoming meeting with Susie to further discuss the details on the *Abundance Now* project. This project had placed me exactly where I was supposed to be, doing that I was meant to do. And it was the beginning of CTM Unlimited, the company I own today.

The loss and anemia left me breathless and broken. But God kept whispering reminders of the vision He'd given me, so I pressed on and traveled to the GLP in February. There I connected with amazing entrepreneurs and visionaries who showed me what was possible. My experience building corporate e-learning proved valuable among my peers in the program. Lisa was my first client, but she referred me to other people in the program who also needed online courses built. Before I could even land on a company name, my client list started filling up.

In one particular working session, Lisa challenged us to get clear about our company's value proposition. That exercise helped me land on the company name: Content That Matters. And the tagline was: We rescue geniuses.

This was the beginning of my current company, CTM Unlimited. In 2017, I merged my corporate consulting business (remember the one that was only a business on paper?) with Content That Matters. In 2020, we rebranded to CTM Unlimited, which encompassed Consulting that Matters, Change that Matters, Communication that Matters, Culture that Matters, and a few other 'C' words that defined our approach to strategic talent and workplace consulting.

The last few years haven't been without challenges, but I've seen so much of the vision God gave me in 2015 come to fruition. David and I married and although I only had one fallopian tube, we easily got pregnant—twice. As our blended family grew by two, we saw God continue to do the impossible.

Many times God has called me to defy the no to make room for a miracle, and even though it always works out eventually, here's the truth—I'm often frightened. But one thing I learned from Lisa was how to dance with fear instead of waiting for the fear to go away before making a move. The heaviest question we often carry when taking risks is: What if it doesn't work out? I'm challenging you to reframe that question and ask, *What if it does?*

So many of my life decisions defied conventional wisdom—graduating from Howard with two babies, leaving a salaried job to pursue consulting, traveling to California just to hear from God, pushing through pregnancy loss and anemia to launch CTM—the list goes on.

For me, the miracles were just past the 'no.' While it's in God's nature to exceed our wildest dreams, He often tells us to do something that doesn't make sense. Ignoring our nagging logic or what society says is impossible makes room for God to work on our behalf.

I finally figured out why my spirit knew Lisa when I first saw her on Periscope. Though I couldn't have known this at the time, God did. He saw how she was destined to be my client. How my life would become a testimony to countless women who have experienced loss. How I would launch CTM Unlimited, and how nine years later, He'd give call me to co-author a book with Lisa on rising above the most dire circumstances and making room for miracles with faithful defiance.

About JeNae

Meet JeNae Johnson, the visionary founder and CEO at CTM Unlimited, a trailblazing workplace consultancy dedicated to transforming organizations from ordinary to legendary. At the heart of CTM Unlimited's transformative approach is a data-driven model that propels clients into the forefront of innovation. Based in Houston, TX, CTM Unlimited's experts immerse themselves in the client's journey, ensuring they are equipped with the essential tools, capabilities, and courage to achieve sustainable success. Specializing in strategic talent planning, people analytics, equity and culture strategy, strategic communications, and change management, CTM Unlimited is committed to fostering environments where every individual can flourish, contribute meaningfully, and drive impactful results to the bottom line.

JeNae's journey is a testament to resilience, determination, and unwavering faith. Her relationship with God has been the driving force behind every career move and business decision. Starting her career as a high school teacher while facing the challenges of single motherhood, she overcame adversity by relying her faith. One such leap of faith was leaving her teaching job to pursue a career in corporate learning and development, where she quickly flourished.

As a PROSCI® certified Change Practitioner and a Fascinate® Certified Advisor, JeNae brings various methodologies to the forefront of her consultancy. Her approach is marked by a profound understanding of corporate culture, workplace systems and behavior change. In 2020, she created Bold x Brave™ Conversations, an action-based framework designed to help leaders navigate workplace challenges.

Notable for consulting with industry giants such as Tesla, Boeing, Chevron, Sysco, and Salesforce, JeNae continues to lead CTM Unlimited to help create workplaces of the future. As a sought-after speaker, trainer, and facilitator, JeNae's consulting expertise coupled with stories of radical faith inspire both corporate audiences and women from all walks of life.

JeNae is a proud graduate of Howard University and a dedicated supporter of HBCUs. With a daughter at North Carolina A&T University and a son at Prairie View A&M University, JeNae continues to engage with the HBCU community, and in 2021, CTM Unlimited launched its own internship program at Howard University.

Her journey is marked by growth and achievement, including graduating from the Goldman Sachs 10K Small Businesses program, Leadership Houston, and the SBA Thrive Emerging Leaders program.

Beyond her professional prowess, JeNae is a dedicated wife to David and a loving mother to five children ranging from age 2 to 20—no, that's not a typo.

CHAPTER 17

A VOICE FOR CHANGE
RISE TO THE CHALLENGE TO MAKE THE WORLD A BETTER PLACE

BY JULIE MEATES

As the four-year cycle of the Olympics again arrives, inspiration and courage meet, and nations of the earth unite with a common vision and hope. Big dreams abound as people overcome barriers within every realm of themselves to vie for a place on the podium—a symbol of hope in a world reeling from challenges, trauma, existential crises, mental health crises, grief, environmental degradation, greed, human trafficking, slavery, and war. Hope reigns supreme for the many who rise up—transcend the chaos—beyond many people's realm of understanding to make the world a better place.

Similarly, the South African national rugby team, the Springboks, "has once again become a tool of togetherness," says Nik Simon of the Daily Mail, having won the Rugby World Cup (the equivalent to the NFL in America), beating New Zealand by one point, in October 2023. The last time these two teams met in a World Cup final was in 1995, when Nelson Mandela presented the trophy. "They delve into their hardships and use it as a force for the greater good, reaching an emotional pinnacle the opposition can struggle to live with." In the words of Springbok Captain Siya Kolisi, "This team just shows what you can do. As soon as we work together, all is possible, no matter in what sphere." As the South African president, Mandela gave the Springboks the motto "One Team, One Country," to help unify the nation.

WORKING TOGETHER, ALL THINGS ARE POSSIBLE

These two examples show that, in the words of Mandela, sport "has the power to inspire. It has the power to unite people in a way that little else does. … Sport can create hope where there was only despair."

These examples also show that if we work together, all things are possible. If we all work together, we actually could create peace and save the rainforests. That's the sort of message that I believe brings hope in a world filled with challenges—a simple, yet complex solution to climate change crisis, allying a beauty with hope beyond understanding, protecting our homes and environment for future generations to come. For sometimes we tear down rainforests like we tear down people. It hurts a lot of people. And let not your harsh words and actions be like killing machines, but soften them so gardens, forests, and people can blossom and thrive, nor allow emotions to create thunder that causes the heart and soul to bleed like the Gaza strip.

For so many others have a fight going on inside of them, like the story told by an American man to his grandson. "It is a terrible fight, and it is between two wolves. One is evil—it is anger, envy, jealousy, sorrow, regret, greed, arrogance, self-pity, guilt, contempt, resentment, inferiority, lies, false pride, superiority, and ego. The other is good— joy, peace, love, hope, serenity, humility, kindness, benevolence, empathy, generosity, truth, compassion, courage, and faith. The one we feed becomes the greater, creating depression as deep as the Siberian sink hole, or anxiety that cracks the soul as fractured as the Antarctic ice cracking—like a doomsday glacier. But we have a choice…

And that's a challenge—to throw down the gauntlet and work together like there is no tomorrow. Helping other people overcome challenges and fulfill their dreams is a passion. Their challenges are our challenges. Their stories are our story.

Empathy and compassion for other people helps, as does love of family and love of people. And when you love people a lot, then you can empathize with what they are going through. We hear the cries of the people. I want them to believe in themselves and see all the goodness

I see in them so they can fulfill their dreams. There's nothing more joyful in life.

A VOICE FOR THE VOICELESS

Literally from the Congo to the Vatican, one of the greatest challenges that the people face is being listened to and not having their common home desecrated for conflict minerals for our disruptive technologies and addictions. Therefore, this story endeavors to help wise people be heard—to be a voice for the voiceless, to give them hope. For example, when the archbishop at the Vatican asked if I could help with the plight of the Congo, I did not hesitate to say yes.

The Democratic Republic of Congo has experienced the loss of seven million lives due to war and conflict as a direct effect of mining to create cell phone and gaming technology. Currently, about 15 billion operate worldwide, double the global population, while in 2022, 5.3 billion cell phones were expected to become waste, up a billion from the previous year (only a small number disposed of properly), poisoning the food supply, according to the WEEE (waste electrical and electronic equipment) Forum. Stacked on top of each other, the phones would rise one-eighth of the way to the moon.

At twenty-six years old, I ended up in the Congo, visiting the rainforest. The beauty, love, and kindness of the people and a rainforest intact are phenomenal. History has a habit of repeating. Why can we not learn from our past? Due to wars, the slave trade, the holocaust of enslavement, deforestation, mining for precious resources to manufacture addictive technology, and other issues, along with the permanent, impermeable scars that are left, people are suffering and dying; whole communities are affected.

Do we sit there in the comfort of our homes, or do we have the courage to speak up? As Martin Luther King Jr. said, "The ultimate measure of a man is not where he stands in moments of comfort and convenience, but where he stands at times of challenge and controversy."

After losing her husband in conflict, feeling she was also in danger, a remarkable woman named Lema Shamamba fled the Democratic

Republic of Congo and lived for two long years with her son as a refugee in Uganda, under a mango tree, having to leave two of her children behind. When the UN saw an interview with her, they enabled her to go with her three children to New Zealand in 2009.

But in the DRC alone, there are over a million refugees. Some are children traveling alone; some are women at risk. Lema's homeland was decimated for the minerals in our phones and other electronics. **On our phones alone, we will spend about nine years** – according to a 2020 study by WhistleOut. The forest in Lema's country is a major carbon sink for the planet, the second-largest rainforest in the world, next to the Amazon. But big multinationals and insatiable human greed mean our modus operandi is disruptive devices. It doesn't even matter if there is a climate change crisis or ongoing wars in many parts of the world. I really wish that our leaders and Elon Musk would listen, for then, the planet would no longer be in jeopardy from our greed.

"It is a beautiful country," she says. "The soil is so fertile—it can grow anything, yet ordinary people are starving. Big companies want the rare earth and precious minerals buried beneath it to make cell phones and other things, and this has made men crazy for money. My country's now divided—and it's the women who suffer most."

In fact, United Nations Women reports that 27 percent of women in DRC are victims of harmful practices, including rape, and they are fueled by financial gains and profits from violent insurgencies for conflict minerals for the electronics industry. Up to 52 percent of women in the DRC are domestic violence survivors, the UN Women report also states.

Lema says people are fleeing daily from their villages; it's hard to have a statistic because they are constantly displaced due to violent insurgency because of conflict minerals. Lema is vehement about the impact of DRC's conflict on women. "They know when they destroy women, they destroy the whole community, they destroy the whole country. They know that there is no one watching them."

In fact, the problem is global. According to UN Women, global estimates of domestic violence published by the World Health Organization show that about one in three (35 percent) of women worldwide have experienced physical and/or sexual intimate-partner or non-partner violence. And some national studies show figures as high as 70 percent.

Also, a 2017 UN report says that the DRC has 2.7 million internally displaced children who are vulnerable to forced labor in mines—diamonds, gold, copper, and cobalt. While international pressure has meant some companies source minerals mined by mining corporations rather than artisanal miners, who are more likely to use forced labor, it's still fraught with violent infractions. Now, the number of displaced people is double that, at more than six million—more than the population of the country Lema now lives in.

A few international companies have signed an international covenant on ethical practice in their mining activities, but these covenants are often breached in practice. "Many groups who have no regard for human life or dignity continue to enslave local people, and rape and murder those they cannot use," Lema says. She urges everyone to remember these atrocities, which continue, especially in the north and east of the DR Congo, because of the mining of coltan and other precious minerals (cobalt, gold, silver—all may be used in our electronic devices), and to take some action as in the movie *Sound of Freedom*.

In the DRC, female slavery and child labor are rife, while education is taking a back seat. In 2014, Lema founded Women of Hope, which connects migrant women through activities such as crafts, growing indigenous foods, children's play groups, and more. Her goal is great—to help humanity. She has a vision. She speaks so wisely. I wish they would listen.

WHAT DOES IT MEAN TO RISE UP?

When I asked this question of a wonderful young person, he answered, "Depends on the context. For some, it could be waking up in the morning."

I asked another young adult, "What does rise up' mean?" She answered, "Sometimes we have so much stress and stuff on our plate that we can't even talk. But we all have a moment of grace. There are many insights. ... If we get to the root of the problem, we might just rise up and help end the enslavement of people mining minerals for our electronic devices and change the world for the fifty million people who are trapped in slavery globally."

The Elders, which Mandela formed in 2007, is an organization of global leaders who work toward peace, human rights, justice, and a more sustainable planet. The group includes former US President Jimmy Carter, former presidents and prime ministers of other countries, and former UN Secretary General Ban Ki-moon, as well as business leaders such as Richard Branson, and seeks to create solutions to global issues including climate change.

In 2017, Oprah told a group of graduates to shift their thinking to service and ask, "How can I be used? Life, use me. Show me … how to be used in the greater service to life."

The answer lies with us—you and me. Let's save this planet. Let's put an end to slavery.

LOVE CAN MOVE THE SOUL

The five interlaced rings that are the Olympic symbol, a visual ambassador of billions of people, represent hopes and dreams for the union of the five continents. The Olympic Movement is underpinned by three values: excellence, respect, and friendship. The goal of the Olympic Movement is to "contribute to building a peaceful and better world…through sport practiced without discrimination of any kind and in the Olympic spirit, which requires mutual understanding with a spirit of friendship, solidarity, and fair play."

The same applies to the game called life.

Sometimes we don't know the answers, our brains and bodies can sometimes feel fried, and sometimes we can feel weighed down and squashed by all the challenges of life. However, like a child, we may fall and graze our knee and we can rise to find the inner joy and laughter with the help of a team, family, faith, a simple hug, and the power of love. Love can move the soul, move a heart to make the eyes water, even a drop, a tear. If we rise with the power of love—if we replace the emptiness, sorrow, loneliness, grief, pain, frustration, broken hearts, broken promises, betrayal, and any other manifestation of heartbreak—it can crack open our true potential.

Rise up and overcome your challenges. Rise up to the opportunities. You are capable of rising up more than you think you can. Live your life with no regrets. Don't sell your soul. Stay true to your values. The world needs hope like no tomorrow, for seeds of change can transform your sorrow.

I've always been one to turn negatives into positives, and instead of complaining about things, doing something about them. Dolly Parton's song "World on Fire" (2023), which speaks of the division in the world today, raises two questions—how we can heal it, and whether we care enough to show kindness and love…and to try to make positive changes.

Mandela said it best: "Sometimes it falls upon a generation to be great—you can be that generation."

About Julie

Julie Meates is a New Zealand-born humanitarian with a diverse career, endeavoring to bring more peace, kindness and love into the world. Family is central to her life, as she is married with three children and a large extended family.

Beginning her career as a teacher, Julie's passion for education and health led her to become qualified as a social worker and counselor. She is now a barrister and solicitor, actively pursuing post-graduate studies in education and health. Her commitment to community wellbeing is evident in her extensive volunteer work, driven by her belief in paying kindness forward.

In 2002, Julie co-founded the Fulfil A Dream Foundation, with a vision, hope and dream of strong and happy families, happy, healthy, vibrant communities, and wise and visionary leadership, uniting high-profile figures from various fields to empower individuals, families, and communities. She also chaired the indigenous Maori learning center, Kohanga Reo.

Julie is a six-time Best-Selling Author, co-authoring books like, *Pay It Forward* with Brian Tracy, *Success, The Soul of Success – Vol. 3, Turning Point,* and *The Keys to Authenticity* with Jack Canfield, along with *Never Give Up* with Dick Vitale. These books contribute to various causes, including nonprofits dedicated to ending human trafficking and modern-day slavery, among others.

Julie joined Abundance Studios as a Producer and worked on notable films including, *The Truth About Reading, Dickie V, It's Happening Right Here, Tactical Empathy,* and *Hero.* She has also been a guest on TV shows such as *Hollywood Live, Times Square Today,* and *The Global Entrepreneurship Initiative's Summer Symposium* at Carnegie Hall. Her appearances have been featured on NBC, ABC, CBS, and FOX nationwide.

Julie has volunteered with Community Law's programme, in community justice panels that facilitate restorative justice to promptly address harm caused by offenders. She also served as the Board Secretary for the United Nations executive in her Canterbury region and is involved with the Women of Hope Wake Up and Help Ourselves Trust Board.

Throughout her career, Julie has volunteered with Women's Refuge, various NGOs, charitable organizations, sport, musical, cultural, social and community-led initiatives, empowering youth, families and communities. She held the position of Vice President at Wairarapa International Communities Incorporated, engaged in community radio with local, national, and international broadcasts, and contributed to homelessness initiatives nationally and internationally.

Julie Meates is a compassionate, kind leader, adept at inspiring, influencing, coordinating, and empowering diverse groups of people to achieve their goals.

CHAPTER 18

THE POWER OF VOICE

BY DEBRA LEE FADER

Without warning, I collapsed, feeling the carpet suddenly beneath my knees. Then, confused and mind racing, I faceplanted against my bedroom floor. I had quite literally fallen out of bed, and I could barely move any part of my body. All I could manage was working my nose to the side so I could breathe a bit better. I was alone in the house and blindsided by my sudden paralysis.

Using what little mobility I had, I pulled myself across the carpet on my belly until, terrified and exhausted, I reached a phone. I immediately called my husband to come get me.

What ensued was months of uncertainty and testing. Even as my organs began shutting down and I became wheelchair-bound, no doctor could figure out what was wrong. They tested for what felt like everything. Finally, Dr. Gary Brunkow thought of ordering an Eastern-Western blot test. Sure enough, the Western blot came back positive for Lyme disease.

With a proper diagnosis, I could start the necessary treatments, but I still had a long and painful journey back. In those early days, my husband had to physically pick me up and take me to my appointments. Over the ensuing months, I regained enough strength and coordination to stand. Then walk. Then dance again.

Slowly, I began to feel like my old self.

I had no way of knowing then, but this was just the beginning of my journey. A path that would test me, try me, and, ultimately, bring me peace in the knowledge that I had reliable anchors in my life. My family, my friends, my faith, and my voice.

THE CALL OF THE SPOTLIGHT

As an entertainer, a singer, and a dancer, courage and compassion have always been present in my life. Getting up on stage, sharing your gifts, and connecting with your audience takes guts.

I started my singing career at thirteen. I was in a polka band (now registered in the Minnesota Hall of Fame). Later, I was accepted to the Juilliard School and USIU-SPVA, a prestigious school of performing and visual arts in San Diego. I chose the West Coast. (I was done with cold winters for a while!)

By my junior year, I had received my Equity card and was playing Hodel in *Fiddler on the Roof*. I then toured internationally as Petra with *A Little Night Music*.

When I graduated from USIU-SPVA, the lights of the Las Vegas strip called. I was the singing star at the center of *Lido de Paris* at the Stardust Hotel and Casino. It was a demanding show, made more difficult by my need to constantly stand up for myself to management and others because of my diminutive stature. It was my first real introduction to using my voice, not as a musical instrument but as a powerful tool to direct my life.

After *Lido*, I worked extensively in Puerto Rican luxury hotel extravaganzas, television, and commercials. For years, sailing both the Atlantic and the Pacific Oceans, I also had my own cabaret act on various cruise lines around the Caribbean and Mexico.

I loved my life. I loved my career. But as I approached forty, I realized I wasn't twenty-one anymore. (Though, everyone around me was!) I didn't know how long I could sing, dance, and perform every single night.

Again, I let my voice lead me. This time it was the voice inside telling me I wanted more out of my life than just my professional pursuits. It was time to go home and start the next chapter of my life.

HOMECOMING

Life has a way of bringing just what you need, just when you need it. True to that idea, shortly after moving home, I met my future husband. (We married in 1997 and have been together ever since.)

For many years, we ran the Sportsmen Inn together while I also put my voice to work in broadcasting and radio. Shortly after selling that business, we decided to start a new life in Savage, Minnesota.

All was going well until that morning I fell out of bed.

After my lengthy diagnosis, treatment, and recovery, we opted to get out of the city. After such a close brush with death, neither of us felt the stress and congestion were good for us.

We ended up buying our business back and moving home to Montevideo. I was feeling better and stronger with every passing month, and I even had the strength to go back to work.

THE REAL STRUGGLES BEGIN

I felt like my old self for almost a full year. Then I began to notice twinges, aches, and stiffness throughout my body. I remember joking on the phone with my mom that I felt like the Hunchback of Notre Dame, dragging my left foot as I walked. More and more, I couldn't move my body. Every doctor had a different idea. Whatever their guess, nothing worked. I continued to deteriorate.

Despite constant hospital visits and intermittently needing a wheelchair, one doctor was adamant it was all in my head. He pulled my husband aside, telling him not to pay any more attention to my complaints.

"Stop pampering her," he said, looking directly into my husband's face. This string of misdiagnoses continued from 2007 to 2013. During

177

this period, I did a lot of listening…to my body…to the limits it was enforcing….to myself. And what I heard was an increasing pull toward civic duty.

In the summer of 2010, I was feeling a little better, and I decided to run for mayor of my beloved Montevideo. Many people dismissed my campaign as a joke, but when the final vote was tallied, I ended up unseating the fourteen-year incumbent.

Meeting and greeting people. Making my town better. It was the perfect position for me. But my lapses in health were becoming more prominent and limiting. I was doing my mayoral duties, but I often needed a cane or a steadying arm to get around. (Still, I went on to hold the position for eight wonderful years.)

It was obvious something was going on in my nervous system, but I was yet to have a formal diagnosis. Then, in the summer of 2013, I became very ill and landed in Montevideo Hospital. By chance (or the intervention of a higher power), I saw a different doctor. Dr. NP Gregg Waylander. He immediately recognized there was some condition going on and recommended me to the Mayo Clinic.

THE LONG-AWAITED ANSWER

When you go to the Mayo Clinic, it's an intensive period of two to three weeks. You do nothing but take tests, provide samples, and undergo experiments. But no one else in the state could get a handle on what was happening to me, so I submitted to the endless battery of needle sticks, prods, and questions.

Accompanying me was a thick three-ring binder containing my complete medical history. Every test I'd ever been subjected to, all the way back to my eventual Lyme disease diagnosis.

I had three female doctors assigned to my case, and one suggested a spinal puncture test. The doctor who had told my family to ignore me had also ordered this test, so I knew the results were somewhere in that massive binder. I also knew it was a painful procedure I wasn't excited about repeating.

The doctors kindly told me they weren't going to put me through that ordeal again, and they examined the results of the previous test. It showed thirteen oligoclonal bands. Starting at three bands, you can begin to assume the presence of multiple sclerosis (MS). I felt a confusing jumble of emotions. Relief at having the diagnosis. Fear of what it meant. Shock at the years of misdiagnosis and medical gaslighting.

After leaving the Mayo Clinic, my sister, Shelley, accompanied me to my next local doctor's appointment. After the solace of a formal diagnosis, I was devastated when the doctor at that visit said the three female physicians had misinterpreted my diagnosis. He wanted to formally write this into my medical chart. He told me to come back in three years. If my condition had worsened, he said, we'd go from there.

With as little strength as I had, I didn't have the physical, mental, or emotional capacity at that point to fight. Luckily, Shelley took control of the conversation. She wrested my medical records from his hands, not allowing him to add any notes that could compromise future doctors' opinions or even my right to claim disability, if necessary.

Shelley knew me and my spirit. She knew what I was capable of, and she wouldn't allow one person's ill-informed opinion to stand in the way of my care. I learned that day it isn't always your own voice that saves you. When you've been through trials and your voice feels weak, it can be the kind, compassionate voices of your loved ones that ring out loudly in your defense.

MORE DOCTORS...AND THE BLESSING OF A NEW FDA DRUG

It was another two full years before I found a doctor to help me. At this point, I could barely hold myself up on a cane. I ended up going to a rural Mayo Clinic satellite location, where I met Dr. Kristen Kelly-Williams. She suggested I go to Edina, Minnesota, to continue treatment. From there, I was referred to Dr. Yelena Usmanova, a respected physician on the cutting edge of MS.

When I met Dr. Usmanova, she uttered one sentence that changed my life. She said I was a candidate for Ocrevus. It was a new drug just approved by the FDA, and it was meant to be good for anyone with primary progressive MS. The first infusion of the drug took eleven hours. The second round took another eleven. I had the litany of unusual reactions, but those cleared within a week.

Since starting in 2017, every six months I've had another daylong infusion. I know with every ounce of my being that had I not had that drug, I would be bound to a wheelchair today. Ocrevus allowed me to halt my symptoms at their 2017 levels.

I don't hurt as much through my back, neck, and hips. I don't seize up like the Tin Man left out in the elements anymore. And I can still sing my heart out, sharing my voice and love with the world.

COURAGE, COMPASSION, AND LESSONS

Before any of my medical issues, I was scared to death of hospitals and shots. Doctors basically had to chase me around the table for a routine blood draw. After the endless tests I underwent, I realized seeing blood can feel scary, but it's nothing less than your life force. It's what's coursing through your veins, sustaining you and keeping you alive.

I also know I couldn't have physically or emotionally made it through the years without the help of God. Genuine angels (family, friends, and doctors) were placed in my life, ensuring I survived all the difficult times.

As a gregarious person who loves people, it's difficult for me not to engage with everyone. But I did encounter toxic people on this journey who brought nothing but negativity. They saw me as a flighty, naïve diva looking for attention.

It's a difficult lesson to learn, but you have to weed out those people from your life. For your own safety, health, and boundaries, you must take those steps of self-protection. Kindness, love, hope, and reciprocity are the keys to unlocking prosperity, and it takes courage to only let people into your life living in those beliefs.

Not once did I let this looming disease stop me from following God's path. When you don't have the connection to something higher, that's when it's easy to succumb to negativity. Sadness. Self-pity. All the things that don't help you.

When you grab that compass of God, you'll still encounter diverging paths, but you'll always be able to discern which way to go.

THE GIFT OF MY VOICE

Through my early career, my days of glitzy stage lights, and my string of misdiagnoses, my singing voice has been the constant. God gave me this incredible gift, and it's been a bridge to get me over and through every obstacle I've ever had. It's brought nothing but goodness and kindness into my life.

In Montevideo, we have an annual festival that celebrates our town and our sister city, Montevideo, Uruguay. Uruguayan dignitaries always attend, and one year, while acting mayor, I learned and performed the Uruguayan national anthem in Spanish for them.

The gesture was so well received it resulted in a fully paid trip to Uruguay sponsored by the US State Department and Partners of the Americas. Over eleven days, I got to meet the mayor of Montevideo, as well as several senators and the Uruguayan president.

Singing has always opened doors for me and allowed me to give back to people. I'm never closer to the soul within me than when I'm singing.

I'm retired now, but I still help Ruth Ann Lee put on performances at Hollywood on Main, the historical theater she renovated in Montevideo. We produce everything from Christmas shows, to multicultural worship shows, to patriotic veteran-awareness shows. Many benefits have gone through those theater doors. We continually use our voices and charitable messages to raise money or goods for food banks, women's shelters, and other worthy causes.

Before my time as mayor, I created and performed a twelve-step show for people in the grips of alcohol, drug, or gambling addiction. This remains one of the most intimate and connective times I've ever had with an audience. Bolstered by the importance and the fulfillment of giving, I also started two nonprofits: Diversity-USA and Queen of Kindness.

My true calling has always been community work and humanitarianism. It's why show business eventually became stifling. A youth-oriented pursuit that didn't allow me to stretch myself and to breathe.

When I gave my life to God, grasping onto that compass and holding tight, I found all the sustainment I sought. I've always loved bringing people solace and peace. By communicating my essence and telling stories through song and entertainment, I've been promoting goodwill throughout my life.

And I know I'll be paying it forward while (yes) singing my heart out for the rest of my life…even if I can't dance as well as I used to.

About Debra Lee

Debra Lee Fader, a Music and Theater Graduate of the United States International University in San Diego, CA, is a multifaceted talent in the entertainment industry. She's been the principal singer of 'Lido de Paris' at the Stardust Hotel and Casino in Las Vegas and performed with Disney, Norwegian, and Carnival Cruise Lines. Debra's versatility extends to principal roles in Broadway Spotlight Musicals across the United States and Canada, as well as appearances on Puerto Rican Television and in films and commercials.

Hailing from Bloomington, Minnesota, Debra Lee Fader served as Mayor of Montevideo, Minnesota, for eight years, emphasizing Good Will and Kindness for all citizens. She also promoted Cultural Exchange as the Official Mayor Envoy to Montevideo, Uruguay, fostering the relationship between the two Montevideo Sister Cities dating back to 1904.

Debra's civic engagement includes roles as an Elected Board Advisor to the Upper Minnesota Valley Regional Development Commission and Vice President for the Minnesota Mayor's Association. Her vision for Montevideo Public Arts Projects brought captivating Public Art Works to the city.

In 2020, Debra was Certified and Ordained as a Chaplain. In 2017, she founded Diversity-USA, a 501(c)(3) Charity promoting Arts, Cultural Preservation, and Inclusion in rural Minnesota.

As a seasoned stage performer and radio professional, catch her Theatrical Revues in Montevideo, MN, and her insightful interviews on Recipe for Kindness and other National Podcasts. She occasionally serves as a Guest Host for Regional PBS Stations.

Debra Lee's upcoming projects include her memoir, 'Walk By Faith,' adapted for a Voyage Media screenplay. She also leads 'Showgirl USA,' offering self-care retreats for women interested in the Showgirl Experience. Debra is currently working on her new podcast titled, *Acts of Kindness—Connecting through Caring.*

Away from the spotlight, Debra Lee is happily married to Brad Fader and previously owned the Sportsmen Inn. They now enjoy their lake home on Lake Minnewaska in Glenwood, MN, with their grandchildren, Jules and Miles, and their son Jason and daughter-in-law, Mandy.

Learn more at:

- www.diversity-usa.org
- www.queenofkindness.org

CHAPTER 19

WHEN YOU HIT ROCK BOTTOM, THERE'S NO WAY TO GO BUT UP
HOW TRUSTING IN THE UNIVERSE CAN HELP YOU RISE UP

BY DEBRA STANGL

I was in Sedona, Arizona, for the first time, with a Practitioner doing a session designed to take me out of my misery. Suddenly, I had a vision of Isis, the winged Egyptian Goddess of healing, magic, and motherhood. She wrapped her wings around me and said, "Everything is going to be OK, but you have to leave your law practice."

I felt safe in her embrace and certainty, even as my mind reeled with all the reasons I couldn't possibly leave the job I hated so much.

"If you don't leave your law practice now, you're going to die like your mother did."

My blood ran cold, realizing I was exactly the age my mother was when she got cancer and died five years later.

But worse than that, I realized I was on the same path as my mother—she had felt stuck, hopeless and helpless, and so did I. I realized if I didn't change my life—and soon—I wouldn't have a life to change for much longer.

HITTING ROCK BOTTOM

This was January 1999, and every part of my life was at rock bottom. I had just started my twentieth year of practicing law, a profession I got into for all the wrong reasons and one that made me miserable. I began in environmental law but ended up in divorce work, which I hated. After spending the majority of my days fighting with other attorneys and the system, I went home to a deeply unhappy marriage, where I was the sole financial support.

Through a series of bad business decisions, we were also $50,000 in debt.

I'd take on more cases. I'd put in more hours. But no matter what I did, that debt remained an albatross around my neck for five years.

The stress of my career and home life quickly affected my body. I was forty pounds overweight.

At one point, the doctors found a tumor. It turned out to be benign, and it was safely removed, but the early death of my mother loomed large in my mind. If I didn't change, something inside me said there could be another tumor, and the biopsy results would be different the second time around.

Every part of my life was a mess—work, marriage, money, my body. There were days I could barely pull myself out of bed. There were even times when I felt so hopeless that I contemplated ending it all. I found myself in the car drinking Jack Daniel's, trying to get up the courage to start the car, inhale the carbon monoxide, and hopefully find some peace. But I couldn't get myself to do it.

During the previous five years I would meditate and pray to God and say, "Please tell me what to do; I'm so unhappy," and I would hear this small voice saying, "You need to leave your law practice." Instead of listening, I got angry and defensive. "How can I possibly leave my law practice when we're $50,000 in debt, we have nothing in savings, and I'm our sole support?" Looking back now, I see that the Universe was telling me exactly what I needed to do; I just wasn't listening.

I finally reached a point where even my therapist was concerned about me (I hadn't told her about the suicidal thoughts, or she would have gotten much more concerned about me much more quickly). She recommended that I go somewhere to get away. When she suggested it, I heard the word 'Sedona' in my head, even though I had never been to the place.

That led me to the retreat center in Sedona where suddenly Isis had appeared and told me, "If you don't leave your law practice now, you're going to die like your mother did."

This time I got the message. I went home to Omaha and spent two weeks with my lawyer brain trying to figure out how I was possibly going to leave my law practice when I was $50,000 in debt, and of course trying to figure it out with your brain never works.

THE MIRACLES START

Suddenly there was a day when I had finished a very deep meditation where I had asked to be shown what I was supposed to do. I was overcome with this knowing, this energy that filled my entire body. It felt like nothing I had ever experienced before. I was filled with this trust that everything was somehow going to be OK. I was weeping, I got down on my knees, and I said, "OK, God, I get it that I have to do this, and I'm going to do it, so if it means selling the house and selling one of the cars and living in the other one and never going anywhere again, OK, I'll do it. But you've got to give me some help here."

Less than eight hours later I got a phone call from one of my former clients. At the end of the conversation, he told me that he had just started a new mortgage refinancing business. I asked him if it would be possible to refinance my house to get a lower monthly payment. He called me back in ten minutes and said, "I can cut your mortgage payment in half, plus I can get you $50,000 in cash."

I had never told him (or anyone else) that I was $50,000 in debt, because I was so ashamed of it. Suddenly, in an instant, the weight of five years of worry and upset was gone. It was gone within eight hours of asking God for help. It was gone within eight hours of going into that energy of knowing, of trusting, that somehow all would be well. I took this as a sign from the Universe that leaving my practice was what I was meant to do.

JUST KEEP TAKING THE NEXT STEP

I spent the next three years going back and forth to Sedona for a month at a time to do deep healing work with different Practitioners I was finding. It was one of the most wonderful times of my life. Sedona is a mecca of the new New Age and incredible Practitioners are drawn here from all over the world to do their work.

Suddenly, in 2001, three weeks before 9/11, I was in Sedona doing a session in the same room where my High Self had appeared to me in that vision almost three years before. My High Self came in again as Isis, and this time she said, "It's time to move to Sedona." I responded, "Why? What am I going to be doing in Sedona?" I got no response. One of the things I have learned over the years is that the High Self doesn't usually show you the complete picture, only the next step. Mine had shown me the next step.

My brain started kicking in, telling me how crazy it was to move to Sedona; it made absolutely no sense from a financial standpoint. Tom had gone to work for his largest client and had a great job in Omaha (along with health insurance and stock options), and I had no idea what I was going to do in Sedona. But over those previous three years of doing all the work I had done on myself, the one thing I had definitely learned was how important it was for me to listen to my intuition and do what I was being told.

Within twenty-four hours of receiving that message, I got a phone call from one of my new Sedona friends, who said, "I hear you're moving to Sedona (note: I had not told anyone I was moving to Sedona). I'm leaving for India for six months to film a documentary. Would you like to rent my house?" It's a fabulous house, and the rent offer was almost too good to be true. I said yes.

I went home and immediately listed my home with a real estate agent, who warned me it could take upwards of six months to sell. Within three days, we had an offer $30,000 over asking.

I immediately moved to Sedona, and every morning for six months, I found myself saying the same thing: "OK. I did what you told me to do. Now what?"

I started having dreams about what would become my work, Sedona Soul Adventures. In my dreams I was being shown that it was me working one-on-one, in private with these incredible Practitioners that had made all the difference. I was shown how I could take what had taken me three years and condense it into three days. Starting a business with no capital was a daunting task. But I've found the best capital you can have is trust in the Universe.

TRUSTING THE UNIVERSE—LIVING IN THE ENERGY OF 'NOTHING IS WRONG'

I started Sedona Soul Adventures twenty-two years ago. Since then, we have helped tens of thousands of people with our private retreats. Each retreat is custom-designed for each individual or couple (nothing is done in groups). I started with ten Practitioners, and we now have over sixty!

In our retreats we help people come back into connection on all the levels—physical, mental, emotional, spiritual. Most people are living lives of disconnection and dissatisfaction, and they feel hopeless and helpless (as I did when I first came here twenty-five years ago). We take them through the same process I went through (my process took three years, but now we do it in three days!), finding, releasing, and healing the Core Wounds, limiting beliefs, traumas, and fears (what I affectionately call 'the gunk') that are holding them back and keeping them stuck and then using processes designed to bring them back into connection, trusting and knowing that All Is Well. When you're living your life in connection, incredible things happen.

MORE MIRACLES

Underpinning all of that is developing a trust in the Universe that everything is happening in Divine Order, unfolding for the highest and best good, that Nothing Is Wrong. That concept came to me one day when I had another incredible encounter and another miracle happened.

My husband and I had an argument. As usual, the argument transitioned to his belief that no matter what he had done or not done, there was never any justification for my being angry with him. The problem was never the issue that I was angry about. The problem was my anger and me. There was something wrong with *me*.

The fight struck something deep. I went home, alone. I began sobbing and sobbing and sobbing. Finally, I was sobbing so hard that I just climbed into bed.

All of a sudden, my body started vibrating. It was vibrating so much that I couldn't move. I just lay there and breathed. Then I heard a voice in my head saying, *"Nothing is wrong with you. Nothing is wrong with you."* The voice repeated those words over and over.

I knew something important was happening. I knew I needed to hold on to this. It felt like this was something that was coming in through the grace of God.

And then I was being shown that there is nothing wrong with me in all areas of my life—my personality, my career, my body—all areas with which I had struggled. I simply *got it* that things were fine just the way they were. In an instant, I saw my entire life in a new way.

At the time I had been on another one of my crazy restrictive diets. I decided then and there to just stop, to stop the insanity. I felt all this love for my body. Rather than hating my body, I was loving my body. The most incredible thing happened. The weight started melting off! It was over a period of fewer than two months. I didn't even realize it until I went shopping for a new pair of jeans. I tried on a size 14, and it was way too big! To my utter amazement, I was a size 6! I went home and weighed myself. Over forty pounds had melted away without diet or exercise. The only thing that was different is that I was eating and drinking whatever I wanted, not worrying about what I put in my mouth and totally loving my body.

The icing on the cake was with my own love life, where another miracle happened. My former husband and I amicably ended our twenty-year marriage in 2010, and he is now happily living in Bali (and became a first-time father at the age of sixty!). I was happily single for six years until something happened that made me realize I wanted to bring in a true soul partner, something I had never had before. I used the principles we teach at Sedona Soul Adventures and did sessions with many of my Practitioners to eliminate any blocks to bringing that in. I utilized the processes I talk about in my book *The Journey to Happy—How Embracing the Concept That Nothing Is Wrong Can Transform Your Life* to manifest the perfect connection. I knew that trusting the Universe was the key—I had a deep belief that if I had such a deep desire for this, the Universe would answer that desire, and I was right!

The day before the book launched, I had the thought, "I finally have time to meet a guy," and two weeks later Richard 'liked' me on Match.com. Although he was living in San Jose, California, he found me, we connected, and one year later we married, surrounded by the red rocks of Sedona. To have found this kind of love with a true spiritual partner at this stage in my life has been such an incredible blessing.

Twenty-five years ago I hit rock bottom. Somehow I was able to connect with my faith and not lose it. Every time I was able to go into the knowing and deep believing that everything would be OK, miracles happened. When we trust, when we have that knowing that All Is Well, we are bringing ourselves into the higher vibrational energies; when our desires align with those higher vibrations, they come into our lives quickly and easily.

About Debra

Debra Stangl is an example of how life is full of second chances. In 1999, she was a divorce attorney in Omaha, Nebraska, hating her work, depressed, overweight and in an unhappy marriage. She came to the spiritual mecca of Sedona, Arizona and had a spiritual re-awakening. Three years later, she founded Sedona Soul Adventures, which has a unique way of doing spiritual retreats. These are retreats for individuals and couples, not groups, and each three to seven-day retreat is custom designed for each person (or each couple) based on the Sedona Proven Process developed by Debra over 20 years ago, consisting of one-on-one or two-on-one sessions with over 60 of Sedona's Master Practitioners.

Sedona Soul Adventures has been featured on *The Today Show, USA Today, Forbes, The Washington Post, Yoga Journal* and *Elle*. They were named 'Best of Sedona' for Retreats in 2020-2023, Best Marriage Retreats in the US (2017-2023) and 'Best Couples Retreats in the World' by *Brides Magazine* in 2022. They were named to the Inc. 5000 List of Fastest Growing Private Companies in the US in 2019 and again in 2023.

Debra is the author of the #1 International Bestseller, *The Journey To Happy—How Embracing The Concept That Nothing Is Wrong Can Transform Your Life*.

Debra received her bachelor's degree in Theatre and Dance from the University of Iowa in 1974. After that, she lived in Washington, D.C. and was the personal assistant to Congressman Edward Mezvinsky, who was on the Judiciary Committee during the Watergate proceedings (and is now Chelsea Clinton's father-in-law). Next, she was the personal assistant to former Supreme Court Justice Abe Fortas who encouraged her to go to law school. Debra graduated from Creighton Law School in 1979 and practiced law in Omaha, Nebraska.

During that time, she was an advocate for women and children, and wrote the 'Children's Trust Fund Act' – legislation which funds programs for the prevention of child abuse. For her efforts, she was named one of ten 'Outstanding Young Omahans' in 1982 and the 'Outstanding Young Nebraskan' by the statewide Nebraska Chamber of Commerce in 1983. Debra practiced law for 20 years before her spiritual reawakening led her to leave her practice and ultimately relocate to Sedona.

Since founding Sedona Soul Adventures in 2002 and helping thousands of people transform their lives, Debra writes and speaks about how it is possible to live a life of joy and ease and purpose.

Debra lives in Sedona, Arizona with her husband and spiritual partner, Richard Kepple, and their two Doodles, Missy and Beauregard.

For more information on Debra:

- Email: Debra@SedonaSoulAdventures.com
- http://www.SedonaSoulAdventures.com

CHAPTER 20

PHOENIX RISING: RESILIENCE AND REDISCOVERY DURING SEASONS OF GRIEF

BY DR. K BLOOM

I've had three major losses since 2016. In the second year of my first loss, I caught a glimpse of myself in the mirror and froze. Who was that woman? I didn't look like me, and I didn't feel like me. Where was the joyful, extroverted person who loved to dance? I love quickly and deeply. Loving makes life worth living. But I'd already gone through losing my soulmate and the embers of grief were still smoldering. I had a second major loss a few years later, when I was still rebuilding my life. How would I find the strength to rise from the ashes once again?

As a therapist, I needed to take better care of myself. I chose an activity that brought me immense joy: riding horses. I find horses to be incredibly healing and magical. Growing up, I'd ridden often. Now I was a woman in her fifties, 5'10", curvy...and heartbroken. I found myself dreaming of horses and wanting to feel the pleasure again. I called the Horseman's Association who directed me to a saddle shop that gave me the names of three stables. From there, I connected with Amanda, a wonderful down-to-earth barn owner.

When she introduced me to Reggie, the beautiful 17.2-hand Chestnut with white markings, it was love at first sight. We formed an instant connection and I leased him for six months. Reggie was being rehabilitated from injuries. Over those months, Reggie improved.

And slowly, so did I. We helped each other to heal, Reggie and me. I asked to extend my lease—or even to buy him—but his owners weren't interested. They moved Reggie out of the area. Reggie leaving created another wave of grief. I'd still go out to the barn to visit, but the sadness of the loss made it hard to connect with another horse.

Grief is a difficult but integral part of life that society doesn't talk about much. Mourners need a path for how to live with their losses. Perhaps reading a bit about my story will inspire those who are grieving to see how it is possible to love again.

A PRINCE AMONG MEN

My grief story begins with a love story. Jim and I grew up together outside of Chicago and dated for several years. He was my first love and my prom date! After high school, we left for different universities. Long-distance relationships were much harder in the 80s before communication was at our fingertips. We wrote letters, but never saw each other. We parted on good terms the following summer.

Years later, we crossed paths again just before starting grad school. This time I was registered in Chicago and he was heading to Texas. Before leaving, he said: "Come with me." But I'd been accepted at a great school. What would I do in Texas? "Just come. We'll figure it out." I was far too practical to accept that answer. So he left for Texas and I finished graduate school.

Fast-forward to 2004. I was living in Florida and going through a divorce. On my birthday, guess who contacted me? Jim had been married and he, too, was in the middle of a separation and divorce. We had been living parallel lives. That night we talked for hours, reestablishing our connection.

I said, "I could have transferred to Illinois or followed you to Texas for grad school. You were always inviting me, and I just didn't know how to do it. I'm not going to make that mistake again. One of us is moving…I love you…I've always loved you." He replied, "I love you too."

As a software engineer, he worked remotely, so he moved to Florida. We fell in love all over again. I was scared of marriage after the first time, but he kept pleading with me to marry him. After three years I said yes, and we began our amazing life together. We took a lifetime worth of cruises and adventures all around the world. We worked hard and played hard. We laughed. The years passed blissfully.

One night in August of 2016, we fell asleep with our feet tangled while watching the Olympics. We planned to wake early and go for a walk. A few minutes before six I woke and said, "Jim, get up," but he wasn't moving. "Come on, quit goofing around." When I touched him, he was cold. He'd had sudden heart failure. I was unable to revive him. I called two friends who immediately came over and so began the next phase of my life without my beloved Jim. I was forty-eight.

REBUILDING

Our friends and family came for the funeral. Everyone was supportive and stayed awhile. My best friend even came to live with me for a time. And then, most people kind of left just as quickly as they arrived. I had one friend who called me every Saturday for a year. That, and a few other close friends and family, made a difficult time bearable. Meanwhile, a deep loneliness had settled into my soul. I looked for a grief group, but the one in my area met at a funeral home. I thought, *That seems awful! I'm not doing that.*

Within the week, I went back to work, running a treatment center. I'm fortunate to do work I love. People asked, "How are you here?" and I'd reply, "How am I not here?" I had a job to do and people to help. That part of me ran on automatic pilot. In those first months, I did my job and fell apart as I needed to behind closed doors.

The heaviness of the grief came in waves and, at times, I felt I was drowning under the weight of emotions. I'd hear a song while getting a manicure, and suddenly start bawling. The grief comes when it wants to; you can't stop it. The heart has its own way of processing. The volcano erupts without warning. But, out of the ashes comes the process of healing.

A devastating effect of grief was my inability to read or write for enjoyment. I started reading early, at two years old, and writing soon after. When Jim died, I'd already had two books published with plans for more, but my ability to concentrate, along with my creativity, seemed to have died with him.

The second year of rebuilding was harder than the first, because the support waned and reality of the loss set in more fully. People seemed to want me to get over my grief because of their discomfort. Unfortunately, the feelings of grief are persistent, and do not magically disappear. Some friendships ended. One person actually said I was too much drama now. Some wanted only the former, blissful me, but I wasn't her anymore.

My true friends and family loved me through my darkest days. Most people eventually stopped talking about Jim, as if he never existed. They may have been afraid to upset me, although the worst had already happened. I enjoyed talking about him, and us. I wanted to keep his memory alive. I was told by fellow mourners who were years ahead of me on the grief journey that I'd always love and miss Jim. That helped me through.

In year two of rebuilding, a friend and colleague recommended I participate in a week-long hypnotherapy training. I'd have the chance to learn new skills and further my healing. I'd done talk-therapy for years; I knew I needed something different to reclaim my joy. I was the subject of the live hypnotherapy demonstration in the class. The trainer conducted a grief session that helped me release some of my grief in a profound and permanent way. Grief had fragmented my lifeforce, but after the hypnosis, I felt revived and reintegrated. I felt my joy begin to break through the fog. I continued deeper healing and advanced hypnotherapy training for two more years.

LIGHTNING STRIKES TWICE

At the end of 2017, I met Paul. He had a big heart that matched his big teddy-bear physique. He was transparent about his long-term marriage soon ending and how I was his first date. I told him about my grief and he shared how he'd lost his two best friends, one to suicide, and one to cancer. Paul was a bit introverted and particular about who he got close to, but the friendships he had were deep and long-lasting.

He was kind and patient with my grief. I burst into tears on our first dinner date before we even got to the restaurant. He held me and told me it was okay. After a few dates, he said, "I see that you have a huge heart. I'm sure there's room in there for both of us. You get to have all your emotions. When my best friends died, everyone told me to stop crying. So I cried privately because nobody would honor it."

After a year, we moved in together. We were in love and integrating into each other's lives, friend groups, and family. Then COVID happened. I started seeing clients online (he worked remotely already). At the end of summer, he started visiting some customer sites. He had struggled with diabetes, but his blood sugars had stabilized. On the morning of September 30, 2020, we ate breakfast together and kissed goodbye. While at work, he had a sudden heart attack. He was fifty-four years old.

With COVID, there were no viable funeral options for Paul. No one could come over to offer me support. I made one new close friend at that time who video-chatted with me daily. She, my therapist, and a few other friends and family were lifesavers through that impossibly lonely time.

People think the depth of grief is correlated to how long you knew a person. I haven't found that to be true. When you lose a person you love, it cuts deep, no matter what. But this second loss hurt differently because I was different.

Less than a year later, in 2021, I lost my best friend of 30 years, Glenda, to cancer. She was a bright light in my life! I honored her with a small beachfront service for friends and family. I felt devastated, and wondered how much more loss I could withstand.

As I continued to heal, I thought about the lessons I could glean from having endured so much grief that could be valuable to others. These losses have helped me empathize with clients and friends who are grieving. Families suffering from addiction and mental health issues, who've lost loved ones to addiction, suicide, illness, or tragedy. We all experience losses as part of the cycles of life and the transitions of death. I hope the insights I offer encourage others in the healing process.

KEEP LOVING

Some people have asked how I manage to get up each morning after so much tragedy. The answer is easy: I get up because of love. I still actively love every person I ever loved, including the guys and my best girlfriend who have died. In all three losses, the last thing we said to each other was "I love you." I live by that. I'm here for a purpose, my life has meaning.

I had days I wanted to give up. Some mornings all I could do was wake up and grab a stale doughnut on my way out the door because I had no food in the house. I couldn't motivate myself to grocery shop or clean. For a year and a half, I wore my hair in a "widow bun" because I couldn't handle blow-drying my hair. Still, I did what I could, and I'm proud of that.

There may be things you aren't able to do while in the grips of grief, but you can do some things. Progress comes in realizing the difference and asking for help. Am I afraid to love again? No, but loving someone is different now. Love has evolved because I have a deeper awareness of the fleeting nature of life. I have an awesome boyfriend that I met over coffee and banana bread in 2021, and he has been loving and supportive. He accepts me – my emotions and my losses – as a package deal. I'm grateful. The friendships and collegial relationships I have now are fewer but much deeper than before, and I'm much happier for it.

Last year I started writing again. I wrote the *Authenticity Playbook* for people in recovery. It's a year-long workbook, and I wrote one page a week. I had to break down the writing process into bite-sized pieces. Later in the year, I was asked to contribute to *The Keys to Authenticity, Unlocking the Code* with Jack Canfield, which became a bestseller! It feels great to write again. Oh, and I'm reading again, too. I joined an executive women's club, making new connections and participating in their book club. I'm singing and dancing again, too. How cool is that?

If you're reading this and you're grieving the loss of a loved one, permit me the privilege of sharing some advice. Love again. Learn to hold close as you learn to let go. Take trips, eat the cake, and dance. Do whatever you can to comfort yourself and ease your suffering. Keep your heart open to the new you and keep loving no matter what losses you experience.

RESTORED

A year after Reggie left, my friend Amanda called. "Reggie's owners contacted me to ask if I could take him. He's suffering in a stall." Reggie's owners had given him drugs and forced him to jump over fences, against three vets' recommendations, so they could sell him for a higher price. I said, "Let's do it—it's Reggie!" Amanda went to pick him up that day. We didn't know if we'd be able to fix him, but we knew we had to try. I couldn't suffer him leaving again at the owner's whim, so Amanda helped me negotiate his purchase and rescue.

The massive, regal, shiny-coated Reggie had been turned into a festering, limping, starving creature. As of this writing, I've had him three months. He is getting stronger, with a special diet and exercise routine, magic shoes I call his Louboutins, and lots of love. He is sound, and being ridden gently. Soon he will be healing others in the equine therapy program Amanda and I started.

When you have love all around you and inside you, you just keep moving forward at your own pace. Giving up was never an option for me. If I gave up, then helping make people, places, and things better than I found them wouldn't be possible. Loving Reggie back to life came with an unexpected gift of reciprocation. Love has a way of doing that, though, doesn't it?

About Dr. K Bloom

K.A. Bloom, PhD, LCSW, ACHT, CST is an exceptional recovery, relationship and sexuality therapist who helps others to have better relationships and lives. Whether they are healing from trauma, or struggling with relationship, grief, or codependency issues, Dr. Bloom brings solutions to help others heal conflict and overcome their blocks so they can thrive in love and in life.

Her approach is gentle, yet direct. She brings fun and great energy to every person she connects with. She has a bold, engaging style and helps people who to reach their personal goals. Dr. Bloom promotes a life of pleasure, meaning, purpose, and happiness. Self-love and care is a much needed and overlooked area of personal development. Dr. Bloom delivers!

Media Presence: She has been featured multiple times as a subject matter expert in various media such as *Cosmopolitan* and *Men's Health*. Dr. Bloom is in demand on multi-media as an expert on relationships, recovery, and sexuality. She has co-authored a bestseller with Jack Canfield, *Keys to Authenticity*, and with Dr. Wayne Dyer in *Wake Up Moments of Inspiration*. She has written several additional books so far, including *The Authenticity Playbook, Relationship Riches and Sizzling Sex Secrets,* and *The Ultimate Compatibility Quiz.*

Speaker and Educator: A sought-after speaker and educator, Dr. Bloom has been post-graduate faculty at prestigious schools – such as Barry University and the University of Peking, Beijing. She has spoken on international stages at professional conferences in the U.S., Europe, and China. She has also been hired to speak on Celebrity Cruises on relationships and sexuality.

Training and Experience: Dr. Bloom is a Certified Equine-Assisted Psychotherapist, Advanced Clinical Hypnotherapist, Trauma Therapist, Certified Sex Therapist, and Licensed Clinical Social Worker with a Doctoral Degree in Clinical Sexology. She has a tremendous healing toolbox and over 20 years of experience serving others. She has been an agency clinical director for over 20 years.

Her passion shines through in all of her work. She leads a private group practice in Ft. Lauderdale, FL where she and her team do individual and couples counseling in person as well as online. In addition, she offers Equine-Assisted Psychotherapy.

Dr. Bloom's Inspiring Grief Journey: after losing her husband, Jim, in 2016, and her paramour, Paul, in 2020, to sudden heart failure, she decided to pursue hypnotherapy and equine therapies to help others heal. She began writing again in 2021 to offer hope and deeper recovery opportunities to thrive through grief and other life transitions.

To contact Dr. Bloom:

- www.healingcouch.com

CHAPTER 21

LOVE YOURSELF FIRST!

BY ANN-MARIE EMMANUEL

I live in paradise.

Trinidad is my home, the place where I began my life and where I once again reside after a 44-year journey to find my way home.

I live in a gorgeous house on a hill, overlooking the sea that surrounds my beautiful homeland. I built this structure to serve a dual role – it's both my sanctuary and Cheryl's Grace Enrichment Centre, a place of retreat for people who come to discover the self-love required to live a life of joy, peace, and success.

I spend much of my time here, writing and in quiet reflection. I travel to the city for a couple of days each week, crossing the mountains to find the groceries and supplies not available in such a remote location. I usually time my travel to coincide with the social engagements that fill my soul, staying in my family home in Central Trinidad, so I don't have to traverse the mountains in the dark.

I really do have the best of both worlds. But it took a long time to get here.

BECAUSE THAT'S WHAT WE DO

After visiting Trinidad twice a year for my adult life, I returned to my homeland full time in 2014, after living the 'American Dream.' I put that in quotes because while I was meeting society's standards for what was supposed to make me happy and successful, I hadn't yet realized that I could set my own standards.

I had gotten pregnant while studying fashion design at the Fashion Institute of Technology and did the 'right' thing by getting married and going to work for the United States Postal Service. They offered me a job, but because of circumstances, it became a career.

Ten years into my career, I started a fashion business on the side, but I kept my 'good' job, because that's what you did. I was successful. It's who I am. But the things that made me successful didn't make me happy.

I was employed but not fulfilled, married but lonely, successful but not happy. It took a divorce, financial cataclysm, a lot of self-reflection, and a good bit of serendipity to lead me to where I am today.

I hadn't been happily married for a long time. When I decided it was time to separate, I didn't want to upset my son's life any more than was necessary. I'd risen to a level at the USPS that allowed me to take a second mortgage on our home so we could stay in it. I couldn't afford both mortgages long-term. I planned to unload the house when my son graduated from high school.

Then came 2008, and the U.S. housing market bubble burst. I was forced to hold onto the house for longer than I had planned. I had always been at the top of my game financially, but this hit hard. It also helped me see I needed to change the goal from financial success to financial freedom, which doesn't rely on things that are outside of your own control.

As I struggled to rebuild, I was hit again when the USPS announced a reduction-in-force that required me to move from a job that I loved to one that I hated. It wasn't long before I changed my focus to building things that can't be taken away: Joy, Peace, and Happiness.

THE RIGHT THINGS AT THE RIGHT TIME

I mentioned 'serendipity' earlier. One of the first examples of that came right around this time, though the seeds of it had been planted six years before, when a friend of mine came back from a course he had taken at the Landmark Worldwide Leadership Program. He was changed, and I saw in him something I wanted for myself. But things in my life were 'fine,' so I didn't make it a priority.

When I found myself divorced, financially stretched, and in a job I hated, I remembered the light I had seen in my friend and said to myself, "Yes, now is the time." I signed up for the intro course expecting to learn some new things. Instead, I had a complete transformation in one weekend. I learned a new way of communicating, of being in relationships, and of seeking the kind success I wanted. What I got from that weekend was so much deeper and richer than what I expected.

When I returned home, I immediately began interacting with my son in a new way. He was 16 years old and filled with anger and defiance. Our relationship had been under great stress. He saw the transformation in me right away, and asked if he could go. Landmark transformed him, too.

His attitude improved. His grades improved. His teachers wanted to know what had happened to him. More than anything, though, our relationship was much better. Where he once would walk fast past my bedroom door, he would now stop and talk, ask me how I was doing. I felt that for the first time, he was interested...that he heard me. He had never talked to me that way before, like a person and not just his mother.

Part of the Landmark process is to have 'clean up' conversations with people so you can move forward together. For my son and me, our relationship has never been the same.

ALL THAT WAS HOLDING ME BACK

Right after Landmark, another bit of serendipity hit when international coach Lisa Nichols popped up on my YouTube feed. Her message was so compelling I listened to her for an hour. I was captivated, completely drawn in. And I realized that all this stuff was coming into my life at exactly the right time.

I was starting to live my life from the inside out. During that video, she mentioned her upcoming Speak & Write conference. I knew I had to go. I went to my first conference. I went to my second conference. Then Covid arrived and everything stopped.

At Landmark, we dug deep to learn about what was running our lives. For me, it was loneliness, a manifestation of childhood fear and insecurity. I thought I had dealt with it, but during the pandemic, I suffered a bout of depression rooted in loneliness.

Trinidad and Tobago closed the borders when the pandemic began. That meant that I couldn't get to my family in the States, and they couldn't get to me, no matter what happened. I was isolated from the people who mean the most to me. It freaked me out.

Fortunately, I had gained the knowledge to recognize what was happening to me and the strength to pull myself together, and finally deal with this childhood trauma.

Just then, I found Joe Dispenza, an international researcher and educator. I immersed myself in his 30-day guided meditation that took me deep into the childhood experience that caused a deep-seated fear from a neuropsychological perspective, to allow me to make changes at a cellular level. It was extremely intense – almost like hypnotism. I even hallucinated. It really got everything out.

As the meditation progressed over the 30 days, I felt lighter and lighter. Eventually I emerged with the fear gone. This kind of work is like treating an addiction. We become addicted to pain and suffering. That's why it's hard for many people to work through it. Pain is a chemical reaction – it's like a 'fix.' Some people would rather be in pain from something familiar than take a chance on the unknown.

TAKING A CHANCE ON MYSELF

My mother was a trailblazer who taught me everything I want to be, and everything I don't.

She struggled in her life. Her mom died when she was 7. She was an alcoholic, which is why I curb my drinking. She had a weight problem, which is why I will always be in control of my body. She accepted abuse from intimate partners.

Even so, she grew up to be the most loving, caring person. When people needed help, they came to my mother. During my childhood, we always had strangers in our house whom she was helping get back on their feet. She knew how to love other people, but she didn't know how to break free of her past trauma in order to direct love back to herself.

Ironically, most of my strength and resilience comes from her. She left her mark wherever she went. I never thought I would be that person, but I am. I am thankful I got that from her. My mother died one week after I broke ground on the biggest chance I've ever taken – a chance I took on myself.

During a vacation to Trinidad, I fell in love with a white house up on a hill overlooking the sea.

"I want a house like that," I told my cousin, as we were driving around. She laughed, then took me to meet her aunt, who knew everyone and everything in the village.

"I want to buy a piece of property in Trinidad," I told her.

"Why?" she asked because people don't know when they live in paradise.

Three years later, she took me to see a piece of land, within walking distance to the beach, and with a beautiful view of the ocean. I bought it and held onto it for a long time before realizing it was time to take a chance on me.

After two years in that job I hated, I took early retirement from the

USPS on Dec. 31, 2010, and moved to Trinidad. In May 2011, I broke ground on Cheryl's Grace Enrichment Center – Cheryl is my first given name. I thought it would take two years to complete. It took seven.

Everything that could go wrong did. First came the chauvinism and culture shock. Contractors would say they'd arrive at 8 a.m. tomorrow which, as it turns out, means they'll be there at 8 a.m. two weeks from now.

I had to build a road up to my property. Trucks would get stuck halfway up. Drivers would dump materials there or at the bottom of the hill and I'd have to get them the rest of the way. I really got beat up, knocked around, and deceived.

When I finally arrived at the grand opening in 2018, my whole family came to celebrate. It was wonderful. When they all went home, I was left feeling isolated and alone without this big project to occupy my mind.

During construction, I lost my mother, my father, and my sister, but I hadn't properly grieved for any of them. Now that the enrichment center was done, I gave myself permission to feel the emotions and pain I should have been feeling all along.

One morning, as I took my daily walk on the beach, I sat on the rock where I meditated and cried for two hours. As I did, I thought, "I'm tired of fighting. I don't want to be here. I don't want to live here."

I wanted to give up.

As I asked, "Where will I go? What will I do?" I heard a voice:

"I gave you everything you asked for. You live by the beach, among nature, in a clean environment. You're your own boss. If you can't be happy here and now, you can't be happy anywhere."

Then, and I swear this is true, I heard Whitney Houston's *'The Greatest Love of All'* playing around me. Not in my head, around me. The lyrics hit hard:

> *"And if, by chance, that special place*
> *That you've been dreaming of*
> *Leads you to a lonely place,*
> *Find your strength in love. ..."*
> *"... No matter what they take from me*
> *They can't take away my dignity. ..."*
> *"... Learning to love yourself*
> *It is the greatest love of all."*

I realized, in that moment, that learning to be happy isn't about a place, it's a state of being.

All this while, I thought I was coming home to Trinidad when I was coming home to myself. I had been searching for something that was inside me all along. This was the turning point when I and my life were irrevocably transformed.

Not long after that, I got an email about earning a certification in self-love and realized that I needed to learn to love myself and help others do the same.

THE GREATEST LOVE OF ALL

One day, I took friends who were visiting Trinidad to a nearby fort on the shoreline. We were sitting on the rocks when a huge wave hit and swept me into the raging water. I thought, "This is how I'm going to die" when I heard an angel say, "Become one with the water and I will carry you."

The next wave took me to another rock, where I was able to grab on and pull myself out, intact and uninjured. It was a miracle. I had called death upon myself, but the universe didn't get the memo. After all I'd been through and all I had learned, there was work to do. These days, I can feel people watching me, being inspired by me. They come to me and want to know more.

Truthfully, I didn't realize how important it is to tell my story until I went on an international tour for my third book, *RelationSHIFT*, and saw how people were reacting to what I'd written. My work is affecting people's lives. I am connected to the world and the world wants to hear what I have to say. As an author, I am guided by something bigger than myself. When I set aside time to write and treat that time with integrity, the words just flow.

Along my journey to loving myself, I have learned to look at love from a different perspective. I know that my family loves me. I don't yearn for them to show it in a particular way anymore. I know it is there. I also see clearly just how bad the first 10 or 15 years of my life were. I went through some traumatic things. I have cried many times for my 5-year-old self, my 8-year-old self.

Now, my response when I see people suffering, is to be an ambassador for self-love. If I see that they're ready to receive this message, I try to help them see the difference that loving yourself can make. If they're not ready, I step back and love them until they are.

I used to be attached to the outcome of my work. I have learned that if I want people to understand the power of self-love, I must embody it, I must be it. When you try to force someone, you come from a space of judging. I need to exist at a higher vibration.

I accept that people are whole and complete wherever they are. And that they, like all of us, will arrive when it is their time.

About Ann-Marie

Ann-Marie Emmanuel is a Trinidadian-American of diverse talents. She is a certified Relationship and Self-Love Coach, best-selling author of three titles, and the CEO of Passion Kairos, a wellness and empowerment community designed to help individuals live passionately and on purpose. Ann-Marie is also the host of the *Ann-Marie's Impact Web Show* featuring inspiring interviews with those who've overcome fantastic odds to shift from survival mode into the grandest vision for their lives through the power of self-love.

Ann-Marie Emmanuel's three titles, *MPower, Bloom Beauty,* and *RelationSHIFT* are dedicated to inspiring readers and clients worldwide to break free of the self-sabotaging voice of their inner critic to design a life lived from compassion and consciousness. The newest edition in her series of self-love books, *RelationSHIFT,* quickly became an international bestseller in the Women's Studies, Women's Personal Spiritual Growth, and Women's Inspirational Spirituality categories. Finally, the Passion Kairos platform is an extension of Ann-Marie's passion for life and people and offers exclusive access to her signature transformative experiences, workshops, international retreats, and meditations.

A highly-driven woman born to break barriers, Ann-Marie proves that when powered by purpose, people are unstoppable. She's built her storied life brick by brick, fighting fears, failures, and setbacks to have the success she's always known was hers to claim. Today, Ann-Marie personifies what it means to ascend above adversity while inspiring countless others to do the same.

Ann-Marie has over a decade of experience in lifestyle and transformational coaching and belongs to The Path of Self Love School of teachers with a presence on six continents. She also trained under world-renowned motivational speakers Lisa Nichols and Suzie Carder. As a result of her training with The School of Self Love and mentorship with Lisa Nichols and Suzie Carder, Ann-Marie now guides thousands worldwide in forming more intimate connections and making more self-empowering, self-loving choices for their lives.

Ann-Marie's work is a testament to what it means to leave an undeniable mark on the world. Extraordinary at walking others through radical transformation, she endeavors not simply to change lives — but to expand them. Her ultimate goal is to elicit a chain reaction of social change, causing individuals to be empowered with renewed confidence and enhanced skills to maximize their potential.

For more information, visit her website at:

- www.passionkairos.com

Follow Ann-Marie Emmanuel @passionkairos on Facebook, Instagram, and YouTube.

CHAPTER 22

COURAGE TO BELIEVE IN YOURSELF FOR OTHERS

BY JENNIFER PERRI

"Stop," I said with conviction. I knew I could simply say "stop," and he would. I could decide whether he inflicted pain on me or not. The choice was mine to make. That was a new reality for me.

He froze, lifted the needle from my skin, and sat with patient understanding. No words were necessary.

As if needing justification, I continued, "Look, you just have to work with me. I haven't been in control of my life for a while now. Being able to have you stop and be in control of the pain in the moment helps."

He smiled.

"Happens all the time. I see people who are trying to take control of something in their life. This seems to work for them too. I get it. Take your time. You're in charge."

"Thank you."

I have over 100 hours of tattoo work on my body. Emerging from a decade of relentless abuse, I grappled with a shattered identity. Despite the searing pain, halting the artist's needle was vital in reclaiming my true self. Scars ran deep, not just on my body but in my psyche.

Stopping him while on the chair wasn't just pain avoidance; it was a declaration of strength, defiance against darkness, and a small step toward rediscovery. In my battle for self, every act echoed my will to survive and thrive, no matter how small.

It wasn't always this way.

Growing up in the small town of Eddystone, Pennsylvania, outside of Philadelphia, in the early 80s was like living in a picture-perfect, all-American storybook. My hometown exuded a serenity that is hard to find these days. Life was simpler, and the community bonds were as strong as steel.

I feel I had incredible role models growing up. My mother, a compassionate woman who worked in healthcare and ran her own cleaning business, represented a harmonious blend of nurturing care and entrepreneurial spirit. My father, with his job at a paper company and occasional forays into law enforcement, contributed to our family's solidly middle-class life.

Eddystone was where dreams seemed attainable, trust was a common currency, and children could enjoy an untroubled childhood. Doors remained unlocked, and we kids pedaled our bikes down sunlit streets, reveling in carefree play until the sun dipped below the horizon. It was a town where neighbors knew each other, forming a tight-knit community where everyone looked out for one another.

I thrived in this nurturing environment. My vibrant personality made me a social butterfly, something I am proud to admit I remain to this day. I couldn't help but lend a hand, whether helping classmates or others in our community. People recognized my intelligence but were equally impressed by my unwavering spirit to connect with others.

Throughout my high school years, I enjoyed a whirlwind of friendships and engagement in various activities. My popularity wasn't confined to one clique. I found myself equally at ease in the drama club, the band, and the company of the football team. My ability to form connections wherever I went became integral to my identity, setting the stage for the warm, caring, and magnetic person I would become.

My upbringing in Eddystone was a time of forming empathetic bonds, experiencing camaraderie, and being part of a close-knit community. These cherished memories of my pleasant upbringing would later serve as a wellspring of strength in my darkest hours.

DARKNESS BEFORE DAWN

The shift began in my senior year of high school. I graduated with honors, spoke four languages, and had a full vision of what my life would look like after high school. In my senior year of high school, my parents divorced, and it shattered my somewhat idyllic world. It was my first glimpse into the harsh realities beyond my sheltered existence. At the time, I didn't realize how much it truly affected my life. Shortly after graduating, I found myself bitter and rebelling, which caused me to get involved with someone my parents would have labeled a 'bad boy.' That's when my life significantly changed.

He didn't start putting his hands on me until probably a month before he asked me to marry him. He was apologetic and convincing. I thought, "Okay, no big deal. You can allow mistakes to happen." We moved on, but it became progressively worse. I became pregnant, we married, and I put my life on hold. As the abuse grew, I thought, "If I go to anyone about what's happening, I would hear, 'I told you so.' So I need to work through this on my own."

The days became months, and months became years, rolling on while my life turned dark. A once confident and vibrant me faded into an unrecognizable shell. I spent an entire decade in an abusive, volatile marriage that nearly took my life on more than one occasion, and eventually, my kids were also in danger. Eventually, a path to safety materialized, and I was able to escape to safety with my two young sons in tow.

COURAGE TO TAKE IT BACK

So, as I sat in a tattoo chair a decade later in the aftermath, I found myself obsessing over the fact that I could take control now. Every moment I decided to stop the needle, despite the discomfort, was an assertion of my newfound autonomy. It was another step, a physical reminder, that I was no longer trapped in a cycle of abuse but was now steering the ship towards my own destiny. Each moment a declaration of strength, resilience, and a choice to shape my life on my terms. It symbolized rebirth and empowerment, a poignant reminder that I was again in control of my story.

My abuser paid for what he had done and found a new existence behind bars, while I had to reclaim my identity and fight to remember who I was before. Emerging from that dark chapter, I was left to raise two young children with no child support and heal from a well of unspeakable trauma. Having no idea who I was or how to make ends meet, I had to pick up the pieces and find a way to move forward.

Today, I am a successful business owner, award-winning coach, and consultant. Back then, I barely made $1,000 a month working three jobs. If you had told me then that I'd be here now, I would have said you are delusional.

Back then, there was no one to show me the way, no mentor or guide to help me rediscover my confidence and rebuild my life. That's when I decided - I had to become the person for other women I desperately needed for myself. This became the primary motivator and driving force for my work today.

The path to regain control and confidence took steps of courage and commitment that may have seemed insignificant to most but were massive milestones in my newfound world. What started with tattoos eventually blended into other paths of rediscovering my courage.

In my path of healing, I found myself in a support group for women in situations like mine and a level of discomfort that I couldn't quite define. As I sat there surrounded by others who had endured their own trials, I reached a breaking point.

"We need more than just a platform to share our stories and compare who had it worse. We need tools and guidance to rebuild our lives after all we've endured. I can't continue down this path." I spoke up, my voice firm.

With unwavering determination, I continued, "I refuse to be confined by my past. I have two little boys who depend on me, and I need to create a future that makes sense for us." As I walked out of that room, it was another significant step in my journey toward healing.

Then came the challenge of dealing with my eight-year-old son's rather unconventional way of expressing his affections—beating up little girls on the playground because he 'liked them,' thinking that was how you show you care. It was an example of behavioral patterns and remnant disorder that needed untangling.

I had to undo many things, both big and small, and it all boiled down to reclaiming power in each of those situations. Even when it came to something as seemingly insignificant as a tattoo gun, it symbolized the control I could assert over my life.

COURAGE TO COMMIT

There was more I needed to decide and a deeper commitment I still needed to make. It took immense courage to stand in that support group and assert, "You're not helping me. This relationship no longer serves me. I'm out." And when I had to recalibrate my children's perceptions, it was a shift in understanding what true courage and commitment meant.

Courage demanded that I take risks, step out of my comfort zone, and confront the inevitable mess. It's one thing to tap into survival instincts during the big battles, but what about the small ones? What about when the worst is finally behind you? In those moments, we face a pivotal choice as we pick up the pieces of our struggle.

There comes a point where we must decide whether we'll settle for something better or push ourselves to reach for the best. I made the choice. I acknowledged that I deserved the best life had to offer. I resolved to summon the courage needed to wholeheartedly commit to the messy process of reclaiming my life.

COURAGE TO STAND FOR OTHERS

I decided to step into the financial consulting arena after experiencing

219

the significant and all-to-common struggle with financial stability for me and other women coming out of these situations. My instinct, after all, is to help. I sat across the table from women, just like me, and told them, "I've been there. I understand your struggles, and I can help." We started with budgets, but we didn't stop there. I wanted to know their stories, to understand their fears, and to help them find the strength to overcome.

As I worked with these women, I realized that my role had evolved beyond financial consulting. It was coaching, but it was also being a guiding light for them, helping them celebrate their small victories. I was now providing to others what I had been missing in my darkest hours, a hand to hold, a profound reassurance that they were not alone in their journey. I do everything I do now because I needed someone desperately to help me sort stuff out 20 years ago, and I couldn't find her. So, I've wanted to become that person.

No matter what life throws your way, a unique sense of fulfillment comes from lending a hand to others on a path you've walked. Knowing you've made a difference in someone else's life is a remarkable reward.

THE EMPOWERMENT BLUEPRINT

Many women come to me deflated. Someone or circumstance determined what their life should look like instead of writing their own story. Often, they have to borrow my beliefs in them at the beginning until we get to a point where there's a handing over of the baton, and they finally believe in themselves. They were conditioned into thinking, "I don't believe I have it. I don't believe I should be successful." So we work together to unpack this.

I developed a system called 'The Empowerment Blueprint: Building Authentic Success for Women.' It's about teaching women how to be authentically successful and empowered. My clients are often at the same point I was. They gravitate towards me because I've been there. I have been through it all. This is a judgment-free zone, and I can meet them where they are and help. It's all about helping them love themselves first, which takes time.

COMMITMENT TO SELF

Today, I'm a Transformational Life coach, and my primary commitment now is to myself. It's a fundamental truth that unless my cup is brimming with contentment, I cannot effectively pour into the lives of others. It took me quite some time to make this pivotal shift – to prioritize my well-being, happiness, and sense of security.

Commitment, as I help my clients understand, begins with the profound acceptance that I may not be precisely where I envisioned myself in life at this very moment. Nevertheless, I steadfastly love and appreciate myself exactly as I am, valuing each step of the journey.

My commitment is layered, starting with my happiness. I'm married to the love of my life, an extraordinary man, Carmine. My commitment extends to nurturing our relationship, serving him with love and respect, and, of course, being a devoted mother to my children. My clients hold a special place in my commitment roster as well.

Every day, I start with a strong promise to take care of myself. No matter what happens, even on hard days or when I'm facing health problems, I stick to my routine. First, I focus on being thankful, then I say my goals out loud as affirmations. Some days, this takes extra effort. Even when I faced tough challenges, like being paralyzed and dealing with Guillain-Barré Syndrome, which made me unable to move from the shoulders down, I didn't give up on my routine. (More about my story on my website at: www.jenniferperri.com.)

Everyone is acutely aware of their position in life and their commitment to crafting the life they desire. It's about actively pursuing the path to your goals. I have been unwavering in my commitment to learning with an unquenchable thirst for knowledge. This commitment extends to the wisdom of those more successful than I am because success leaves clues.

Now, I have a beautiful life, an incredible husband, a rewarding career, and a loving family. I may not be perfect, but I am whole. I tell everyone I'm "great from the waist up," and my legs might never fully recover, but I'm still here. As long as I am, I'll keep changing the world, one woman at a time.

I've arrived at this profound realization, which I leave with you as a personal challenge:

Have the courage to commit to prioritizing your own well-being and personal growth. Doing so will make you better equipped to impact the lives of those you serve.

About Jennifer

Jennifer Perri is a Transformational Life Coach, a Certified Divorce & Empowerment Coach and 3x Best-Selling Author and she has spent over two decades helping women transform their lives. Jennifer's mission is to empower women to live financially fearless, embrace their inner worth and become the sheroes in their stories.

Jennifer stands as a living testament to the indomitable human spirit. With a beautiful life, a loving husband, and a fulfilling career, she has triumphed over adversity and emerged stronger than ever. Jennifer's journey, though marred by hardship, has equipped her with the unwavering resolve to effect change in the world. With each client she empowers, each life she touches, she continues to rewrite the narratives of resilience and triumph, proving that we all have the power to craft our own destinies.

Jennifer has been featured in the media as a thought leader, appearing on or in ABC, NBC, FOX, CBS, *Vanity Fair* (February 2022, Atlanta Woman Feature), *The Tycoon Magazine, Newsweek, Fortune,* and *Forbes.* She has been a contributor to two international best-selling books, *Dare to Succeed* with Jack Canfield, creator of the *Chicken Soup for the Soul* series and her most recent book, *Quiet and Badass.*

For more information or to connect with Jennifer, visit:

- www.jenniferperri.com

CHAPTER 23

TURNING PAIN INTO PURPOSE
DELIVERING THE VOICE AND CHOICE I DIDN'T HAVE

BY DR. TABATHA BARBER, FACOOG, NCMP, IFMCP

At sixteen, in eleventh grade, I got pregnant and then got married. A school counselor suggested I leave school so I wouldn't set a bad example for the other girls at school. I thought, *How is staying in school a bad example?* So, rather emphatically, I said, "Uh, no," and I finished out the school year. I did have to drop out before my senior year to take care of my daughter.

My pregnancy was traumatic—I was on Medicaid and food stamps. Medically, I went through the motions—enduring endless pelvic exams with a doctor who looked to be on the verge of retirement, taking pills, getting shots, having procedures. These things were so routine, not one doctor or nurse asked my permission or gave me any options. No one explained why they were doing these things.

When it came to my body, I didn't have a voice or a choice. Things didn't get easier with my labor and delivery. I had gone forty-two weeks—what felt like an eternity—without any signs of labor. So, I finally went into the hospital to be induced. When my water broke, it was pea-soup green. Timidly, I asked, "Is it supposed to be that color?"

I wasn't in the habit of questioning anyone during my pregnancy because I thought the doctors and nurses knew what was best for me—after all, they were the ones wearing the white coats. But now, it wasn't just about me; it was about my baby, and seeing my water green scared me. So, I started asking questions. The nurse pointed to the monitor and said, "Don't worry about it. Your baby is fine." Her attempt to 'assure' me did not.

At my age, I didn't know what to expect or what was normal. "What do these squiggles on the paper mean?" The nurse snapped back, "That your baby is fine. Do you think we would just sit here if it wasn't?" "I guess not," I answered, not convinced.

I had pushed for three and a half hours, crying in pain, alone—my husband was sick, and my mother had to leave while I was in labor to take care of my three young siblings at home. I begged the nurse, "Please give me a C-section!" Finally, a doctor came in. And I thought, *Finally, someone is going to help me! Thank you, God!*

But he was a family doctor, not an obstetrician, and could not perform a C-section. I didn't have a choice. He prepped me for the delivery, draping my legs wide open over cold metal leg holders. Suddenly, the pain became burning, searing, unbearable.

Clang! Clang!

As the metal forceps hit the floor, it felt like knives piercing my spine. He had used them to deliver my daughter, tearing me front to back. I spent the next hour biting a wet washcloth, tears streaming down my face, while the doctor sutured me back together. I changed my focus to my crying daughter and thought, *What a beautiful, soothing sound. Oh, I wish they would let me hold you, my sweet baby Ellie.*

Through tears of joy, I vowed to never let her go through this alone or without options. I would do whatever it takes to give her a voice, a choice, love, and support.

ON A MISSION

The disrespect of the medical community toward young girls was really eye-opening. It sparked in me the desire to help other women. I thought, *I don't want anyone to have to go through what I went through.*

In my small Michigan town, I had been a wild child who cared more about hanging out with my friends than school. Detention and Saturday school had been familiar places. I had wanted to be a rock star when I grew up. I wanted to be anything but what my mission became: a gynecologist.

But God spoke to me that day. He clearly told me, "You need to get your life together for you and your daughter. You need to use your voice to ask for the respect you deserve." My daughter needed it. Women needed it. And the Holy Spirit was with me, showing me my purpose.

Over the next many months, God repeatedly whispered to me, "Take care of your body—it is a gift to be cherished. Find your voice. Help other women find their voice. Help other women keep their bodies safe. Figure out how to help women feel heard, safe, and supported."

BACK TO THE CLASSROOM

Suddenly, I felt a reason to be in school. I got the courage to go back and get my GED and then attend a community college. I had plans to become a nurse. I learned how to study—and that I was capable of way more than I had thought. After getting Cs and Ds in high school, I got straight As for two years in college!

I told a professor I didn't want to be a nurse and take orders, but I dreamed of becoming a doctor instead. "I want to make those decisions for myself."

"You can," he said with confidence. Those two words changed my life.

I remember feeling shocked at his reply. "You believe I could do that?"

"Without a doubt," he said. "And God put you on this path to do great things, to help women, so I know you will succeed. You could go to Michigan State like I did." And he offered to write me a letter of recommendation.

His belief in me and the reminder from God as He spoke through my professor brought me clarity. After two years at the community college, I transferred to Michigan State University with two scholarships. There, I took another four years of undergrad coursework, majoring in physiology—the study of how the human body functions down to the cellular level and in response to the environment it's exposed to. I earned my bachelor's degree with high honors.

A DOCTOR IN THE HOUSE

Since my daughter was in second grade then and I didn't want to move her, I applied to only one medical school. I wanted to go to an osteopathic medical school because they seemed to stress the importance of the mind-body connection.

The road was rough. I had to take out loans and work multiple jobs, but I felt like I had made the right decision. I was determined to show women in my care, especially my daughter, that you don't have to settle for substandard. You can live a better life with more responsive care. I got accepted and became the physician I needed a decade earlier.

I became the doctor my daughter and other women needed—one who would talk to her patients and let them know about available options and that they are not alone in their journey. This all happened because I listened to God when He said, "Help other women," and relied on my faith. As Martin Luther King Jr. said, "We don't have to see the whole staircase, just the first step."

A decade later, I was living the life of an attending physician, the life I worked so hard for, the life I thought God wanted for me. But I was exhausted, sleep-deprived, and addicted to sugar and caffeine. I would wake up at 6 a.m. from a short nap after a long night of working, rush around waking up my two babies, feeding them, packing their bags for daycare, taking a quick shower, and then do everything I could to get to the office by 7:30 a.m., though I was usually fifteen to thirty minutes late. By the time I got settled, answered questions for my nurse, talked with my manager about the day, and started seeing patients, I was already a half hour behind and I hadn't even really started my day.

The whole day, I would try to catch up seeing patient after patient, only to end up further and further behind because I didn't really have the time to listen to my patients and actually try to help them the way I wanted to. I churned through patients as fast as I could, in the interest of keeping my bosses satisfied. I rarely ate lunch and often got even further behind, frustrating my patients, when I had to go deliver a baby during my workday.

My nights consisted of often scrambling to find someone to get my kids from daycare because I was working late, caring for two rambunctious toddlers, and regularly lining up a babysitter to sleep at my house when I was on call and had to leave during the night to deliver babies.

I found myself following the conventional path, handing women birth control pills and scheduling them for surgery. I was never really able to treat their core issues. It was not rewarding for me, nor was it sustainable. I had reached a point where I had constant back pain while doing my job, and it eventually became unbearable. Here I was, a women's health care expert, but unhealthy as it gets.

Finally, I went to the doctor. I had a herniated, ruptured disc in my lower back and was told I needed surgery. "How in the world am I going to not work for six weeks?" I said. "Who's going to take care of my patients? Who's going to take care of my kids?" It seemed impossible, but I accepted it, had the surgery, and took six weeks off—only for the problem to reoccur. *I just went through all of that for nothing.*

The surgeon said, "Yep, you re-herniated. Now we need to put hardware in your back—rods and screws," adding, "Back surgery is like Lay's potato chips—you can't have just one."

I thought, *Dear God, I can't do this again. Please help me.* God answered, shouting, "Use your voice!"

I woke up and remembered how I told God I would protect my body. So I told my surgeon there must be another solution. "Nope, not really," he said flippantly, "unless you just want to live with the pain."

MY KIND OF DOCTOR

I did not—and I didn't want to accept his only choice. Then I heard God say, "I have already given you the tools to heal your body and be well. Trust me." I realized conventional medicine was failing me, so I started researching outside of my normal sources and was amazed to find an entire world of wellness and prevention out there that I knew nothing about: functional medicine.

I began absorbing everything I could from Cleveland Clinic's Institute for Functional Medicine. I had a renewed hope—and a reminder that I am a child of God and that through Him all things are possible.

So next I enrolled in that institute. I applied what I learned to my own life and found amazing results. I could remember things, I had energy, I lost twenty pounds in three months, and my back pain was lessening. After taking four months off to focus on my own health, I was a changed woman. Also changed was the way I approached my patients' problems.

I had found hope. I would no longer cover up symptoms with pills and surgeries, creating even more problems. I now viewed my patients' complaints as signs that something was going on that wasn't being addressed, that there was dysfunction.

I finally understood and believed what I was told on the first day of medical school: Dr. Andrew Taylor Still, the founding father of osteopathic medicine, said the body has the innate ability to heal— the physician just needs to guide that process. Studying functional medicine, I focused on how the body functions; how it interacts with the world around it; how the bacteria, viruses, yeast, parasites, and environmental pollutants affect us; how the body reacts to physical and mental stressors, and how all of our systems are intricately interconnected.

Our conventional medical system is designed to keep us sick and focused on disease. I did not accept a fate of disease, and I don't want you to either. We need to focus on true return of function (healing), wellness, and prevention. We must ask why. When a patient tells me her complaints, rather than spending five minutes finding a drug that will treat her symptoms, it's my job to ask, "Why is she feeling that?" Together we work on solving root causes of problems. I help patients work on core issues like balancing out their adrenals, cleaning up their diet, and most importantly, healing the gut.

I truly believe that God wants us to leave this world better than we found it, and caring for your body first is critical for you to glorify the Lord and live out your purpose.

If you haven't already, I promise an opportunity will present itself for you to step into your purpose, and God will give you the chance to grow into the person you are meant to become. I believe you get as many chances as you need to step into your greatness and shine the way you were born to shine. You may just need a guide or someone who believes in you. If you aren't living your best life because of hormone, weight, or gut issues, then I would invite you to check out my podcast, *The Gutsy Gynecologist Show*, or reach out to me. My team and I help women all over the country, through our virtual medical practice, get to the root cause of their issues – so they can become the women they are meant to be!

About Dr. Tabatha

Dr. Tabatha Barber has dedicated her life to giving women a voice and a choice when it comes to their health and well-being. Overcoming struggles as a young girl, including self-esteem challenges and the hurdles of being a high school dropout and teenage mother, she emerged as a successful physician through faith and perseverance.

Her unwavering commitment to women's health is evident through her triple board certifications in obstetrics and gynecology, menopause, and functional medicine. As the driving force behind her thriving medical practice, Dr. Tabatha and her team provide compassionate support and care to women nationwide.

Through *The Gutsy Gynecologist™ Show*, her Gutsy Gyn supplement line, and her international best-selling book *Fast to Faith*, she shares insights into the importance of gut health, hormone balance, mindset, and most importantly, nourishing the soul to truly heal and become whole. She is a beacon of light in a sea of medical darkness.

To contact Dr. Tabatha:

- www.drtabatha.com

CHAPTER 24

GAME, SET, BALANCE

BY DR. HEIDI GREGORY-MINA

"Game, set, match." For years those words echoed in my mind, propelling me forward and igniting my love for the game. Tennis wasn't just a hobby for me; it was my lifeblood. So, as I approached the pivotal moment of considering college, it was only natural for me to envision continuing my tennis journey at the next level. The thought of competing for a university and pushing my boundaries filled me with excitement and determination.

Visiting various colleges shattered the idyllic image I had of collegiate tennis. I witnessed the grueling training sessions, the demanding schedules, and the intense pressure that seemed to surround every aspect of the sport. The pure joy and love I once associated with tennis began to fade, overshadowed by the constant focus on performance and results. Emotional intelligence, time management, resilience, and numerous other skills essential in tennis are surprisingly similar to those required to excel as a CEO—though such parallels were far from my teenage mind. Closer to reality was the transformation of my once passionate source of joy into a daunting job, where every decision overshadowed my initial love for the game.

Amid the overwhelming intensity of collegiate tennis, I realized I needed to prioritize my well-being and happiness. With a heavy heart, I made the courageous decision to put down my racket and explore other opportunities. It meant reevaluating my dreams and embracing the uncertainty that lay ahead. While the dream of playing tennis in college took a backseat, I found solace in pursuing other passions and interests. I discovered a well-rounded college experience that went beyond the boundaries of sports, nurturing my personal and academic growth in ways I hadn't anticipated. College was a time of discovery, meeting new people, exploring new experiences, and challenging my perspectives.

NAVIGATING BURNOUT AND REDISCOVERING BALANCE

Throughout my academic journey, I was no stranger to hard work. Balancing school and employment became the norm for me. As I embarked on my career path, I initially worked in the field of accounting and finance. I eventually found myself transitioning into the health care industry. I led a significant grant portfolio worth over $120 million, but the weight of responsibility took its toll. Silent indicators started to surface, and I gradually felt the grip of stress tightening around me. My productivity waned, I sought to escape early and arrived late, and additional time off became a necessity. It was inevitable—I had hit burnout. This experience served as a stark reminder of the importance of self-care and the necessity of taking time for myself.

Prioritizing my mental and physical health became nonnegotiable. I recognized that to be effective in my career and personal life, I needed to nurture myself first. I embarked on a journey of self-discovery, exploring activities and practices that brought me joy and rejuvenation. Whether it was engaging in hobbies, spending time with loved ones, or simply indulging in moments of solitude, I found solace in these acts of self-care.

Recovering from burnout required more than just time off; it demanded a reevaluation of my priorities and the creation of a healthier work-life balance. I learned to set boundaries, both for myself and for others, to prevent the encroachment of work-related stress into my personal life. By adopting self-care practices as a regular part of my routine, I regained my energy and enthusiasm. The journey to recovery was gradual, but the transformation was profound.

A NEWFOUND PASSION AND PURPOSE

During the challenging period of burnout recovery, I welcomed Hazelnut, my second pug, into my home. It was during this time that I decided to pursue a long-held dream: participating in agility training. The dynamic sport of agility, with its obstacle courses and teamwork between handler and dog, brought immense excitement and fulfillment to our lives. It became a shared passion that not only strengthened our bond but also ignited a newfound sense of purpose within me.

As time passed, Hazelnut and I continued our agility journey, participating in various competitions and events. The challenges we faced together taught me invaluable lessons about patience, perseverance, and the power of teamwork. The agility community provided a supportive network, fostering friendships and shared experiences. Through this pursuit, I discovered a deep passion for not only the sport itself but also the connections and personal growth it offered.

As my love for agility blossomed, I began to reflect on my career in health care. While I had dedicated many years to the field, a growing desire for change started to stir within me. I yearned for a profession that would align more closely with my newfound passion for personal growth and education. It was during this period of introspection that an opportunity arose—a position in higher education opened up.

I took a leap of faith and seized that opportunity. The decision to pursue a career in this field was driven by my passion for learning, personal growth, and helping others unlock their potential. It felt like a natural fit, as I could combine my previous experience with my newfound enthusiasm for education and agility. The opportunity to support students in their academic journey, foster a love for learning, and witness their personal growth became incredibly rewarding. Each day brought new challenges and opportunities for me to make a positive impact on individuals' lives.

LEARNING TO BALANCE PASSIONS AND PRIORITIES

Driven by my love for dog sports, I embarked on an exciting venture by opening my own dog training business. This decision allowed me to share my passion with others and create a meaningful impact. However, I soon discovered the delicate balance between running a business, teaching, and consulting work. With the unexpected arrival of my daughter coinciding with the onset of the pandemic, my priorities underwent a significant shift. As a result, I made the difficult decision to close my business, realizing that the boundary between pursuing what I loved and turning it into work had become blurred once again.

Closing the business served as a moment of clarity and self-discovery. I understood the importance of maintaining a healthy balance between passion, work, and personal life. I learned that turning a passion into a business venture required careful consideration and an understanding of the potential consequences. It was essential to preserve the love and joy associated with my passions while still allowing space for personal growth and fulfillment.

As I closed the chapter of my dog training business, I carried forward valuable lessons. I realized the significance of maintaining a healthy balance in pursuing what I love, ensuring that it remains a source of joy and fulfillment. While the business may have come to an end, my passion for dog sports and teaching remained intact. Armed with newfound wisdom, I sought to strike a harmonious balance between pursuing my passions, nurturing my family life, and pursuing meaningful work in the future.

EMPOWERING WOMEN

As I contemplated my future steps, it became clear to me that I desired to make a substantial impact on society. I had a deep-rooted motivation to demonstrate to my daughter that women have the power to achieve success and should never allow anything to hinder their progress. Recognizing my aptitude for engaging others, imparting knowledge, and assuming leadership roles, I resolved to expand my personal brand.

While my involvement in higher education had played a significant role in my life thus far, I yearned to broaden my horizons beyond the confines of the classroom. I aspired to acquire knowledge and expertise that transcended traditional educational settings. By doing so, I aimed to amplify my influence and make a more profound contribution to society.

To embark on this path, I decided to take a series of deliberate actions. First, I committed to defining my long-term vision with utmost clarity. By pinpointing the areas where I could truly make a difference, I sought to align my passions with the causes that resonated most deeply with me. This strategic approach would allow me to focus my efforts and channel my energy effectively.

Furthermore, I acknowledged the importance of recognizing and leveraging my existing expertise. Reflecting on my skills, knowledge, and experiences, I identified the domains in which I possessed a wealth of insights and unique perspectives. This process enabled me to carve out a niche for myself and establish my credibility as a thought leader.

With my vision and expertise firmly established, I understood the significance of cultivating a robust online presence. Through various platforms such as social media, blogging, and maintaining a personal website, I planned to share valuable content related to my areas of expertise. By doing so, I could engage with a broader audience, provide meaningful education, and forge connections with like-minded individuals.

Recognizing the power of collaboration and networking, I committed to actively seeking opportunities to connect with fellow professionals, experts, and influencers in my field. By attending conferences, joining professional associations, and participating in online communities, I aimed to expand my network. Through these connections, I envisioned fostering collaboration, forming partnerships, and ultimately magnifying my impact.

MY JOURNEY OF EXPANSION AND INFLUENCE

In the ever-evolving landscape of personal branding and professional growth, I have emerged as a trailblazer, taking my role as CEO of Dr. Heidi to new heights. With a relentless drive to make a significant impact, I have expanded my horizons, explored diverse avenues, and embraced various mediums to extend my reach and influence. From expanding my client base to launching workshops, increasing speaking engagements, starting a podcast, publishing books, and appearing on television shows, I have continually demonstrated my expertise and commitment to empowering others.

Public speaking has not come easy for me. In fact, it stirred up a profound sense of fear in me—until I learned to see it in a positive light. When I was asked to present at my first conference, I was excited and honored. When I arrived, I headed toward the door, but as I grabbed the door handle, I froze in fear. I did not go in, and I did not give my speech! It was at this point that I had hit rock bottom and knew I wanted to change. So with my newfound self-awareness, I started to surround myself with people who pushed me out of my comfort zone and challenged me to be the best version of myself. This fear was not new; it went all the way back to when I was five years old and in a play. I had only one line, yet when it came time to say it, there was dead silence. I said nothing.

I have come to realize that fear is just an emotion. Every situation I put myself in would have only one of two outcomes: I would either learn, or I would succeed. So I really pushed myself out of my comfort zone and decided to pursue a job in higher education—of course realizing I would have to talk to people. I promised myself I would not leave my students sitting alone in a classroom, as I had done with the conference participants. I would enter that room. The first class I taught was hard but so rewarding! It taught me that I loved teaching, I loved seeing people get that 'aha' moment. I truly began to develop my speaking ability further as I went through my doctoral program and continued to change my mindset around public speaking. Though initially, all my associations with public speaking were based on negative thoughts, I had flipped the script and began to see fear as a positive catalyst—even developing a model to overcome this fear of public speaking.

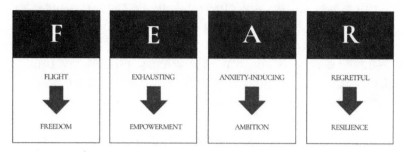

Further, recognizing the power of education and personal interaction, I have taken the initiative to launch my own workshops. These workshops serve as platforms to engage with participants, impart knowledge, and inspire personal and professional growth. In addition, my commitment to expanding my speaking engagements has allowed me to connect with even larger audiences, spreading my message of empowerment, resilience, and success.

With a wealth of knowledge and experiences to share, I have authored impactful books that resonate with my audience. My written works offer practical advice, inspiration, and valuable perspectives, positioning me as a thought leader in my field. Additionally, I have contributed numerous articles to prominent publications, further establishing myself as an authoritative voice in my industry.

ADVICE FOR WOMEN CEOS: EMBRACE CHANGE ALONG THE JOURNEY

For women who aspire to become CEOs or currently hold CEO positions, my journey serves as a testament to the significance of embracing change and prioritizing well-being throughout the pursuit of success. Transitioning from a career in tennis to one in higher education taught me that our passions often lead us on unconventional paths, and it is essential to align our professional pursuits with our core values.

Furthermore, nurturing our mental and physical health is of utmost importance, as burnout can undermine our effectiveness as leaders. I came to understand the value of striking a harmonious balance between our personal and professional lives, ensuring that our passions remain a source of joy rather than mere work, and that we can achieve growth in both areas. By openly sharing our experiences and seizing new opportunities, we can inspire others to pursue their passions, shatter barriers, and make a lasting impact in their chosen fields. We always possess the power to choose our own paths, and I too ventured down the less-traveled road. I confronted my fears, pushed my limits, and challenged myself. Along the way, I discovered that the emotions that accompany courage and commitment are well within our control.

Now, I have the privilege of assisting nonprofits, businesses, professionals, and students in enhancing their performance and achieving their goals by delving into the science of human behavior. As I mentioned, every endeavor yields only two possible outcomes: either you achieve success or you gain knowledge from your experiences. When you shift your mindset and view criticism as a source of growth, as a means to enhance yourself, the path forward becomes clearer. These moments cease to be setbacks; they transform into steppingstones leading to self-improvement. Dig deep and summon the courage to believe that there is no loss, only progress.

About Dr. Heidi

Meet Dr. Heidi Gregory-Mina, the once-shy 5-year-old who transformed from struggling to give her single line in a play to captivating thousands from diverse stages. Her passion lies in sharing knowledge and witnessing the 'uh-huh' moments that ignite understanding. Early in her professional journey, she discovered the profound importance of mentorship in leadership, a lesson that would guide her throughout her career. With extensive experience in management, she became renowned for her exceptional ability to foster employee engagement.

Dr. Heidi boasts an impressive portfolio, with numerous publications in peer-reviewed journals and other esteemed publications. She is also a best-selling author and has graced the screens of FOX, NBC, CBS, and NBC. Beyond her professional endeavors, Dr. Heidi is a dedicated mom, loving wife, cherished daughter, and supportive sister. In her spare time, she finds joy in the world of dog sports.

To connect with Dr. Heidi today to tap into her wealth of knowledge and experience, to delve deeper into her transformative journey and the lasting impact she continues to create, visit her website at:

- www.drheidigregorymina.com

CHAPTER 25

TURN OFF YOUR AUTOPILOT!
I DIDN'T KNOW I WAS ASLEEP
UNTIL I WOKE UP

BY RHONDA LYNN DAVISON

I woke up each morning, looked in the mirror and didn't recognize the reflection staring back at me with those sad green eyes. I opened my mouth to speak...only to realize the words were stuck in my throat. My heart was in so much pain that...I began to pray that I would feel *nothing*.

My 'inner bully' screamed cruel and vile words on repeat, looping over and over in my mind. Sometimes, we listen to negative voices and just check out on life. Sometimes, we use food or wine, TV or social media...*simply to numb out*.

Have you ever felt so desperate to change your life but just didn't know how? That was me. On that day, my car's AC was working. Everything else in my life, though, was not. I was stuck in New York City traffic on a Saturday morning in 95° F. heat, taking a 40-mile journey from Staten Island to Long Island that might as well have been 4,000 due to a three-lane chaotic artery of frustration and stagnation. My life, too, was chaotic and my life, had also screeched to a halt.

My father had died, sending me into a valley of grief. My relationships were faltering, only furthering my sense of hopelessness. The job that once brought me fulfillment now was no longer fun. Meanwhile, the handful of friends that were left in my life were facing the same struggle that I was facing: a sense that we were stuck on the hamster wheel of life, with no purpose, no direction and no joy. Simply put: I felt dead inside.

The sun on that August day was beating down on the Belt Parkway, transforming the surrounding landscape into a depressing mirage of concrete and metal. Waves of heat rose from the pavement, mingling with exhaust fumes to blur the view of the Empire State Building, the Freedom Tower, and well, every other part of the iconic city skyline.

Our destination that morning was a wellness event at Hofstra University, some 40 miles to our east. But thanks to bumper-to-bumper traffic and countless New Yorkers who, too, were trapped in a vehicular purgatory, my friend Robin and I had plenty of time to commiserate about our respective midlife crises.

As the car's AC did its best to cool the car -- not to mention our conversation – we bounced a series of seemingly unanswerable questions off each other.

- *Why do I always feel depressed and lack energy?*
- *Why can't I lose weight no matter how hard I try?*
- *Why is the world against me?*

At one point during the conversation, the subject turned to therapists:

"Maybe that would help," Robin said.

"I guess," I responded.

Neither of us, though, knew a good therapist. None of our friends had been to one – at least, not from what we knew.

It took three hours to travel 40 miles that day – three hours at roughly 13 miles per hour on a stretch of highway that had suddenly been transformed into a slow-moving parking lot. Up ahead at Hofstra, I would find the help I so desperately needed. I felt stuck in a deep abyss of darkness. My life seemed like a dead-end road.

My midlife crisis began five years earlier when my father, then 70, traveled to the Pocono Mountains with my nephew for a fun weekend of sledding and tubing in the freshly-fallen snow. That's the type of man he was – always thinking of others, always placing the needs of others before his own. He even chose a career where he regularly placed his health and life on the line as a firefighter in the famed New York City Fire Department. He entered burning buildings when others were fleeing. He climbed tall ladders that would send fear down your spine. He also climbed the career ladder of success, claiming the title of battalion chief before retiring from the job with disability after sustaining an on-the-job injury when he dislocated his shoulder and his knee, ending his 28-year career of service.

He had battled a few health problems in his later years, but his doctor had cleared him to travel that weekend to enjoy a few peaceful days in the mountains away from the big city's sights and sounds. I was at work that day when the phone rang. It was my sister, her voice trembling.

Honestly, I don't recall everything she said. I only remember my reaction. I screamed. I sobbed, the news hitting me like a sudden gust of wind. My father had died in his sleep. Time stood still as I grappled with the surreal reality of losing the man who had been my pillar of strength.

He had always provided emotional support and even financial assistance – and the day before he died, was helping me escape an unhealthy romantic relationship that had been detrimental to my well-being. The daily drama seemed too much to bear. My fiancé and I had been together for 10 years. We shared a daughter, a car and an apartment.

The breakup, or rather the dissolution of the living arrangements, combined with my father's passing, was a 1-2 punch to the gut. A short time later, life hit me with a third blow – and this one nearly killed me.

I was packing boxes and moving out of my old house when a small, unseen spider bit me on the leg. That's what the doctors later said. I never saw the tiny creature. I only saw its aftereffect: a high fever that had me bundling under blankets in summer with a painful, swollen, red leg that prevented me from walking. Unable to drive, I asked a family member for a ride to the hospital. Once there, I hobbled through the doors.

"You'll be here for a while," a nurse told me in a friendly yet matter-of-fact tone that seemed cruel after all I had endured. I had cellulitis. Days earlier, I had seemingly turned the corner in life, moving out of a home filled with dreadful memories and into a new home full of hope and the promise of a fresh start. And now, thanks to a spider bite, I was confined to a hospital bed.

A few days later, I developed sepsis, a life-threatening condition that is triggered by an infection and shuts down the immune system. It is, I later learned, the No. 1 cause of hospital deaths. Doctors couldn't control my fever. They also couldn't find an antibiotic that worked. For a brief moment, I was ready to die. I even whispered a prayer: "You know what, God, if you need me, I'm ready to embrace whatever comes next, because I want to be with my father."

Friends later told me they thought I might die. Nurses later told me that my name was on the short list of patients whose condition was grave. The turning point came when my daughter visited me in the hospital, her face filled with cheer and a warm smile that cut through the hospital's sterile atmosphere. She was a ray of sunlight and optimism.

Thanks to her, I chose to fight. Like a boxer down for the count, 1 got up off the canvas, clinging to life and chasing this thing called hope. If nothing more, I told myself, my daughter needed me. She had lost her biological mom before the age of 4 months old. I wasn't going to let her lose me, too.

Gradually, I recovered.

Less than six months later, I started my life over again, this time as a 40-something student in the esteemed Villanova University. Two decades earlier, I had started work on my bachelor's degree but had never finished. This time I was determined to cross the finish line. I loaded up on classes – too many at once if I'm honest – graduating near the top of my class with *magna cum laude* honors. I was beaming with pride. *This girl barely graduated high school.* But the joy didn't last.

Even with a degree, I felt like something was missing in my life. Even with a degree, I felt disconnected. Deep down, I was also angry. I would argue with friends at the drop of a hat. I would snap at coworkers over the most mundane matters. Much later, I discovered that my mood swings were tied to feelings of abandonment and rejection from a childhood of being bullied.

I felt lost, scared and depressed, all at the same time. I would indulge in food – snacks and chips and junk food of every kind – for a quick carb and sugar 'high.' I would drink several glasses of wine, just about any kind of red was fine, the cheaper the better, to escape the reality I no longer wanted to face.

That's where I was in life that day on the Belt Parkway in the extreme summer heat. I was sitting behind the wheel of my gray Hyundai Santa Fe, and yet, I felt as if my life was on autopilot, ready to crash over the guardrails of life.

I felt dead inside.

I wasn't taking care of my body. As I soon learned, I wasn't caring for my mind and soul, either. Three hours after we left home, we arrived at the Hofstra campus, the air filled with the aroma of grilled food and the sounds of high-energy music. That alone briefly lifted my spirits. It was a family-friendly event for parents and kids alike, with thousands packing the outdoor stadium for the main event to discover whether their team would be picked in the raffle. The grand prize: a trip to Paris!

As I walked across the field to find a better view of the speaker, the voice of a bubbly, pony-tailed woman with a contagious ear-to-ear smile caught my attention. She was bouncing up and down on stage, urging the massive crowd to stand to its feet and join her over-the-top workout. I didn't need another Covergirl fitness doll telling me how to 'thrive.' I had been there, done that. I had tried the diets. I had gone through the workouts. It may have helped her, but it didn't help me.

But then I listened to what she *said.* "The diet and fitness industry has lied to you!" She had my attention. "You're the master of your own mouth. You're the keeper of your own health." That was new. "I want you to roll your wrists forward as fast as you can right in front of your heart and repeat after me...I am powerful beyond measure." With a bewildered look on my face, I repeated: "I am powerful beyond measure" again and again and again.

That, too, was different.

Her message was simple yet powerful: You're not just a *body*. You're a body, mind *and* soul. She called her spiritual fitness program 'intenSati,' telling us it was a combination of cardio exercises, high-emotion mantras and affirmations. Her name: Patricia Moreno. She had launched it some two decades earlier, her program embodying the belief that the language we speak to ourselves matters. Patricia's tagline: 'Exercise Your Power!'

Her program hooked me. Her story did, too. Like me, she had struggled with fear and shame. Like me, she had been stuck in a deep, dark valley that seemed inescapable. Patricia believed there was more to life than this physical world. That's what I believed, too. I just didn't know how to express it. I cried all the way home.

Days later, I signed up for her class. A few weeks after that, I signed up to be an intenSati leader. It was a whirlwind of events that changed my life for the better. Until then, I had never understood spiritual development. Until then, I believed the world's lies about happiness. They say when the student is ready, the teacher appears. Through Patricia's coaching and mentorship, I became a voracious reader and student of implementing an intenSati way of life.

She taught me how to live life fully even through her terminal diagnosis of stage IV cancer. I was not ready to lose her. It did not feel fair. I made her a promise a few weeks before she died to live my best life in her honor and that I would share intenSati with the masses. Shortly after Patricia's death I found author Laura Lynne Jackson who wrote *The Light Between Us* and *Signs*. These books changed the way I view death and grief. Energy never dies. We are all energy transformed – and there is a way to communicate and interact with our team of light on the other side.

Life hasn't been a breeze since then, but it's been much better. Less than three years after I began intenSati, my mother lost her four-decade battle with cancer. She taught me what it is to be a tender-hearted warrior, to be strong. She often shared her life motto: *The grim reaper can come for me, but he must play: 'catch me if you can.'*

I continue to process through my grief journey without my best friend, and it didn't push me off a cliff as so many past tragedies had done. I miss my mama every single day and am equipped with tools to work through difficult emotions without shutting down. I communicate with her by asking for unique signs. I ask and she sends them. It's our new language. She's in a better place. I am, too.

I developed a new program – the Break Wide Open Program – introducing the '5 Pillars of Ease' to help others find healing at life's breaking points. These five pillars are simple and impactful:

1. **Elevate**: Place yourself around people who are evolving themselves. Read books with innovative ideas in them.

2. **Energy**: There are so many rituals that involve energy that can change your state of being – breathwork, crystals, hypnosis and meditation.

3. **Exercise**: Move your body, move stuck energy. For me, It's my intenSati practice. I need that each day. Movement and speaking affirmations to feed and heal my soul.

4. **Embody**: Immerse yourself in the stories of your lost loved ones. Hear them, accept them. Feel gratitude, look at pictures and videos. Imagine them here with you.

5. **Evolve**: Open your mind to new ideas. Learn what you need and have love and compassion for yourself. Take time to explore your feelings, to feel your feelings.

My story is simple: Although we may feel shattered, none of us are broken. Healing is possible at any age. Sometimes, you must hold on until you get there. Sometimes, you just don't know what you're holding on to … until you get there.

If you want support navigating from your breaking point to your next breakthrough…I got you.

About Rhonda

Life is a symphony of pivotal moments—those breathtaking crescendos where we stand at the crossroads of choice:

- *To numb or to grow...*
- *To hide or to soar...*
- *To belittle or to become.*

Rhonda Lynn Davison, a soul deeply immersed in the dance of life, intimately comprehends the profound beauty held within these breaking points. Having traversed her personal pilgrimage through these transformative instants, she now holds them as sacred whispers from the universe, urging us all to 'break wide open.'

As the CEO and founder of Spiritual Fitness Warriors with Rhonda, she leads a soulful tribe on an extraordinary journey towards healing and breakthroughs. With a career spanning over 30 years in IT project management for one of the largest healthcare systems in the Northeast, Rhonda knows the toll of corporate burnout and the yearning for soulful transformation.

Rhonda passionately commits herself to guiding others through their breaking points, gently urging them to embrace growth, to soar, and to embody their best selves. Certified as a Lisa Nichols Transformational Trainer, Spiritual Energy & Healing Guide, intenSati Leader, and Quantum Healing Hypnosis Technique (QHHT) practitioner, Rhonda's mastery creates a nurturing cocoon for individuals on their transformative expedition.

As a radiant light in the sphere of Grief Education and Food Freedom, Rhonda illuminates the intricate relationship between emotional well-being, spirituality, and our nourishment. Rhonda's essence further radiates as a Manifesting Maven and Mindfulness Meditation Trainer. She ardently believes in the power of intention and mindfulness, guiding others to unveil the boundless potential of their minds and manifest abundance and purpose in their lives.

In her role as a Soulful Speaker, Rhonda shares her story and insights, inviting others to embrace their breaking points as gateways to soul expansion. She embodies the truth that from these pivotal moments, breakthroughs can be attained, paving the way for a life imbued with purpose and fulfillment.

As a result of the sacred space Rhonda cultivates, those leaders and organizations she guides experience a profound metamorphosis. Rhonda's clients learn to trust their intuition, to awaken the warrior within, and to witness an expansive landscape of possibilities before them. They gracefully transform into the conscious co-creators of their lives—more awake, more aware, and more aligned with their purpose. Through Rhonda's love-infused guidance, they wholeheartedly 'break wide open' to a life of transformation and empowered expansion.

To connect with Rhonda:

- www.spiritualfitnesswarriors.com

CHAPTER 26

IT'S DARKEST JUST BEFORE DAWN — NEVER GIVE UP!

BY PAULA WILLEY

I pause and look around—a rarity in my hundred-hour workweeks. Strings of small colored lights line the borders, neon signs add color and fun, and outdoor covered seating and umbrella tables bring the fresh air to the customers in nice weather. "This is a blessing," I say to myself. I'm reminded of how far I've come to get here, at the restaurant and bar in Barberton, Ohio that I have owned for the past two and a half years.

I have faced a lot of trials and tribulations in my life, and I've gotten to this point by always overcoming them by facing them head-on. The reason for my perseverance and success in my life has been my belief in God, having been raised a Christian—my dad's side was Catholic, and my mother's, Baptist. My dad, my mother, my Grandma Leona, and many family members were big factors in molding my life as a child and young adult.

FROM MANAGER TO HARDLY MANAGING

In 2009, while working as a manager for a restaurant/bar, I was physically assaulted by a twenty-six-year-old employee when I asked him to leave due to his odd behavior. He punched me in the face in front of an entire roomful of people and then fled the scene. This was someone I trusted, someone I waited with at night to ensure his ride showed up to take him home. He was the age of my children. I couldn't understand it. When I arrived at the emergency room, I began to pray for him. It was then that I knew God had instilled something very special in me. Here I was praying for someone who had just assaulted me, breaking my nose, and I still felt the need to pray for him.

Shortly after the assault, I was clinically diagnosed with PTSD. The BWC therapist recommended medicine for my anxiety. I am very anti-drug, so I became offended and walked away from any help. Later I would realize that it wasn't the best idea. PTSD is very real with triggers, and I could have just received counseling without medicine. I am still in counseling now, which has helped me to understand the diagnosis over the past fourteen years. Now, I am able to help others too.

My recovery lasted approximately thirty days. Once I was ready to go back to work, I found out the owners had closed the business. I was lost. I was on my own without a job. Feeling desperate, I took a job for eight dollars per hour. I realized that wasn't enough money, so I got a position as a manager at Subway—making ten dollars per hour. Looking back, I didn't even realize what I was doing. Here I was used to making $48,000 a year, and I was working for the same wage I made in 1986.

Unfortunately, due to my bewilderedness, I lost my home of twenty-two years, a home where I raised my children, my grandchildren. All of my memories were being swept away, and there was nothing I could do about it. I didn't know what to do. I was mentally hurt and didn't know how to fix it. I was homeless for the first time in my life.

I WANTED THE LOVE STORY

Since I met my current husband in the midst of losing my home, I didn't have to be without shelter or on the streets. After I shared my story with him, he told me, "I'll be the best husband you'll ever have." I believed him; I thought God had sent him to me. I wanted the love story. I was a damsel in distress, homeless, and he showed up just in time. We were married on March 26, 2011.

Shortly after we married, I found him treating me differently. Three months into the marriage I asked him, "Why are you mistreating me? You said you would be the best husband I would ever have." He replied while looking me dead in my eyes, "I fooled you, didn't I?"

I stayed with him for another ten years, until I had had enough. We are now in the middle of a divorce. I feel he only married me because he could see the brokenness and knew that he could use me. Looking back, I believe he had narcissistic tendencies, and I never knew the word existed until last year.

During the marriage, I was abandoned by him several times. I believe that we have the choice of being pitiful or powerful, but we cannot be both. I chose powerful. I started working on me. I first learned of Lisa Nichols, founder and CEO of Motivating the Masses, by watching *The Secret* during my recovery. Now, years later, I was offered an opportunity to spend a week with her on a retreat in Mexico, and I took it. It was amazing!

I vowed that I would never be homeless again. I became licensed in real estate in Ohio and started investing in properties. The first two properties my husband and I invested in were two houses side by side. We bought them by land contract. That's where the owner holds the note and you pay a down payment and make payments until it's paid in full. My husband remodeled one property, and I remodeled the other. It was at this time that I knew I couldn't count on him. He cut corners on everything while I was doing what was right by us. I realized he was just using me, though I truly loved him.

We continued buying houses, most of which I purchased and all of which I maintained. He would help me as long as I paid him. Now, he wants half of what I built. I am leaving his share up to God. He's in control, not us.

FEELING BETRAYED

One of the most difficult things I've had to overcome involves my daughter, and it's something I am still going through. I haven't seen her or my two grandchildren for over one and a half years. She entered the USMC at the age of seventeen, where she met and married the kids' dad. She came out of the Marine Corp once my mother was diagnosed with cancer. Once her grandmother passed, she reenlisted in the Navy Reserves. A few years later, she was placed on a medical hold in Virginia. Since she had shared parenting with the kids' dad, I stepped in to take care of my grandchildren on her week. She was gone for approximately one year. When she returned home, I moved into a seven-hundred-square-foot home on her property until I could find something else.

Within a year of her return, her home caught on fire. She wasn't speaking to me at the time, so her dad phoned me. The call didn't go well. Upon my arrival home, I found my door open. When I asked her who was in my house, she responded with insults and verbal abuse. A friend she knew for only a few years grabbed my arm and told me to leave. Then, a fireman came out from her home and grabbed me too. I couldn't believe what was happening. I called the police. Once the police arrived, it wasn't long before I knew something was wrong. They were doing nothing to rectify the situation. Later, I found out that my daughter and her friends all lied and said that her friend didn't grab me and that I grabbed the fireman. It was like I was living in a dream and someone needed to wake me up. The police ended up arresting me, placing me in handcuffs, and taking me to jail for the first time in my fifty-six years.

After being released that morning, I knew God was going to right this wrong. I knew He was my vindicator. Ten months later they dropped all of the bogus charges, and now they are all in a civil lawsuit. The Bible says your children will come against you—but I never thought it would be mine.

BEAUTY FROM ASHES

I know God has a purpose in my trials with my daughter, and this too shall pass. Even though I'm emotional now, I am good with it because it has to be done. God gave me the role of being 'the mother,' and now I must teach her some tough lessons. Parents are set in place to guide their children, not enable them to lie, cheat, or steal. She must be accountable for her actions. I am her mother! To have access to me, you must show respect, or it's best you go away.

God gave me the ability to say, "If I don't have any control over the situation, I must let it go!" That's strength. I'll pray for her, but that's all I can do right now. There's peace in my heart—God provides the peace that passes all understanding. I have to go forward. I have to move on.

The divorce is moving forward, and I learned I had to be accountable for my own actions, my part in it. He showed me who he was three months into our marriage. I chose to stay for ten more years. That's not his fault. Now, I know better, so I'll do better.

I've also come to realize that after my assault, I was building a cocoon in my home. I believe God said, "Oh, no, little girl. I have bigger plans for you." I believe I am working out those plans. Today, I own two restaurant/bars. I have several properties in my name. I have a book published on Amazon. I have hopes of getting my Willey's Gourmet Kraut Ballz to the market. I am doing all this while dealing with trials and tribulations. God is my strength. He provides all my needs. I just show up!

I physically work one hundred hours a week. That may seem a lot to most; however, if God brings you to it, He will see you through it. Being busy helps me with my PTSD, the divorce, and not seeing my children or grandchildren. Oh, yeah, I have a son too, who just stopped talking to me for no reason. There's nothing I can do. Obviously, he doesn't want a relationship—there's nothing I can do about that, so I just go away. As long as I keep my mind moving in a positive direction, I'm good. And God just keeps opening up doors.

People tell me that I need to have more fun. I say, "This *is* fun."

Because of my determination to never be homeless again, I now have several homes. Even though my husband may receive some of them, I will always be good. When I was rehabbing and flipping houses, I wrote a book titled *God Given: Rehabs, Rentals & Reality—From Me to You*, published in 2021, to help others in the investment industry as well as those who have always wanted to rehab or rent properties. Jack Canfield, author of several *Chicken Soup for the Soul* books who was also in *The Secret* with Lisa Nichols, personally interviewed me about my book. I've written *God Given: Poetry—From Me to You*, as well.

Through everything, I've learned it's true what they say, that it's darkest right before the dawn—so don't give up!

IT'S NOT ABOUT ME

Beyond my achievements, I want to encourage people, to strengthen them and give new hope, because every level we go up, we face a new devil. New level, new devil. And I want to help others overcome them. That's who I am. It's automatic with me. I'm a born giver.

There are also things I would like to experience. In all things I just ask for the Lord's will to be done. I believe I've developed a strong relationship with God. Once while driving, I asked God if He had anything to tell me. I instinctively turned my radio on, and a song was just starting at that very moment. It was a song by Cody Johnson, 'Till You Can't. I highly suggest you look up the song, and you'll understand what I'm talking about.

I know why God has me here. He has me here as a beacon of light. I didn't intend on owning a restaurant/bar. I believe He plants me where He wants me. Now, I get to speak life into others. I've met so many people who've lost children or are broken in some way or have life tragedies they are dealing with. I will try and help them—that's my heart, no matter the circumstances. God provides all my needs. I just show up every day. I know that I'm way stronger today than I've ever been, and I'm not easily moved—and that's huge in life. I love life. I love people, and all the things I've gone through have made me who I am today. I pray that in some way I've helped you too. You matter. You're worth it. Never give up!

The customers and employees have all gone home. I unplug the lights and close up for the night. Another long, hard day has ended. But I smile knowing that this is much more than my restaurant/bar where I work over one hundred hours a week—it's the memory of my overcoming, and it will always live on. It will always be my *why*!

About Paula

Paula Willey was born in a small town in Northeast Ohio. She is the mother of two, Eddie and LeAnne, and grandmother of seven – Alyssa, Aiden, Kadence, Paul, Jordy, Kenadie and little Eddie. She was blessed with her father, Rich, and her mother, Darlene, who set great examples for her to follow. Even though they passed at young ages, they continue to inspire and guide her from above.

Paula has an older brother, Rick, and a younger sister, Laura. Grandma Leona taught her how to sew, crochet, and cook starting at the age of five. Paula fought and persevered many personal battles over her 58 years. She will always give God the credit for instilling everything within her to overcome any fiery darts sent.

Some of her experiences include becoming a mother at 17 years old; raising her children as a single mother from their ages of two and six; Broker, Realtor, and a real estate investor; current owner of 'pw Cheers' restaurant/bar in Barberton, OH; current owner of Tomaso's Italian restaurant in Norton OH. She physically works over 100 hours a week but enjoys every single day. She loves helping people but will not enable them to remain in negative patterns or situations.

God has blessed her with a creative mind that she uses to advance the world in positive directions. She is the author of *God Given...Rehabs, Rentals & Reality ... From Me To You.* Her poetry book, *God Given Poetry...From Me To You* is scheduled to be published in 2024.

She doesn't tell you this for you to be impressed. She would love to impress upon you that where there is a will, there is a way! She sends much love to ALL who reads this, knowing that we are ALL connected and what we put out will be returned to us.

Paula can be reached at:

- paulawillhelpyou@gmail.com

You can also find her on Facebook at:

- https://www.facebook.com/PaulaWilley333

CHAPTER 27

THE WOMAN WHO SMILES

BY SABRINA E. GREEN

THE TALKING BABY OF TURKS & CAICOS

My daughter, Jalesa, could speak fluently when she was just seven months old. It was remarkable. In Grand Turk, the island where I was raised, there are still people who remember her as 'the talking baby'. It was from that age that I knew my daughter would be special.

I did not envision raising my daughter as a single parent, but Jalesa's biological father abandoned me the moment I told him I was pregnant. Just like that, he was gone, leaving me alone in the world to figure out how to raise a child. I was 18 years old. I was hardly more than a child myself.

My mother was a single parent as well. She worked hard to raise seven children all on her own. The man who was my biological father was an American, serving in the United States Navy. I grew up never having known my father, making this a life path that my daughter and I would share. Many times, I could have let that get me down, but I chose not to.

One of the earliest decisions I made as a parent was that I would do everything I could to give my daughter endless freedom to speak her mind; as long as she did so respectfully. When I was a child, talking back to adults was considered rude and out of order. My mother would reprimand me for my insolence. Not in our household, I decided. Anything Jalesa wanted to say, I would permit it.

I was very lucky to have a strong support system that I called 'my village.' Recognizing that my daughter was gifted, I was comforted to know I had help harnessing those prodigious gifts. Many people were willing to lend a hand, helping me raise my daughter. While I was out working two jobs at a tourist resort, trying to make sure there was enough food on the table for us to eat, there was always someone to babysit. In one particular case, help was offered through granting her a two-year scholarship to a private school. Whatever support I needed, it was there for me. Not everyone is fortunate enough to say that.

I feel blessed that my daughter grew up to be a very smart woman. That was obvious early on in how quickly she learned to speak, but she became more than just that. She developed an inner drive and a strong sense of morality.

However much freedom and strength that I gave Jalesa, growing up without a father still proved a challenge she needed to overcome. It is difficult for any child. When I was a girl, I knew that my father lived in America. He was far enough away that I never had to worry about seeing him. In my daughter's case, however, her father was here in the Turks and Caicos. That meant he was close enough that she could expect to run into him.

When Jalesa was eight, I remember she said to me, "Mommy? What would happen to me if you decided to treat me the way my Daddy did? I'd probably end up a welfare case."

"No," I told her. "That would never happen to you."

"Why not?"

"Because I could never be that kind of mother." I said.

My connection with Jalesa grew into something more than mother and daughter: we developed a relationship resembling a dynamic duo. Raising her became my greatest contribution to the world. She is a person from whom I am almost inseparable, and who has helped me every step of the way throughout my rise.

CLOSED DOORS

Turks and Caicos is a tiny nation. Most people have heard of our country but very few know much about it. Our way of life would seem foreign to most.

A British overseas territory, Turks and Caicos consists of seven inhabited islands in a small archipelago southeast of the Bahamas. The island of Hispaniola, home to the countries of Haiti and the Dominican Republic, lies less than one hundred miles south across the Caribbean Sea.

The most important thing to know about Turks and Caicos is this: it is among the most stunningly beautiful places in the world. The islands are home to some of the most beautiful beaches you will ever lay your eyes on. The city of Grand Turk is home to just under four thousand people. In most parts of the world it would hardly qualify as a city, but here, it is the center of government and the country's capital.

The most important thing to understand about how our country works is that, aside from the always flourishing tourism industry, we don't really have any other means of employment outside of government and other private sector entities. The largest employers here are the government and the hospitality industry.

Island tourism leads to constant immigration. As a result, many complicated humanitarian issues have become common. Once, twice or sometimes even three times each week, marine vessels intercept boats containing immigrants fleeing the impoverished country of Haiti. Those boats are filled with people looking for the opportunity for a better life by seeking to work in our tourist industry or construction trade. Boats are often intercepted but there's no telling how many go undetected.

In 2008, the Turks and Caicos Islands Human Rights Commission was created. The United Kingdom, whose laws govern our nation, believed we needed a special commission to deal with vulnerable persons and other pressing issues surrounding equality and gender.

One day, my daughter and I were together. She pointed out a sign announcing the newly formed commission. With a very knowing tone, she said to me, "I wonder what sort of qualifications are required for a job like that, Mommy?" My daughter said I would be perfect for the job. Even though I lacked the necessary qualifications on paper at the time, she still believed it to be the ideal role for me.

At a very early age I was approached about entering politics. Many people thought I had what it took to represent their interests. My daughter on the other hand had different viewpoints. She believed that I was too good for politics, as it was messy and a nasty game.

People continued saying, "Sabrina, you need to step forward. You need to get into politics." Feeling wanted by my constituents felt very empowering and left me with a lot to consider. I was only a high school graduate though, and I wanted to give my country and the world the best version of me.

The decision was made to start working hard. I would commit myself to earning the degrees and certification necessary to represent Turks and Caicos domestically and on international platforms. In 2012, I began Law School where I obtained my bachelor's degree from the University of Buckingham. Though law was interesting and I was doing well in the course, I felt the pull toward my first love: tourism. I decided against going to bar school and instead pursued a Master's Degree in International Hotel and Tourism Management. I was going to be the best Minister of Tourism my country has ever seen. Or so I thought.

Returning home, I made the application to my party of choice to be a potential candidate in the 2016 general elections. Even though I had the experience, the backing of the people, and had prepared myself academically for the demands of the position, I did not get one of the candidate spots. After emerging as a viable, popular candidate, my party rejected me.

This led to a very rough time.

Unbeknownst to me, a group was formed for the election of Sabrina Green. I was added to the 2016 ballot as an independent candidate. I had an amazing time campaigning throughout the country. On Election

Day, however, no independent candidates were successful – myself included.

Losing the election brought me to my knees with sadness. Perhaps the country didn't need what I had to offer. I badly wanted to serve, which made the rejection sting even more. I wanted to help facilitate change. For the time being, however, I was not able to. My own party and the people I thought would support me, did not.

SOMETIMES GOD OPENS A WINDOW

For most of my adult life, I have suffered from back problems. The depression of losing the election brought on a surge of pain. I experienced the kind of debilitating anguish that often knocks a person off their feet, putting them onto the floor.

Each day, my daughter would come home and beg me, "Mommy, Mommy, you're still on the floor. You need to rise up. You need to get back into life." Her words of genuine encouragement were difficult to hear. The country I so desperately wanted to serve had moved on without me. That was too painful for me to face.

Life went on like this for quite a while. I was alive but I hardly felt like I was living. Disappointment and pain consumed my every waking hour. I slept on the floor because of constant back pain. I felt terrible all the time. All I could see was that my friends and some family members didn't support my campaign. My daughter pleaded. She insisted that I had to forget about the past.

Then one day my daughter came home and said, "In my eyes, Mommy, you are this beacon of light. Someone that so many people look up to for inspiration, motivation and encouragement. Now, when I come home, Mommy, I see that light dwindling. Are you going to let politics do that to you?"

I wasn't. But I also didn't know how to move on. Then Jalesa said, "I have a surprise for you." I wasn't ready for any more surprises, but I listened. My daughter got down on the floor beside me and said, "Sometimes when God closes a door, he opens a huge window."

I had heard that kind of talk before. What could that window possibly be?

My daughter opened a newspaper and forced me to look at an advertisement. The Human Rights Commission was looking for a Director/CEO. As I listened, my daughter read off the criteria for the position:

- *A law degree.*
- *Management skills at master's level.*
- *Someone in touch with social issues relevant to Turks and Caicos.*
- *Fluent in English, Spanish and Creole.*

I felt myself stir inside. These were all things I could do. I was absolutely perfect for the job description she had read.

"What do you want me to do?" I asked.

"I beg you, Mommy," my daughter said. "Apply for the job."

"Why?"

"Because this job is even greater than going into political office," she replied. "In this job you won't just serve in the government. Don't you see, you will be able to direct it."

Jalesa was right. There was no question that I was perfect for the position. I began to feel like I had no choice. I was down and right here before me was a path to rising up.

OK, I decided. I'll apply.

Soon after, I was hired for a Director position in the Human Rights Commission. All it took was a handful of years of preparation, a persistent daughter, and the courage to accept the call to rise.

ADVOCATES FOR ALL

I have been told that I am the woman who smiles. When I ran for office as an independent candidate, I wanted to use my bright, smiling face as the symbol of my candidacy.

Finding a way to affect change in Turks and Caicos has been a great achievement. But on October 31st of 2023, I officially ended my career in human rights by formally resigning my position with the Commission. Six long years in office with all of it under heavy public scrutiny, was enough for me, and I recognized that it was time to finally do something else.

I have decided to return my attention to Advocates For All. This is a company I have independently owned and operated for a number of years. Experience has taught me that government positions present barriers to truly affecting change. There are always boards and higher ups to answer to, in addition to the constant pressures of seeking re-appointment, all of which and more I experienced during my term serving on the commission.

Turning my focus back to this company will allow me to continue advocating for issues in the Turks and Caicos that matter to me – education, health care, immigration and social justice, just to name a few – but in a freer, more natural way.

This change will also allow me to devote more attention to something more personal: the imminent publication of my book, *Raising Royalty.*

In this nostalgic memoir, I tell the story of raising Jalesa, my daughter, up as a single mother. I take the reader through all of the highs and lows, pitfalls and triumphs, revealing how I brought up the girl, once known as the 'talking baby' to become a powerful force who continues to back my rise.

About Sabrina

Sabrina E. Green, known for her bubbly persona and her megawatt smile, is from North Back Salina, Grand Turk in the Turks and Caicos Islands. The trilingual Sabrina learnt both Creole and Spanish at the age of nine years in the diverse and underserved community she hails from, known as the Garden.

She is a multi-hyphenate. Sabrina is a graduate in Law from the University of Buckingham in the United Kingdom; she holds a master's degree in International Hotel and Tourism Management from Oxford Brookes University (also in the U.K.), and she is also the recipient of a Certificate in Women's Leadership from Yale University.

Sabrina is an entrepreneur, and as an activist in her community, she dedicates her life to the service of humanity through her personal philanthropic initiatives. She is the author of *Cracking the Code – Raising Royalty: A New Legacy.* In her memoir, she shares her journey as a single mother of her beautiful daughter, Cyprianna. Together, like two peas in a pod, the pair overcame many of life's obstacles in this walk down memory lane.

Sabrina is the former Director of the Turks and Caicos Islands Human Rights Commission. In this transformative role, she was a key player in the promotion of a more just, equitable and inclusive Turks and Caicos Islands.

Sabrina now continues her work in being a voice for the voiceless as the CEO of Advocates For All, an organization that was created for the sole purpose of championing the causes of the most vulnerable in the Turks and Caicos Islands.

To learn more about Sabrina, please go to:

- www.sabrinaegreen.com

CHAPTER 28

RISING STRONG
REVOLUTIONIZING BRAIN HEALTH, ADHD, AND ANTI-AGING

BY SIMONE FORTIER

What if slowing down the aging process is real? What if, buried within the intricate workings of our brains, lie the solutions to some of the most fundamental challenges we face, from weight management and digestive health to the quality of our sleep and the ever-persistent presence of anxiety?

This relentless pursuit of knowledge and understanding has driven my life's work—exploring brain health and its profound connections to these common yet vexing problems. After years of rigorous clinical research, I've unveiled remarkably straightforward protocols that yield astonishing results. But, like the narrative arc of countless triumphs, my journey toward these revelations was fraught with adversity, trauma, and an insatiable quest for answers.

As a child, I often found myself sprawled out on the ground, the aftermath of a spectacular tumble. Whether climbing a fence, walking a tightrope, or jumping a chair, this fall down the stairs was different; I stopped and breathed. In that split second, a singular thought pierced my consciousness: "Is my leg broken?" Returning abruptly to reality, I gingerly assessed my limbs for any telltale signs of fracture. Fortunately, no broken bones marred the landscape of my body.

Remarkably, it turned out that individuals like me, who grew up contending with ADHD (Attention Deficit Hyperactivity Disorder), often possess a peculiar trait – hypermobility.

This inherent hypermobility rendered me unusually flexible, a quality that acted as a protective barrier against the menace of broken bones. However, this blessing in disguise was not without its share of challenges. Hypermobile ADHD children frequently find themselves walking into walls or succumbing to tumbles and falls, often culminating in concussions or mTBI (mild traumatic brain injury) that, in turn, exacerbate the symptoms of ADHD.

Thus, an ominous cycle of head trauma silently weaves its web, often eluding detection, much like my own experience during my formative years. I was constantly attracted to drama/trauma in my life, like a weird magnet, car accidents, skiing or snowboarding, or any extreme sport I did. Also, attracting people who tried to hurt me or prove me wrong was all I knew: an unwitting connection between ADHD and the recurring head trauma that would persist throughout my life.

Growing up, I was a whirlwind of energy, perpetually in motion.

As a child, it felt as though my mind and body were engaged in a relentless race, with my thoughts frequently outpacing my physical self. With every challenge, I developed a steely resolve that fueled my determination that my parents would never break my spirit, a characteristic trait often synonymous with ADHD.

Little did I know then that both my parents had some form of ADHD, a genetic legacy that shaped my turbulent upbringing. The intersection of my obstinate nature and their undiagnosed conditions led to an ongoing clash of wills, a fierce battleground marked by defiance and an unyielding thirst for independence. The friction, kindled by these hidden familial disorders, ultimately fostered an environment marred by dysfunction and, at times, even abuse. Verbal and physical abuse ensued as far back as I can remember. Close friends, relatives, and energy workers have often asked me how I survived my family.

My family never acknowledged the abuse, and discussing it was forbidden. I vividly recall a moment at age ten, bloodied face and nose, as I secretly marked the back of my door with my blood, my silent proof of the abuse no one acknowledged. No one shielded me. Parents are supposed to protect, but mine didn't. They provided necessities - food, clothing, shelter, admittedly out of obligation. My mom, once fiercely independent before the men in her life quashed it, instilled in me the values of hard work, honesty, and self-reliance, laying the groundwork for my journey as an entrepreneur.

Despite my physical and mental strength, I often had dark thoughts. I was conditioned to conceal my emotions, becoming emotionally detached and numb, as it was the expected norm for me always to maintain an unwavering facade of strength.

I wanted a way out, but there was none; no one was saving me – no teacher, friend, or parent. I was alone. Thoughts that started at the tender age of ten: "I wonder how many people would go to my funeral?" The weight of suicidal ideation shadowed me throughout my life, even though I held steadfast to my faith, rejecting the notion of taking my own life. Each day, my prayers pleaded with a higher power, "God, please take my life today." What I considered normal with such thoughts, was, in reality, an enduring struggle.

The physical abuse I endured spanned from ages four to fifteen until I said no more. Yet the dark cloud of suicidal ideation persisted. My research discovered that children like me lacked the resources to recover; this lack of resources shaped our thoughts. This realization ignited a passionate commitment within me to fill that void.

Living in a perpetual state of heightened anxiety or fight-or-flight mode over the years led to a numbing of the mind, freezing it in a place where decision-making became an insurmountable challenge. Through the years, I witnessed this in others – high-performing individuals, children, women, and men trapped in abusive relationships, unable to take that critical step towards seeking help, even when their lives were at stake.

In high school, amidst playing basketball and volleyball and excelling academically, I faced multiple head injuries in sports, adding to the cumulative toll of a lifelong journey marked by head trauma. The turning point came in tenth grade when I entered a contest, securing a year-long educational adventure in Australia. Living with five different families during this transformative year, I gained a profound perspective on the dynamics of healthy homes – the warmth of hugs, affectionate interactions, and genuine care for one another left an indelible impact. It opened my eyes to a world vastly different from the trauma and disconnectedness I knew.

Today, my life's work is focused on preventing suicides and healing trauma among both children and adults, particularly those grappling with the aftermath of head trauma compounded by the challenges of ADHD.

THE START OF A DREAM

After returning from study abroad and my first year of university, I had to find my way without help or guidance. Faced with the challenge of forging my path, I took on the responsibility with determination. Juggling three jobs, attending school year-round, and embracing the label of an overachiever became my *modus operandi* – a testament to my insatiable love for learning. It was in those moments that I found true fulfillment and confidence.

During this time, I dedicated my spare hours to volunteering at a naturopath clinic, soaking up valuable knowledge. As my graduation approached, a burning desire ignited to establish my wellness clinic. Upon graduation, my goal and focus was to open a holistic clinic, the first of its kind at the time. The hurdles loomed large – substantial student loans and an empty pocketbook. The quest for suitable leasing options became an overwhelming challenge, as affordability seemed like an elusive dream. After looking at many leasing offices or clinics, I was overwhelmed with the cost, and thought, "How do I make this happen with no money?" I went home and bawled my eyes out in desperation. "Look, Lord, it's not like I'm sitting on my butt doing nothing. If this is meant to be, I need help, and I need help now."

The next day, I was volunteering with the naturopath, and the phone rang. The receptionist, on her way to lunch, left the duty unclaimed. Seizing the opportunity, I decided to take the initiative and answer the phone – a task I had never undertaken before.

Adopting a professional tone, I confidently declared, "Naturopathic Association." On the other end of the call, I heard, "Hi, I'm a medical doctor, and I'd like to put an ad in your newsletter."

"Oh! Okay," I said politely.

He continues, "I've been trying to sublease this space. I'm moving, and no one in the medical community wants to take it over. It has three treatment rooms, and it has its own bathroom."

Then he said something that grabbed my attention, "Six months free rent."

"I'll meet you today," I said emphatically. We met and made a handshake deal. He put the money into my bank account, and that's how my clinic began over twenty-five years ago.

FROM INJURIES TO ANSWERS

In 1999, a major car accident marked a turning point, my first significant adult head injury in a life marked by such traumas and changed my career path from studying to being a lawyer to physical sciences. Subsequently, migraines became a constant presence. Over the years, more head injuries from car wrecks and extreme sports followed, taking a toll on my well-being. By 2014, I faced a culmination of neurological issues stemming from six major concussions in about fifteen years.

The aftermath manifested in brain fog, memory lapses, and a disorienting struggle to distinguish left from right. My mind was embroiled in chaos wrought by these head injuries, with chronic pain and debilitating effects on the left side of my body becoming the norm. Faced with this cacophony of challenges, I recognized the pressing need for a solution, yet none existed. Thus, I committed to forging my path toward healing. Guided by inspiration from a higher source, divine channeling, and insights from the best sports professionals, I embarked on the journey to create a solution.

In 2010, I pioneered a manual treatment for concussions, a technique I teach to healthcare professionals. Transitioning to 2015, I initiated the development of a groundbreaking brain nutrition program. Working individually with people, I meticulously honed the system, solidifying its effectiveness over time. These innovations have provided answers crucial for my personal quality of life and assisted others in getting their lives back.

The incredulity of witnessing my high functionality and freedom from pain often prompts statements from neurologists or functional medicine doctors who do brain mapping or scans to share, "We have no idea how you manage to be so high-functioning and pain-free; your brain insists that you shouldn't be." After 15 years of results, I'm unveiling 20 case studies highlighting my teaching's remarkable effectiveness for new practitioners. Individuals see impressive 30% to 60% improvements in just two treatments. My protocol is an undeniable success and exhilarating as we look to share this knowledge with a broader audience.

FAILURE IS NOT AN OPTION

I have a deep-rooted mindset or innate belief that failure is not an option; success is the only path. I never had a safety net or entertained the idea of a plan B. Relying on my inner faith, I recognized a shared experience with others like me who faced challenges without a readily available solution. This realization spurred me on to pose the necessary questions and seek answers.

Now, at this juncture, from the program I created, my brain functionality, memory, and sleep quality continue to improve and are better than when I was a child. Every facet of my life radiates with a vibrancy previously unmatched. This program de-aged my brain and my body. Remarkably, I find myself free from pain despite enduring extensive nerve damage. My passion for work is unwavering, and retirement never crosses my mind because I see it as a life of service. It's almost an inherent part of my being, much like individuals with ADHD.

For those grappling with ADHD or anxiety, overwhelming perfectionism and even words or events tend to trigger specific reactions. However, the program I crafted offers a solution to symptoms of ADHD: the busyness and the lack of focus can all melt away, creating balance and space in the brain. It's a game-changer. The most rewarding part, personally and professionally, is witnessing a transformation in my life and in others. The sense of fulfillment is immeasurable.

DE-AGE YOUR BRAIN

My clinical research delves into neurotransmitters, revealing compelling evidence: the foundation of quality sleep lies within the brain. It's not just about getting rest; you can slow aging, ease anxiety with simple nutritional adjustments, and kickstart weight loss.

Enter the Brain Health Assessment, a rigorously-tested diagnostic tool crafted by a specialized psychiatrist versed in neurotransmitters and their impact on performance and aging. This assessment unveils the current state of your brain – the epicenter of how you perceive the world, manage your weight, react or overreact, and determine your overall body performance. Dive deeper into our Brain Health Assessment and discover additional supportive products at: www.fasciatraininginstitue.com/products.

Consider this program your missing link – a transformative force giving people their lives back, enhancing memories, and improving sleep quality. Anxiety sufferers, often plagued by sleepless nights, find relief. I, too, grappled with lifelong insomnia due to ADHD, seeking help from countless doctors. However, since incorporating this program into my life, I've experienced the joy of uninterrupted sleep for the first time in six years. The swiftness and effectiveness of the results are remarkable. I extend an invitation to explore how our assessment, protocols, and brain nutrition can assist you in revitalizing your brain and reclaiming your life. It would be an honor to be part of your transformative journey.

CHOICES THAT BRING EASE, GRATITUDE, AND JOY

Life is inherently challenging; pursuing ease often leads to disappointment, as true simplicity is a rarity. However, we've uncovered a path that offers a semblance of ease. My brain nutrition program serves as a catalyst, providing the capacity to make decisions from a place of centeredness and presence. My current journey involves substantial transformation, and while it's far from easy, it signifies continual growth.

Despite the inherent difficulties, there should be a space for joy and enjoyment. Often, individuals caught in the throes of fight-or-flight responses, anxiety, overwhelm, and perfectionism neglect to rediscover the joy in life.

Gratitude becomes paramount. When you reach a goal, make a discovery, or attain a certain level, take a moment to sit with it. Acknowledge the hurdles overcome, the sacrifices made, the creations brought forth, and the lives touched. Genuine gratitude for the journey and the lessons learned is essential. While it's acknowledged that life will never be easy, deliberate decisions can be made to introduce more ease into one's life and circumstances.

It all boils down to gratitude. Sitting with and acknowledging the challenges overcome, the sacrifices, the creations, and the impact on others provides the fertile ground for joy to reemerge. With a heart full of gratitude for the journey and understanding, though the road ahead may not be easy, it paves the way for a life imbued with more ease.

RISE UP OVER YOUR CHALLENGES AND INSECURITIES

My unwavering dedication to helping others has fueled a journey marked by a relentless pursuit of passion, ultimately propelling me to become an unparalleled expert in pain management and trauma healing practices. Clients trust my profound, intuitive comprehension of pain's root causes and my extensive knowledge of human anatomy.

Rise up over any abuse or suffering you've endured; the brain and body can triumph with the right resources and support. My story provides hope that overcoming challenges is achievable. Embrace resilience, choose to prevail, and you'll find your path forward. Doubt your insecurities, acknowledge greater possibilities, and summon the strength to persevere. Your moment to rise up is now!

About Simone

Simone Fortier is a leader in healing and transformation, pioneering innovative methods to foster lasting change. Her mission is focused on guiding individuals struggling with the unseen challenges of trauma, concussion symptoms, mTBI, ADHD, and unresolved pain toward an optimal, pain-free existence. As a renowned International Trainer, Concussion Teacher, and ADHD Consultant, Simone's expertise transcends conventional therapy, positioning her as a beacon of hope for many.

Her role as a Fascia Brain Treatment and Course Creator has garnered international acclaim, with professionals from diverse fields, including elite athletes from the NHL, MLB, NFL, and Olympic competitors, lauding her transformative results. The Fascia Training Institute, Simone's brainchild, epitomizes her pioneering spirit. This institution offers groundbreaking approaches in Brain Nutrition, Concussion Treatments, and Fascia Treatment and Training (SFT), presenting a revolutionary therapy that goes beyond the ordinary, offering a lifeline to those trapped in the grip of chronic pain and neurological distress.

Simone's journey, marked by relentless innovation and a commitment to excellence, spans over three decades of experience in business, training, and treatment. Her intuitive approach in therapy sessions weaves a tapestry of relief and recovery, precisely targeting the core of her clients' suffering.

Beyond her therapeutic expertise, Simone is a celebrated author. Her works, such as *How to Beat Brain Burps, How to Heal Plantar Fasciitis*, and *11 Transformative Beliefs*, are invaluable resources for those seeking to support their brain, business, and body. Her upcoming titles include *How to Sell Like a Cat,* and *Concussion Recovery – A Guide to Getting Your Brain Back.*

Her online course, "Younger by Tonight" - is more than a beauty regimen founded on a concussion self-care program; it's a revolution in self-care, intertwining beauty with brain health. Simone's holistic approach delves into the intricate interplay of mental, physical, and emotional wellness, offering a comprehensive solution to well-being.

As a Master Brain Health and Wellness Coach, Simone empowers her clients through knowledge, blending Neuro-Linguistic Programming (NLP), hypnotherapy, and a deep understanding of neuroscience to reshape lives. Her techniques are transformative tools, from brain nutrition programs rejuvenating neural pathways to strategic business coaching leading to success.

Simone Fortier is more than a therapist, author, trainer, or coach, she is a visionary committed to unlocking human potential. In a world often mired in pain and confusion, Simone stands as a clear, guiding voice, offering a path forward for those brave enough to envision a life not constrained by limitations but defined by limitless possibilities.

CHAPTER 29

ENDING THE CURSES

BY GINA JONES

SINGING AND SLINGING

I've been on stage, performing for an audience for about as long as I can remember. Performing with all your heart in front of people was something you had to do.

At nine years old, I learned a valuable lesson about the music industry. That was, a girl could sell a heck of a lot more records sitting on the old man's lap. Some of my family had the gift of music. My brother was one of those people. He could play the guitar like nobody else and sounded just like Merle Haggard. He almost made it big but he missed. His fate ended up like so many others who try to break in.

I remember getting all dressed up for show time. Putting on boots and the cute clothes my Mama used to make, getting ready to go on stage. Always with curlers in my hair, in the green room, hurrying to make call. Even though I was nine years old, I looked a little older. Maybe twelve or thirteen. Before I had the foggiest idea of who I was as a person, they were teaching me how to work the crowd. To turn those dimples and a smile into money. Compromise anything to make another buck. I call it prostitution of the gift.

My Mama's last name, before she got married, was Moses. I always get a laugh out of that. Never, in all the time I was growing up, did I feel any connection to Biblical, or spiritual, matters.

Simply put, my Dad came home from the Korean War a different man. He was chock full of anger that he ended up taking out on most of us on a regular basis. We all suffered the consequences in different unbearable ways. I don't remember that he ever hit Mama, but when it came to the kids, whether it came in the form of violent whippings or verbal abuse, we all experienced his wrath.

I remember my sister, who was just ten years old at the time, told the teacher that her nickname at home was 'slut'. The teacher was terrified. It was an awful thing to say to anyone, least of all a child. But we didn't think there was anything wrong with it. Daddy called me that name too from time to time. That was just how he talked to us. Neither my sister nor I knew what that meant.

All of us kids either ran away or got married before the age of sixteen. They had sent me to live in a Foster Care home when I decided to run away from home. I was pregnant, too young and scared to know what to do about any of it. It all ended badly. I ended up miscarrying in a Greyhound bus toilet. That is a painful memory for me to think about now. But that kind of pain was what my siblings and I were raised with. We endured because we thought it was normal. We had never experienced any other kind of life.

THE WORD OF GOD

Childhood trauma bred one heck of a rebellious streak into me. While being a run away, I ended up being trafficked by a well-known drug dealer in California. He would send me out to sling hard drugs and to strangers saying, "Just be nice to men, and if you are extra nice, you might make us extra money," to try coaxing me into sleeping with them. One year later, I married at age sixteen so I wouldn't have to go home to my parents.

Landing in Nashville, Tennessee, the heart of country and western music, in my twenties I ended up in the oldest business in the world: running a brothel, the kind of place everyone in the industry knew, right there at the heart of the country music scene, in a historic building that's still there today.

I was the Madame of Music Row. That's where I came up with the title of my first book. At that time, I knew how to do two things to take care of myself. I knew how to get up and sing and I knew how to deal drugs. Got to be pretty good at both of those. As a criminal, I made a heck of a lot of money. Looking back, that's all that lifestyle is good for— making money and making it quick. Forget anything with any meaning or spiritual elements. Those never came into play.

No surprise my first husband and I didn't last forever. I had already been married twice, with two children by the age of twenty-four. The marriages both ended in abuse. I rebounded over a prolonged period, six or seven years, of criminal activity. I was in a vicious cycle.

I still remember the morning I was saved. It was after six o'clock. The morning sun was just coming up on a particularly long night where I had been partying with the head of a Nashville record label at my place. We had gotten into everything, cocaine and meth, heavy drinking. The guy was a good friend but nothing special. Wild nights like these were part of our routine.

He left around five-thirty or six. Seeing that I had to get back up for work at the brothel later on that morning, I thought I would lie down and rest. I told myself that I would just close my eyes and catch a little sleep. I remember laying down on my bed and right away, I felt life bleeding out of me. My flesh got ice cold. I started feeling numb with a tightness in my chest that kept me from breathing. Panic washed over me and I sat up. I looked into the mirror and saw that my flesh was turning gray.

I can't die like this, I said to myself. I started thinking of all the things I had to live for. I had two beautiful children. I could not bear the idea of them growing up, knowing that their mother had died of a drug overdose. Soon after, I felt a presence come over me. I got goosebumps up my neck and down my arms.

Then I heard a disembodied voice.

"Get on your knees and pray for the desire to leave you," it said. "Or you will die like this."

What else could I do? I obeyed. I hit my knees and said that exact prayer. Immediately, I felt this massive weight lift off of me. I discovered I could breathe again. My breath came back and I knew, right then and there, I had been saved from something. I had been touched by God.

But my heart was hardened. Even though my life had been saved by divine intervention, I was not ready to fully accept that. I had committed every sin, from selling drugs and women to sneaking moonshine into my sister's wedding to spike the punch. With all the hell I had been through, it was going to take a lot more than just coming back from the brink of death.

I always say, looking back, that God treated my heart like an onion. After saving me that morning, he started peeling back layers. He worked his way toward the center one addiction at a time. First it was the drugs. Then it was the lure of easy money. At last, I found myself in a hotel shower, scrubbing myself clean after turning a cheap trick with one of my sugar daddies. Suddenly, a deep, dreadful feeling came over me and I started asking some really hard questions.

Why am I like this?

I was on fire for Jesus, going to church every chance I got, but I still clung to this one addiction. Why, God, am I like this? You delivered me from other things, why not this?

Then he said to me, in a voice I had by that time become familiar with, "Get on your knees and pray for the desire to leave you, or you will die like this." Once again, I obeyed. I hit my knees in the shower, said that prayer, and felt myself restored.

BREAKING THE CYCLE

Being an extreme sinner like I was, God does not strip you down all at once. After an entire life when you've grown accustomed to getting things the easy way, having to do the work makes for a tough adjustment.

There was a time when, if I was broke, or I needed out of a jam, all I had to do was make the call to one of those sugar daddies. Nothing has ever been that reliable. One call and I would have whatever I needed. Rent. Food on the table. When you're someone who always believes in love, it's hard to turn away from easy comfort. Hard though it has been at times, I have to be vigilant, staying anchored in what God passed onto me.

A large part of my rise has been finding the courage to live. To endure the pain of neglect, addiction, and my own health problems. Now, I see my rise, finally, as a path to really thriving. In order for me to take a big step forward, I have had to learn very precious lessons. Some of the most important have been about negativity. Specifically, how to break its vicious cycle.

My family can tend toward the negative side. Often, when we get together, there is a lot of gossip going around the kitchen and the dinner table. Seems like everyone has something to say about everyone else, often focusing on what's wrong with that person. It's hard for me to be around now. Growing up and into my young adult years, however, I believed that was what everyone did.

After what I have been through, I can see that negativity is not just normal talk. I realize that when a person focuses on negativity it has a way of keeping people down. I know that it did for me. That is why I've learned to see it as a generational curse. It took a nurturing connection with God for me to see things clearly. Since that night in the hotel room, once the messages came, I heard them loud and clear. Through a lot of prayer, I have discovered a way past the backbiting and gossip:

- Dwell where peace is not worry.
- Everyone has their shortcomings. Don't judge, but love them.
- Take captive every thought or confusion and speak out the exact opposite of it – canceling it in the Spirit Realm.

The cycle of negativity and confusion runs far back in my family. It's deep like the roots in an old oak tree. Although I have not abandoned hope of bringing that positive change to them, I know the path to breaking that cycle comes through affecting the next generation.

A lot of what God has shown me, I am passing along to my children and grandchildren. I have worked hard to bring the message of forgiveness and positivity to the people I meet around the release of my book. My family isn't the only one suffering through such a curse.

If I can reach enough people, someone will learn to see that cycle in their life. Maybe they'll enact the necessary changes to break their cycle.

I'M JUST GINA

I have experienced a lot of different versions of myself over the years. When I was a little girl, I was 'performer Gina.' Later on, I became 'drug dealing Gina' or 'Madame of Music Row.' Currently, I'm happy to say, I'm just Gina Jones. I'm myself for maybe for the first time.

Some of the people I used to run with didn't make it out. Later on, the man I was getting high and partying with on the night I heard God, died of a heart attack. I don't know if drugs directly led to that, but the lifestyle is hard on a person's body. I know my body has suffered the scars.

Sadly, one of my niece's didn't make it out either. Her name was Jill. The hard life got her too. For a while I spent time with her in the afternoons reading the word of God on the porch. She even got away long enough to get clean, but you know how old cycles are. They're hard to break. My sister and I wrote a song for her. It's called, *I'm Lost*. From time to time I perform that song and it always brings a tear to my eye.

Many of us are lost. Only some of us get found. We can't go back and do everything we got wrong. If we are wise, we realize the blessings that came from our messes and Rise Up above the past to make a better world.

About Gina

Gina Jones' life has been anything but easy, but one thing remains constant: her love for writing, singing, and performing music. Gina began her musical career at the tender age of 9, singing and playing bass in her family's band, the Ozark Rhythm Aires. A natural talent, she performed with the band from the age of 9 up to 15-years-old, entertaining audiences at fairs and festivals, and touring the Ozarks in Missouri, including Branson. By the age of 9, Gina had already cut her first record with the Ozark Rhythm Aires, and at 33, she opened for over 42 Grand Ole Opry Stars, discovering her true identity in the process.

However, Gina's journey was marked by unfathomable challenges, including abuse, near-death experiences from a medical illness, overdosing, ten car accidents, and even a prison sentence. Gina overcame these trials when God intervened in her life, saving her in her darkest moments. Over the next 20 years, Gina wrote her story, evolving from a victim to a victor, 'rising from the ashes' to embody true beauty and stepping into her own.

Gina Jones is now a best-selling author, with her book *Madame of Music Row* released in September 2023 quickly becoming an Amazon Best-Seller. In addition to writing her book, Gina composed a song for every chapter, adding a musical dimension to her inspiring journey.

Despite the tragedy in her life, Gina's story is triumphant. Today, she embraces life with a smile, sowing seeds of inspiration on college campuses, in bookstores, and listening rooms—anywhere she can share her transformative story.

Gina's narrative resonates with people from all walks of life. Her wisdom, love, and grace shine through the darkness, carrying a message of hope. Her purpose is clear: to teach others that with God, there is hope, and one can transition from a victim to a victor. Gina emphasizes that God can save anyone, encouraging others to rise above their circumstances and believe that all things are possible.

To learn more about Gina's incredible journey, visit:

- www.musiccitycartel.com

CHAPTER 30

I'M NOT GOING OUT LIKE THAT

BY LORENA BELCHER

I opened the letter with trembling hands, already anticipating what it would say. Even expecting the news, I felt shocked seeing it in print. I was officially suspended as a Tuskegee University student. If I wanted to remain there, I needed to pull a minimum of two As and one B. I'd also have to write the dean a letter expressing why I deserved to continue being a student at that university.

At the time, I was an emotional mess, and my grades had plummeted. Living in the heart of Alabama, therapy was not available or culturally accepted. You didn't do counseling. You sucked it up, pushed it under the rug, and got on with it.

My sexual assault was several years behind me at this point, but I carried the burden of it alone. In all the intervening months, I hadn't spoken a word of it to my father, mother, or aunt, whose best friend's son was my assailant.

The attack happened during my senior year of high school. I went to his house as a naïve girl, thinking he was a potential prom date. As it was happening, I had one thought. Get through this…and get out. Just survive.

I heard a quiet mantra start in my mind. I'm not going out like that.

Afterward, the fallout wreaked havoc on my life. It shattered my sense of self, self-esteem, and ability to trust – both others and mostly myself. I struggled with weight issues. Without mental health support, I fumbled. Choosing Tuskegee, more than two thousand miles from my home in Los Angeles, was very much an act of escape. Although I was excited about attending an HBCU, I was still fleeing from the scene.

As a third-generation college student—and a Black woman—I took great pride in my education. Reading that letter, I heard the mantra start again.

"I'm not going out like that!"

No way, I thought. I'm not disappointing my family. I'm not disappointing myself. I'm not letting that one day dictate my entire life.

I buckled down and made the grades, pulling the B out of a particularly tricky statistics class. I wrote my letter to the dean. Putting my words on paper gave me a sense of power. I knew this was my chance. I was writing for my life and future.

When the dust settled, the dean made his decision. I was reinstated.

Getting my bachelor's degree took seven years. I changed majors (several times), but I was never on probation again…because I wasn't going out like that!

DISCOVERING MY VOICE AND LIVING IN A WORLD OF NORMALIZED VIOLENCE

I grew up in a household where domestic violence was normalized and accepted. We didn't experience physical violence at my father's hands, but my parents' constant arguing was unsettling and scary. I remember being no older than ten and waking to the sound of the back door slamming. I peeked out to see what was happening, and my father locked eyes with me.

"Don't you let her in," he said.

That's when I heard my mom pounding on the window to be let back inside out of the cold. I was always the cooperative kid, but in that moment, I knew I had to make my own decision. My mother couldn't stay out in the cold all night. I unlocked the door, turned the knob, and let my shivering mother in.

My father just looked at me and walked away. We never talked about that night again. In that moment of uncertainty, I felt equal parts dread and giddy defiance. I did have a voice, and I was smart enough to let it guide me through adversity. I knew to get out of the pool if I was drowning, and that wisdom would carry me through.

When my parents divorced, I was twelve. The stress caused my hair to fall out. At the time, tiny afros were not the thing, and having short, unstraightened hair was not the beauty standard. I felt ugly and different, and this laid the groundwork for many underlying self-esteem issues. Already I was questioning whether I was pretty enough or smart enough—questions that reemerged painfully after my assault.

UNPRODUCTIVE RELATIONSHIPS, UNFULFILLING WORK

Months before college graduation, I narrowly escaped another assault. It became apparent my choices required greater consideration and a dose of reality. I was clueless about how I deserved to be treated.

After graduating with a degree in economics, I bounced around aimlessly. I still hadn't dealt with my past, and no matter how many miles I put between me and that house my senior year, my angst, anxiety, and depression followed. I was constantly swinging the pendulum, and I soon found myself in and out of unproductive relationships.

During this time, I quickly fell in love and became engaged to my oldest daughter's father. But before she was born, the relationship ended. Although he ghosted me, we managed to integrate both families. My daughter's grandparents on both sides adored her. All these complicated events added layers of complexity to my trauma.

Looking back now with the benefit of therapy and tools to embrace and reconnect with myself, I realize I attracted traumatic people into my life because of the way I felt about myself. I'd taken on a victim mentality, and it had made me a victim.

In 1990, I took a radical career turn and became a police officer. It was a poor fit from the start, and I only did it for two years, but I can see it came from a place of simultaneously wanting to help and take back power and control in my life.

I was angry and saddened, and those emotions were only amplified and complicated by the Rodney King brutality, which happened when I was on the force, but while I was away at a wedding in Alaska. After that, I realized I didn't want that life anymore. I didn't need it anymore. It wasn't fulfilling, and I got back into education.

When my daughter was about seven, I met a man. We had a whirlwind romance and married much too soon. That marriage ended up being a toxic and unhealthy relationship. His temper tantrums introduced constant emotional upheaval into our lives. I had to have left what felt like seven times before finally leaving for good. This whole time, I was also pursuing my master's degree in education. I knew I needed to take care of myself and my (now) three children. I needed a financial means to survive on my own.

Throughout that marriage, I framed my life in terms of escape... financial escape...physical escape...emotional escape. Leaving my daughter with a neighbor the morning of what I thought was our final departure, I covertly secured a restraining order against my husband. Having him out of the house allowed me to think in peace and strategize my next steps.

Going through these motions felt surreal. I repeatedly reminded myself, This isn't a movie. This is your real life. During that time, three things became clear:

- One, everyone wants to hurry up and heal, but that's not how self-actualization and self-love work.

- Two, I had made some great decisions: resigning so I could work on my emotional mess, leaving my husband, and starting the healing journey for me and my children.

- Three, I couldn't help any child until I got my life together.

I also knew my children and I needed therapy to support our time of transition. Two of my daughters suffer from chronic autoimmune disorders, and my life was in chaos. (One daughter has sickle cell anemia and has been in and out of hospitals since she was one, and my youngest developed autoimmune hepatitis at thirteen.) My pre-teens spent many of those early sessions with uninterested, get-me-out-of-here expressions and folded arms, but in time they began to share their heartbreaking truths.

I eventually returned to teaching, becoming a K–eight special needs educator for several years. I wanted to make a difference, and I thought I could do that best by catching kids before they entered the system. Yes, I taught the state-mandated curriculum (math and science) to my students, but I also taught a hidden curriculum.

I taught my students to feel important and valuable. To learn what they could control—and give up the rest. To confront the lies within themselves. To realize they were the only people they could control.

LIVING THROUGH THE DARKEST HOUR

In 2013, I got a call from a dear church friend. "Have you got a minute," she asked. "I need to tell you something…and you should sit down to hear it." She proceeded to tell me my fifteen-year-old daughter had 'been with' a trusted adult member of our church for six months. Immediately, I almost fell. Then I thought, "He groomed my baby!"

The news broke across my body like piercing glass shards. I had known something was wrong for months. My daughter used to love school and track. She'd even been a freshman on the varsity team, but she'd taken a 180 in her schoolwork, interests, and personality.

As traumatic as my own assault was, this hellacious revelation was twenty times worse. My daughter initially denied it, but I knew. After putting in that puzzle piece, everything else made sense. I'd recently graduated with a second master's degree in psychology and marriage and family therapy. I kept asking myself, How did I miss this? The layers of guilt, shame, and anger were almost debilitating.

Within a few weeks, my daughter admitted the truth. The depth of her shame was palpable and painful to witness. Even though it was difficult, I had to give her the space to decide if she wanted to file a formal report. Eventually we did go to the police station to name names and file that paperwork, but the DA couldn't take the next steps. Without physical evidence, it was he said/she said. It was another kind of hell having to learn to live with that injustice.

But God, my faith, and prayer held me when I was empty. And, yes, we did return to therapy to regain our footing and begin again.

FINDING MY LIGHT IN THE DARKNESS

After experiencing my own assault and dealing with my daughter's, I felt compelled to work with sexual trauma survivors. As soon as I had the idea, I knew it was part of my calling and what I was supposed to be doing.

In 2022, I began my own coaching business, H.E.R.story Reimagined, to help mothers who are sexual trauma survivors and who also find their daughters in the same situation. In addition to coaching, I also created an online course, *Not My Daughter Too*, to help mothers struggling in this situation. "H-E-R," or heal, emerge, recreate, is the three-step process that underpins H.E.R.story Reimagined.

My greatest mission is to meet each client where she's at and for her to walk away with a greater sense of self and worth. I want every client to know she's enough and has power—not to change what's happened but to rewrite her own narrative moving forward.

TO THE MOMS: THE GREATEST LESSONS I'VE LEARNED

By helping mothers through this unthinkable time, I've found tremendous personal solace and healing.

If I can offer any guidance to mothers in this situation, it would be this:

- **Put on your own oxygen mask first.** If you don't carve out a life for yourself and work through your own healing journey, you'll be in no position to help your daughter. As you heal, it'll serve as a healthy model for your child. Remember, you're not here to rescue anyone. Not even your own children. Your capacity to love outside yourself is never greater than your capacity to love yourself. Grow that, and your ability to love and help others will flourish too.

- **Give your daughter space to heal differently than you.** Everyone deals with intimate and sexual trauma differently. Your daughter's survivorship journey won't be exactly your own, and that's OK.

- **Give yourself grace and stop judging yourself so harshly.** Blame. Guilt. Shame. All these emotions are natural, but don't forget to give yourself grace, leeway, and space to reconnect to yourself. At the time, you did the best you could with what you had in an impossible situation.

- **Love life the way it is right now.** Even in the midst of chaos, there are good times. Hold onto those. I'm always pushing hope, and part of that is realizing nothing is ever perfect. Love it anyway.

- **Validation doesn't come from the outside.** If you think you'll be complete when you have that relationship or job or accomplishment, you'll forever be chasing happiness. Your validation comes from you—and nothing and no one else.

- **Remember and honor that little girl inside you.** That little girl is often put in the background and told to be quiet, but you take her with you wherever you go. Hold her instead of scolding her. Let her know you're the adult, and you're making the executive decisions, but you see her, and it's safe.

- **Normalize getting help.** Whether you're pursuing therapy, coaching, or counseling, there's no shame in getting that help. Normalize asking for the guidance you need.

- **Learn to feel safe in your bodies again.** Get comfortable in your own skin. In the world of social media and comparison, find a way to look in the mirror and love and value what you see. Take the microscope off your imperfections and embrace and celebrate the good. Know you're valuable and deserving of anything and everything positive in your life.

- **Forgive...so you can live**. I forgave my ex-husband. My daughter's father. My assailant. My daughter's perpetrator. I had to in order to live. To stop them from having unlimited power over me and my future, I had to forgive and live my life. That's how you come back.

That's how you live in resilience and transformation. That's how you can be as powerful and bold as you are.

- **You have the power.** You can have an entire community of support, but ultimately you're the one who can change your life. You're the one to love you. You're the one to rescue you. You—and you alone— have the power to create a life by design and pursue the future you want.

When you're met with a traumatic event over which you have no control, it's easy to turn to anger and to take up residence there. Choose patience and grace. Find the joy you can take with you moving forward. Brace yourself. *Know and choose to believe you're not going out like that.*

For me, I'm a mother who's raised three loving human beings, and they are the very best I can give to this world.

About Lorena

Living a full life of intention and purpose, while expressing the best version of yourself, is the only way to live, according to Lorena. Lorena Belcher, CEO of H.E.R.story Reimagined, is a Resilience and Transformational Coach, Author, and Consultant. H.E.R.story Reimagined is a global movement for women to Heal, Emerge and Reimagine a new story with brand new chapters of excitement and triumph. Lorena believes it's vital for women to know they have the power to do so.

As a Resilience and Transformational Coach, Lorena's clients have changed their lives by building meaningful boundaries, crushing limiting beliefs, and taking steps to become someone new. Lorena is a Lisa Nichols' Certified Transformational Trainer. Also, she created an online course, *Not My Daughter Too*, featured on Tony Robbins' and Dean Graziosi's platform. The course supports women ending generational sexual trauma. Lorena works with moms to cope, thrive and navigate both their own sexual trauma, while discovering their teen daughter's sexual trauma, to create a life they love, without losing themselves.

Recently, Lorena collaborated with 29 authors to create an anthology of real-life stories: *LIVE. LOVE. PROSPER: A Positive Mindset Can Change Anything.* All royalties go to authors' local charities. Lorena authored *Yes Girl, Yes You Can: Affirmations to Elevate Your Self-Talk*, an affirmation book to support women in changing their inner self-talk that supports a greater vision for themselves. Her first book, *Fly Girl! A Journey from Darkness to Daybreak* was written under the pen name: L. Anne Belcher. This is a powerful memoir that shares her struggles and triumphs from sexual and intimate partner trauma.

Lorena was an Educational Specialist-Case Manager/ Middle School Math Teacher of students with special needs and general education students K-8. She integrated best practices of mental health strategies and social-emotional learning with multidisciplinary teams.

As an Associate Marriage and Family Therapist Intern at Peace Over Violence, Lorena was a Trauma Therapist Intern. She volunteered as a speaker with Voices Over Violence. She spoke throughout Los Angeles, including at Mount Saint Mary's University's "Take Back the Night" – speaking to college student survivors of interpersonal violence. Lorena was a Los Angeles Police Officer briefly. She realized working with trauma survivors offered greater connection to the core of people.

Lorena holds a BS in Economics and two master's degrees, in Education and

Psychology. Lorena resides in Southern California with her mother and two of her daughters.

Learn more about Lorena at:

- herstoryreimagined.com